W9-BGP-712

KNOWLEDGE MANAGEMENT AND NETWORKED ENVIRONMENTS

KNOWLEDGE MANAGEMENT AND NETWORKED ENVIRONMENTS

Leveraging Intellectual Capital in Virtual Business Communities

Alfred J. Beerli
Svenja Falk
Daniel Diemers
Editors

AMACOM

American Management Association

New York • Atlanta • Brussels • Buenos Aires • Chicago • London • Mexico City
San Francisco • Shanghai • Tokyo • Toronto • Washington, D. C.

This publication is designed to provide accurate and authoritative
information in regard to the subject matter covered. It is sold with
the understanding that the publisher is not engaged in rendering
legal, accounting, or other professional service. If legal advice or other
expert assistance is required, the services of a competent professional
person should be sought.

Library of Congress Cataloging-in-Publication Data

Knowledge management and networked environments : leveraging
intellectual capital in virtual business communities /
Alfred J. Beerli, Svenja Falk, and Daniel Diemers, editors.
    p. cm.
    Includes bibliographical references and index.
  ISBN 0-8144-0742-0
  1. Knowledge management. 2. Virtual reality in management. 3.
Electronic commerce. I. Beerli, Alfred J. II. Falk, Svenja III. Diemers, Daniel.
    HD30.2 .K636848 2002
    658.4'038--dc21

                                    2002009129

Printing number

10 9 8 7 6 5 4 3 2 1

CONTENTS

FOREWORD

We are at a critical juncture in the short but impressive life of knowledge management. In one sense, nothing whatsoever has diminished the importance of managing knowledge. More than ever, we live in an economy that values and rewards knowledge. We need to use it to differentiate products and services, extract efficiencies from shared learning, and to make better decisions and to take smarter actions. We certainly still haven't mastered Peter Drucker's challenge, which is to make knowledge work productive in the 21st century in the fashion in which the 20th century dramatically improved the productivity of industrial work. In this regard, it's important business as usual for knowledge management.

But something has undeniably changed in the business environment for knowledge management (KM). Like many novel or ancillary activities in corporations today, the movement is beginning to struggle a bit. As the case studies in Chapter 1 illustrate, some companies have reduced their investment in and commitment to managing knowledge. Some companies view KM services as a commodity, and are even exploring the possibility of moving them offshore to India or the Philippines. The subject is no longer regarded as new, and the broad array of conferences, journalistic accounts, and impassioned followers has narrowed in the current difficult economic environment.

Knowledge management came of age at a time of unprecedented boom in many leading economies. To persist on the business scene, however, it needs to survive the current bust. It needs to become mainstream, pervasive, and common. The concept needs to move beyond a few committed enthusiasts to become a broad organizational capability. In short, it needs to become more like the idea of quality, which has become so persuasive in many companies that it can hardly be noticed; it is fully integrated which the day-to-day activities of many organizations, and has moved to almost all functions beyond its origins in manufacturing.

To do this, KM must change considerably. Instead of being a separate activity from normal work that requires knowledge workers' motivation and spare time, it must become "baked in" to their daily work processes. Instead of being a strategy in itself, it must support other business strategies. Instead of being justified on hunches and faith, it must prove its worth in conventional economic terms.

The lessons in this book are timely, and can provide the key to the "mainstreaming" of knowledge management into organizations. Several of the book's foci will help to increase the alignment between KM and the business:

- ❏ Several chapters of the book have a strong orientation to customers and knowledge about them—an important resource for any business, and one that is relatively easy to prove the worth of.
- ❏ There are strong links in the book between KM and the pursuit of innovation; this is, of course, a much more familiar and accepted topic in business, yet one that could use some new perspectives.
- ❏ The role of knowledge and KM in strategy and strategizing is addressed directly in Chapters 5 and 7.
- ❏ The book concludes with a section on the relationship between KM and the roles of knowledge workers, which will have to be addressed directly if we ever see productivity and performance improvements in knowledge work.

While there are many examples in the book, the primary case study is perhaps Accenture itself, the employer of most of the contributors. Accenture is certainly a bellwether among knowledge-managing organizations. It was one of the first large organizations to make a significant investment in the concept, and has seen numerous ideas and technologies for KM come and go over the past decade or so. Accenture's KM activities are highly regarded, and the company has just been named to the "Hall of Fame for 'Most Admired Knowledge Enterprises'" by a KM consulting firm, Telcos. But Accenture is also struggling with how to maintain a strong focus on managing knowledge in the midst of a global recession for consulting and professional services industry. What better group than a collection of Accenture knowledge management thinkers to identify both mistakes and promising approaches to knowledge management?

Most of the Accenture contributors are particularly well suited to discuss the integration of KM with work, because they are practitioners themselves. They work on the front lines of both consulting and knowledge management, and they know how best to combine the two. They can present a real-world perspective on all of the issues addressed in this book.

In summary, I believe that the perspectives described herein are critical to the eventual success of knowledge management. Because of the importance of knowledge and the continuing growth of knowledge workers in organizations, I'm optimistic that knowledge management is here to stay. Assuming I'm right, the lessons in this book will be of great long-term value.

Thomas H. Davenport
Partner and Director, Accenture Institute for Strategic Change;
Professor of Information Technology and Management, Babson College

Part 1

CONCEPTUALIZATIONS OF KNOWLEDGE MANAGEMENT IN THE eFUTURE

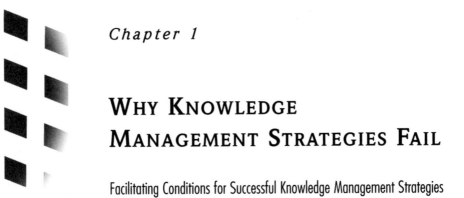

Chapter 1

WHY KNOWLEDGE MANAGEMENT STRATEGIES FAIL

Facilitating Conditions for Successful Knowledge Management Strategies

Dr. Alfred J. Beerli
Accenture, Zurich, Switzerland

1. Introduction

Information, knowledge, and intellectual assets increasingly drive innovation, which gives companies new opportunities to compete. Knowledge can be regarded as the only unique resource that grows when shared, transferred, and managed skillfully. Many knowledge-based companies (such as Microsoft, Intel, Cisco, Skandia, among others) increase their market share by the fact that they leverage their intellectual assets for innovation, growth, and care (Edvinsson and Malone, 1997). Therefore, the new economics of information and knowledge, coupled with the increasing technological complexity, create dilemmas for traditional established companies that rely still on internal technological development to meet their knowledge and innovation needs (Christensen,

1997). Many companies today are finding themselves paralyzed and unable to respond quickly to time-paced market shifts, because they had concentrated on making their pool of knowledge and technology more and more specialized, hoping that this would preserve their competitive edge. Exploiting achieved advantages does not seem to be sufficient in a competitive environment that calls increasingly for speed and creation of novelty.

Since more and more multinational companies fail in achieving significant benefits from investments in global knowledge management programs, shareholders and analysts become critical for survival in the new world of uncertainty. According to a poll report of *CIO* magazine, 56.7 percent of all responding companies have a knowledge management initiative underway (Rutherford, 2001). But if you ask those executives if they are dabbling in knowledge management, the majority are likely to say yes. Knowledge management projects and initiatives can be found on a spectrum ranging from the simple—such as the setting up of mailing lists among workers with similar interests—to something as sophisticated as building intranet platforms that facilitate collaboration.

This chapter seeks explanations why knowledge management initiatives have not delivered the promised returns to shareholders. Further, our goal is to discuss common barriers to knowledge management initiatives and the facilitating conditions for successful knowledge strategies and their underling initiatives.

The following case studies will show potential cleavages and failures of knowledge strategies. We have to consider that many barriers of knowledge facilitation initiatives might hinder the success of knowledge transfer even more if some of these barriers coincide and the resulting effects increase. Therefore, the final section of the chapter summarizes important concepts that will help support effective organizational knowledge transfer.

2. Knowledge Facilitation

The ability to identify, acquire, enrich, apply, and transfer knowledge is an increasingly important capability for successful companies. This is particularly critical in knowledge-intensive industries, where rapid innovation and proactive knowledge transfer mechanisms are a *conditio sine qua non* to corporate survival. Many companies attack this challenge through intensive efforts to "manage" information, intellectual capital, knowledge, and organizational learning more effectively. Since many researchers discussed the possibility that managing knowledge is unrealistic, the most commonly used term for this process is enabling knowledge creation (Von Krogh et al., 2000). As the number of practitioners and academics multiplies in this field, so does the number of definitions and discussions with regard to these knowledge activities.

2.1. Definition of Knowledge Facilitation

For a better understanding, I use the term *facilitating conditions* to describe the enabling principles around knowledge transfer and the organizational structures of the firm to ensure effective knowledge transfer (Beerli, 2001, p. 34). Von Krogh (1998, p.148) recommends looking for enabling conditions for the fragile processes of knowledge creation and knowledge transfer, which have not been well explored, especially not in dispersed settings like new business structures. Von Krogh et al. (2000) analyzed the organizational activities that positively affect the knowledge creation aspect and focused their work on enablers, which make knowledge creation possible. Furthermore, not enough attention has been paid to the organizational governance and their impact on knowledge transfer. Nonaka and Konno (1998) suggest that the structural and cultural features, which govern the relational and communicative processes in an organizational setting, should be studied in further detail. In this context and within this chapter, the emphasis is on facilitating conditions for making knowledge transfer actually possible.

Thus, the main difference between enabling and facilitating can be seen in the nature of the condition itself. Whereas, for example, the enabling condition makes the knowledge activist capable of communicating and supporting the knowledge creation process, the knowledge facilitator supports the knowledge transfer process and makes the sharing, the dissemination, and the learning in an enabled environment actually possible.

2.2. Facilitating Conditions

From previous studies conducted in several industries, I believe that the technology and technological systems that provide knowledge transfer platforms are the easier parts of the knowledge facilitation process. Business processes and the business model built upon technology therefore have to be in sync with the changing environmental business conditions and the evolving needs and demands of the knowledge workers. This is the more challenging part in justifying and legitimating the vast amounts of money invested in knowledge management systems and their supporting processes. The most difficult but also the most important facilitating condition seems to be the culture, which is not only necessary but is essential to providing the trust among the actual knowledge workers to collaborate effectively.

3. What's Wrong with Knowledge Management

Many managers continue to believe that knowledge strategies and knowledge transfer processes matter to the overall success of their companies. Some of them even made "knowledge management" a company-wide priority through dedicated workshops, new processes, assignment of new functionalities—like chief knowledge officer or knowledge facilitator—, the deployment of information technology platforms, and so forth. Aligned to the strategies of the companies, all knowledge-based organizations share the intention to generate profits from the initial investments in knowledge management. The following examples show the similarities between two completely different players in different industries.

3.1. Case Study: Asea Brown Boveri

Asea Brown Boveri (ABB) is a global engineering and manufacturing company, which employs about 160,000 people in more than 100 countries and has revenues over $23 billion (ABB Group Annual Report, 2001). Research & Development is an important part—with $1.6 billion, or 7 percent of revenues, invested in technology innovation and $654 million, or 2.8 percent of revenues, spent on research and development.

To support its eight research centers located around the globe, ABB uses Lotus Notes databases to make corporate research resources available across all business units. By better managing and leveraging knowledge about on-going and planned research activities, ABB wants to be able to conduct a greater number of distinct research projects and respond faster to market needs and technology trends, with the same number of people. Corporate Research controls $200 million worth of funds, and ABB estimates that in the first year of its knowledge initiative the company has realized an effectiveness gain equal to 2 percent of its research budget.

ABB had been led by CEO Percy Barnevik, who formed and significantly influenced the strategy of ABB for many years. During the 1990s ABB acquired multiple companies in various businesses, became a knowledge company, and transformed itself into an e-Company at the end of the 1990s. Since then ABB's market capitalization and revenues went down, the company lost more than 50,000 employees, and the debt increased (Clausen, 2002). What this actually means for knowledge facilitation programs is obvious. Many of the key people involved in knowledge facilitation have left, and as a result the program will lose its strategic anchor to the overall strategy.

3.2. Case Study: Zurich Financial Services

Zurich Financial Services is a global insurance company of integrated financial services with offices in more than sixty countries, over 70,000 employees, gross premiums of $50 billion, and about 38 million customers. Zurich is a provider of financial protection and wealth accumulation solutions and related services. It has a strong presence in the key markets of North America, the UK, and Continental Europe, and follows the strategic goal of enhancing its presence in the Asian region. The management of the New Zurich Group heads for growth and opportunity, and toward leading and shaping the insurance industry. In doing so, Zurich formulated three main goals to achieve in the near future:

❑ Triple the customer base.
❑ Double the product density.
❑ Intensify the customer relationship significantly.

These strategic challenges required powerful support for critical information exchange. This support was partly defined through knowledge transfer programs. To support its many projects, Zurich has sought to align all its core capabilities and built up the "Knowledge Management Framework." This framework set the foundation of all knowledge facilitating activities, processes, tools, and knowledge initiatives. Based on a thoroughly developed knowledge-enabling methodology, an internal division called Corporate Development Services was established to help all internal organizational units identify and close knowledge gaps in order to implement the group's strategy.

The strategy was based on a new vision mainly defined by Rolf Hüppi, former chairman and CEO of Zurich Financial Services. The vision, which reflects the new pace of business, was to extend the company's Web presence, to transform the company to enter the New Economy, and to offer its customers totally new and innovative products and solutions. After the implosion of the Internet hype, the combination of massive financial losses and the loss of employees presented a continuing challenge for the company. Due to the departure of Mr. Hüppi, who was the main sponsor, the knowledge facilitation program will lose its importance.

Major changes influence the implementation of much of the so-called knowledge management strategies. Many multinational companies are suffering the consequences of the decline of the stock markets and face ever-increasing cost bases. Most of the recently launched projects in multinational companies include goals for reducing the cost base and decreasing overhead cost or nondirect-value-adding activities. Many cost-cutting projects these days include also knowledge facilitation programs, which have been underway for some months but whose financial effects will not be felt for some time in the future. For that reason, and because many executives had to leave their positions, projects with a long-term focus are in danger of being stopped and should be assessed separately as long as they are part of a company's overall strategy.

4. Common Barriers to Knowledge Management Facilitation Initiatives

The high failure rates of knowledge facilitation programs indicate the need for a more thorough and critical analysis of the possible root causes of such failures. The literature review and case analysis provide the following insights:

4.1. Missing Connection to the Company's Strategy

Businesses are increasingly competing on the basis of information. Building a knowledge dimension into a company's strategy tools is a first step toward developing and implementing a knowledge-based strategy. Knowledge facilitation initiatives that are not based in a company's strategy will, obviously, not produce the desired effects. In the increasingly market-oriented environment, knowledge facilitation activities must bring immediate value to customers and shareholders. Thus, vision from the top must be translated into tactical plans that ensure that the right knowledge will be captured and optimized to ultimately raise the company's intellectual capital and shareholder value.

4.2. Top Management Support

As with most other key business initiatives, knowledge facilitation initiatives require top management vision and support, particularly for firms shifting from a nonknowledge-based culture. If top management support is not proactive, firms should not attempt to implement large-scale, organization-wide knowledge facilitation programs. Instead, focus should be placed on "managing" knowledge on a smaller scale with specific attention on a specific process or function. Involving senior managers who have served the company long enough to be familiar with various operational and strategic issues of the business will also enhance success. Senior managers enjoy the essential level of respect and are able to bring together the necessary people, who are key links in the vital networks of knowledge professionals and who have to be involved and convinced in championing programs such as knowledge facilitation.

4.3. Trust in an Appropriate Culture

The culture of authentication and trust enables knowledge workers to share and transfer knowledge, to collaborate effectively, and to apply their human and social capital in the knowledge facilitation process. The company that develops the right set of incentives for its employees to work collaboratively and share their knowledge will go a long way toward developing a successful knowledge facilitation effort.

> Turn up the heat on your people and they will leave. Change the forces that bind people, and they will regroup.
>
> (Tapscott, Ticoll, and Lowy, 2000, p. 171)

There are many cultural factors that influence knowledge transfer, including lack of trust, differences in cultural backgrounds, perceived loss of status and rewards, lack of time and conducive meeting places, and intolerance for mistakes.

4.4. Lack of Understanding of Knowledge Facilitation

In large organizations where business scope and geographical distribution can be very diverse, the lack of a common understanding of or a working definition of knowledge can be confusing. Also, where top management fails to articulate clearly the benefits that can be derived from its knowledge facilitation initiatives, employee support is not likely to be voluntary.

4.5. Knowledge Facilitation is Not an IT-Driven Thing

A great misconception about knowledge facilitation is that it is all about technology. As Markus Raebsamen, director of corporate development at Zurich Financial Services, observed, "pure technology-led knowledge facilitation initiatives have a high failure rate." Companies that pursue an IT-driven approach in their knowledge facilitation programs tend to rely on concepts from information technology theory in their understanding of knowledge facilitation. Thus, it also follows that most chief knowledge officers (CKOs) come from a predominantly IT background. As a result, they tend to neglect the other key aspects that are critical to the successful implementation of knowledge facilitation programs. Alternatively, they may lack the necessary people skills to cope with the human and other key aspects of knowledge facilitation.

We cannot deny the very fact that knowledge resides in people, not in technology. In practice, knowledge facilitation requires a combination of many disciplines, from human resources and personnel development to corporate reengineering and information technology.

4.6. Lack of Training in New Knowledge Facilitation Systems

Some companies invest huge amounts of money toward developing state-of-the-art information systems to enable and support their knowledge facilitation activities—without training the users of the systems. Without training, users are unable to optimize the processes underlying the information systems. In some cases, the intended users might not even attempt to use the systems. Additionally, technical training may not be enough; companies should also provide training sessions to impart the benefits of knowledge facilitation and its relevance to the business.

4.7. Performance Management

The fact that there is no agreement on the definition of intellectual capital and intellectual assets can pose a major problem. Although most companies are still using a traditional accounting framework to report performance, there is evidence that this framework does not adequately account for intellectual capital and intellectual assets. This is particularly true of companies in knowledge-intensive industries. The lack of standards for performance management of intellectual capital and intellectual assets poses a problem for management, since return on investment for knowledge facilitation initiatives may be rather challenging to calculate.

Further, the lack of nonfinancial measures may lead management to think that there has not been improvement in performance and to declare the knowledge facilitation initiatives as failures. The lack of measurement could also deter companies from investing in training and other programs to enhance or increase employee competencies. This is danger-ous, since intellectual capital and intellectual assets are increasingly being recognized as the drivers of future performance.

4.8. Replacing Technological Contact with Human Interface

The use of information technology in knowledge facilitation programs is quite rightly justified. However, there is widespread tendency to overem-phasize information technology in knowledge facilitation. A pivotal error underlying some uses of information technology, which severely limits its potential contribution to organizational knowledge, is that firms tend to equate technological contact with face-to-face dialogue. For knowledge facilitation to be effective, human interaction is indispensable. Companies do not realize that often the transfer of knowledge requires the right combination of timing, place, processes, and people.

Failure to differentiate between codified and tacit knowledge is also one reason why some knowledge facilitation programs fail. Companies have to realize that not all information or knowledge can be codified. Where it involves tacit knowledge, ambiguities can only be overcome in face-to-face communication or interactions. In this sense, over-reliance on information technology can be detrimental to effective knowledge transfer. Further, environmental factors can also affect the success of knowledge facilitation programs, such as the failure to plan space for war rooms or for cafeteria-talks. Physical distance and space planning are also factors that can contribute to effective knowledge transfer.

4.9. Lack of a Common Information Technology Platform

While IT should not be the primary driver of any knowledge facilitation programs, it is obvious that technology plays a vital role as enabler of knowledge facilitation. In addition, a common technology platform must exist in the organization so that knowledge repository and sharing can be carried out efficiently, especially for organizations with wider business scope and with units spread geographically.

For instance, in the early years of Accenture's knowledge facilitation implementation, multiple technologies were allowed to proliferate. As a result, dozens of local applications and databases were developed around the globe. The consulting firm has since streamlined its information systems to a common standard that allows ease of use across the diverse scope and geographical distribution of its knowledge base.

4.10. Trusted Open Relationships

Shared communication infrastructures enable partnering and trust. The faster information and knowledge moves between partners, the better. This networked social capital may be strategic, and irreplaceable, and therefore it is powerful. Every new business model is a unique system, which has its own dynamics. As a result of these relationships, the openness, the pervasiveness, the speed, and the sheer volume of information are redefining the way people work together. (This statement is from an interview with Eugene Polistruk, CEO of Celestina, by Tapscott; see Tapscott, Ticoll, and Lowy, 2000, p. 178.) Another fact is that managers who either hide or lack information cannot facilitate the most effective use of human and social capital and build upon the transparent relationships within companies.

These barriers do not consider poor project management techniques, which often can be found as a main reason why knowledge facilitation programs fail. Last but not least—in times when every dollar counts and time is the scarcest resource—patience is necessary, especially for knowledge facilitation programs. Many project managers responsible for knowledge facilitation programs experience missing patience. Since knowledge transfer and knowledge facilitation programs deal with trust among human beings and should investigate and enhance the effectiveness of social relationships, project results and the master plan of such projects should consider the fact that human beings have to get used to changed conditions, processes, and rules, and that this might take some time.

5. Conclusion and Implications for Management

Although knowledge facilitation initiatives fail for a variety of reasons, we have singled out the most common ones. Each situation requires separate attention simply because there is not one best solution for all organizations attempting to use knowledge as a strategy differentiator. For example, the significance of tacit knowledge tends to be more pronounced in service or knowledge-intensive industries, such as consulting firms, software, or biotech, where intellectual capital is manifested through the daily interactions of their staff members.

Finally, knowledge facilitators should place balanced emphasis on several key components, which have varying degrees of influence over the success or failure of each knowledge facilitation initiative. These include strategy, culture, technology, organization, and people.

There are important considerations in making the commitment to have knowledge facilitation taking place. Described in more practical terms, executives and management of knowledge-based companies, but also project managers of knowledge transfer project teams, should consider the following recommendations that support organizational knowledge transfer:

❑ Secure the commitment of senior management for knowledge facilitation initiatives.

❑ Incorporate intangible asset conversion into the organization's overall mission, strategy, and proposition of value.

❑ Establish that the primary objective of knowledge management initiatives must be to convert intangible assets into organizational value, not to convert intangibles into traditional measures of value.

❑ Appoint a leader in the organization who has the authority and responsibility to leverage the organization's intangible assets, and the understanding and ability to make it happen.

❑ If there are significant questions regarding the organization's commitment or ability to execute, do not proceed. Unsuccessful efforts waste resources and can inhibit future success at a time that might have otherwise been appropriate.

❑ Should this be the first knowledge facilitation initiative, establish a pilot project that offers significant high-visibility benefits if successfully executed, and employs knowledgeable cooperative constituents.

❑ Appoint knowledge facilitators in areas where knowledge has to be leveraged and transferred.

❑ Have knowledge facilitators identify sources and uses of knowledge that are closely linked with the value proposition also from potential partners.

❑ Have knowledge facilitators establish a process for putting this knowledge into context.

❑ Develop business and technology plans that outline measurable objectives and progress milestones, and consider the unique characteristics of intangible assets and knowledge transfer.

❑ Establish constituent goals and rewards that are consistent with sharing what is known, and take steps to ensure these goals and rewards embrace the concept.

❑ Report and communicate findings and use these results to make adjustments and to increase the organization's commitment.

Chapter 2

CUSTOMER KNOWLEDGE MANAGEMENT

How Does My Customer Look and Feel?

Thilo Schotte
Accenture, Munich, Germany

1. Introduction

Some decades ago, shopping was a pure relationship experience. The salesperson—in most cases the owner—in the little neighborhood shop did know his customers well. He knew a lot more than just what the customer bought last time; he knew about the customer's family environment, his job, his personality, and his likes and dislikes. This enabled the salesperson to customize the relationship and even the offers: bringing baby clothes into the assortment when a customer was pregnant, asking about the health of a customer's husband after not having seen him for a while, and many other situations.

This was knowledge management on a small scale, but the model ran into a dead end as soon as the shop owner wanted to expand the business. The customer potential was limited to the neighborhood, and the capacity for personal relationships was limited by natural limits. Expanding was directly linked to physical assets. One hundred customers could be served by one shop and one salesperson. Five hundred customers required five shops with five salespersons in several neighborhoods.

This law of "returns from scale in assets" has been invalidated by the rules of the new economy. Physical assets, human resources, and geographical centers no longer determine market limitations. And even though technologies will probably never be able to replace personal touch and feel, a fundamental pillar of personal relationships can be managed by technologies on a large scale: knowledge about individual customers.

The purpose of this chapter is to discuss relevance and guidelines of effective management of customer information. After we have defined "knowledge management" and "customer knowledge management," we will discuss fundamental trends affecting customer knowledge management. We will then present several theoretical models and illustrate their application to today's business through short case studies.

1.1. Definitions

Knowledge management can be defined as the process of offering the right knowledge to the right users at the right time and helping people share and put information into action in ways that strive to improve organizational performance (see Figure 2-1).

In comparison to knowledge management, customer knowledge management (CKM) means the business-oriented gathering and organization of data on customers or prospects. The gathered data are focused on the customer, in order to make the right data available at the right time and place in the right situation.

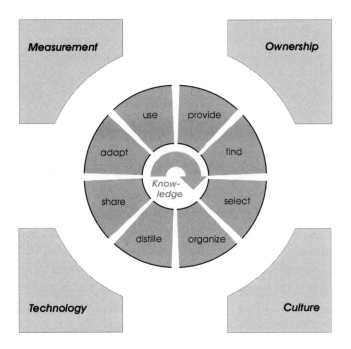

Figure 2-1. Knowledge Management.

2. Current Situation

2.1. Fundamental Trends

2.1.1. Trackability of Customer Behavior

The Internet is a fully technology-based channel. In contrast to traditional contact channels like mass advertising, call centers, retail stores, or showrooms, how customers search for information, services, and products can be tracked directly. Each click leaves an electronic footprint. Additionally, the documentation of the customer's searching and buying path can be documented without any IT breaks. This means that companies are generating masses of customer information through the Internet. Of course, it needs to be considered that this information about consumers is in many cases anonymous, if the consumer does not identify himself, but even anonymous data offers tremendous insight into general behavioral patterns.

2.1.2. Technology Availability

Technology becomes a commodity. Technological innovations lead to only short-term advantages. The basic technologies are available to almost every market participant. The underlying technological evolution can be summarized by three dominant trends:

1. *Ubiquitous Computing:* Many more everyday things will become computerized, or, the other way around, computers will become available in many different forms and shapes. For example, in your future home, the refrigerator, the windows, the coffee machine, and even the coffee mug will have computerized eyes and ears—for everyone.

2. *Ubiquitous Communications:* Everything that is computerized will be able to communicate with each other. Internet, broadband, and wireless technologies allow this connectivity at any time at any place.

3. *Digital Abundance:* There will be almost no limitations in digitalizing content through computerized eyes and ears, and content can be communicated to everywhere immediately. Digital information is becoming more and more realistic, almost undistinguishable from the real object or situation.

2.1.3. Information Overload

Consumers have to deal with an enormous information overload. It has to be considered that approximately 98 percent of the information items that come to the consumer's attention are not memorized. Consumers select information according to its current relevance. In this context, the situational involvement dominantly determines the consumer's information selection. Many companies ignore this fact—especially in advertising—by assuming that consumers are as involved and interested in their products and related informative messages as the producer. This is a fatal misunderstanding, since already in the early 1970s Kiss and Wettig (1972) observed that people look at print ads for an average of 2 seconds. This, of course, has even decreased since.

2.2. Influencing Factors for the Usage of Internet Technologies for Knowledge Management

❑ Based on the trends listed above, descriptive knowledge of directly observed searching and buying behavior in the long run is not a competitive advantage. The "information democracy" allows everyone to have the same access to information.

❑ Although historical data allow explaining general behavioral patterns, they do not offer exhaustive tools to anticipate future behavior with regard to the specific consumption situation.

❑ Being "glassy" generally means a condition in which the consumer feels uncomfortable (e.g., need for privacy). On the other hand, customers are willing to share information about themselves if they observe a clear advantage or value-add in the purpose of the data.

2.3. Key Question for Customer Knowledge Management

Based on the described influences, managing knowledge about the customer becomes crucial. Just storing the information that occurs over the customer contact process is not sufficient. Customer Knowledge Management needs to answer the question: How can customer knowledge support the development of customer relationships?

This question can be divided into three elements:

1. What information is needed in order to generate relevant insight into customers' consumption behavior?
2. What are the right sources, processes, and mechanisms for gathering the specified information?
3. How can the gained customer insight be made operational and implemented into sales and customer relationship processes?

These elements are very specific to a company's market environment, to the products or services offered, to the customers, and to the nature and intensity of the relationship.

In the following sections, some general considerations will be described and illustrated by specific case examples.

3. Models

In order to understand the importance of Customer Knowledge Management, the general dependencies between customer relationships and behavioral patterns need to be clarified. Therefore, the topic will be integrated into the *CRM Capability Model* as an overall framework with a broader Customer Relationship Management context. Then, the *Involvement Model* will be explained. This model shows, from the customer perspective, how specific situations and buyer values interfere with consumer behavior. This is the basis for the *Customer Knowledge Management Model* that combines the customer and company perspectives. Finally, the core process of data mining will be described as the evolutionary stages in *Sophistication of Data Mining.*

3.1. CRM Capability Model

From Accenture's point of view, Customer Relationship Management (CRM) represents the heightened need for companies to orchestrate all of the activities that bring them into contact with their customers. The core CRM objective is to deliver a consistently differentiated and personalized customer experience, regardless of the interaction channel chosen by the customer. CRM brings together a company's efforts in marketing, sales, and service that would traditionally have been pursued in separate, ad hoc ways, and therefore it constitutes a more comprehensive, methodical approach to identifying, attracting, and retaining the most valuable customers.

The Accenture CRM Capability Model (Figure 2-2) summarizes the core capabilities a company needs to establish in order to maximize its customer equity. We define *customer equity* as the economic value that is determined by taking the aggregate value of 1) share of the market ("increasing the number of high-value customers"), 2) share of the customer ("selling more to each of those customers"), and 3) customer lifetime value ("extending the length of each customer relationship").

Figure 2-2. Accenture CRM capability model.

❑ *Customer Insight* allows a company to define its most valuable customers and to determine how to work with them to maximize mutual value. Creating a valuable customer experience is highly dependent on establishing a single view on the customer, generating insights and applying these insights. The customer insight capability is the source and the designer of a company's CRM activities. This is the capability in which Customer Knowledge Management needs to be established.

❑ *Customer Offers* is the capability to develop highly relevant bundles of products and services tailored for individual customer needs based on customer insight knowledge. The most important tasks are to focus on crafting compelling value propositions and developing new products and services that are coveted by the customer. This needs to be embedded in the process of building strong brands and the process of managing the product and service mix.

❑ *Customer Interaction* is the capability to enable customers to interact with the company seamlessly across all contact points. This means to consistently provide insightful, integrated interactions that reflect the customer's value to the company and that demonstrate insight into customer needs and preferences. Therefore marketing, selling, and customer service need to be integrated in order to provide consistent messages across each type of contact. Overall this is a shift from managing point-in-time interactions to managing the customer experience.

❑ *High Performing Organization* is an enabling capability for CRM. Especially in industries where the primary core offer has a service character, human performance—more than specific products or services—delivers a customer experience so unique that it cannot be replicated. Four distinct areas significantly impact human performance: organizational structure and roles, culture, talent management, and learning.

❑ *Enterprise Integration*, the second enabling capability, creates a customer-driven enterprise that forges two aspects:

1. Intra-enterprise linkages across its organization
2. Extra-enterprise connections outside its own borders

3.2. Involvement Model

Involvement is the key for the determination of information search processes. Therefore we need to understand the different types of involvement. Celsi and Olson (1988) distinguish three categories of involvement toward sent information: personal involvement, stimulus-based involvement, and situation-based involvement. Personal involvement is determined by specific attitudes and beliefs of the recipient that leads to a general interest into specific products or information. The second involvement category is triggered by stimuli in conjunction with the presented product or information. The product itself can also lead to stimulus-based involvement (e.g., sports cars or holiday destinations).

Finally, situation-based involvement is by far the most important category, since it dominates all other types of involvement. The recipient's current situation can be determined by the current need for a decision or by time pressure. For example, many people have a personal involvement in cars. Nevertheless, most people rarely show a particular interest in car advertising (e.g., measured by the time people spend looking at a print advertisement for cars), especially if they are under time pressure.

Arranging the car in an attractive environment can create stimulus-based involvement. Many car manufacturers especially make use of landscape scenery or attractive women. But this does change the consumer's attitude toward the brand more than directly affecting the buying behavior. But if the consumer is in need of a new car, how he looks at advertising often changes dramatically.

Therefore it is crucial to understand the customer's current situation in order to make sure that the information sent to the customer is relevant.

Although involvement theories are first a discipline of advertising research, they can be applied as well to Customer Knowledge Management: Depending on the customer's situation, specific information or activities might become tremendously relevant at this point in time. Figure 2-3 shows the dependencies.

Another aspect of the involvement theories needs to be taken into account: the customer's decision-making behavior. Basically, three categories can be distinguished.

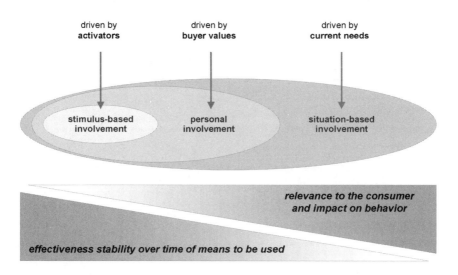

Figure 2-3. Involvement model.

1. *Cognitive Decision Process:* The consumer extensively searches for alternatives and follows a rational evaluation process. This especially takes place if the consumer perceives a high risk in conjunction with his decision.

2. *Emotional Decision Process:* The consumer is driven by emotional activators and personal beliefs. This phenomenon is very common, especially with low involvement products like laundry detergent or with socially observable products like cigarettes or beer.

3. *Habitual Decision Process:* The consumer is driven by habits without using distinctive cognitive or emotional factors for the decision. An example of this behavior is commuting daily by bus.

3.3. Customer Knowledge Management Model

As described above, Knowledge Management is about managing the process of gathering, structuring, filing, and placing valuable information at someone's disposal. In this process, the most important task of Knowledge Management is to make information easy to find and to increase the hit rate of finding the right information easily (Figure 2-4).

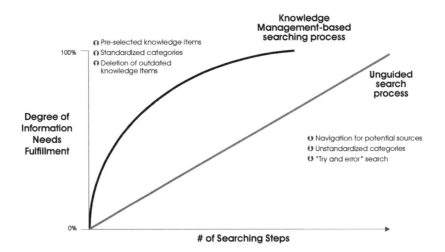

Figure 2-4. Knowledge Management purpose.

The trigger of the information processing is an important characteristic of Knowledge Management. The starting point is the occurrence of the information need of the information addressee. This is a fundamental difference from Customer Knowledge Management, which needs to anticipate the future behavior of the customer. If the company waits until the customer asks for information, it is not able to influence the process where and whom the customer asks. Therefore CKM needs to focus on means to anticipate the occurrence of a potential need (Figure 2-5).

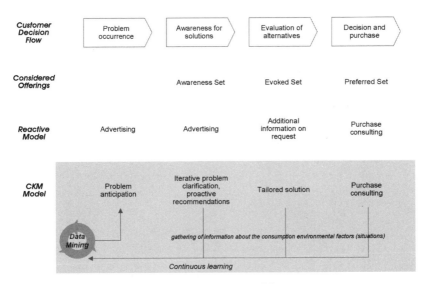

Figure 2-5. Customer Knowledge Management model.

3.4. Data Mining Model

Over the last two decades, organizations have been collecting and storing masses of data. For all these years this data has languished in dusty archives until such time that regulators or lawyers deemed it safe to destroy—data have been a burden for companies and not a valuable asset.

The view on historical data now has changed, and its value as a proprietary resource to discover patterns and hidden meanings to help manage customer relationships has become recognized.

New technologies are enabling efficient and fast access to large volumes of data. In addition, analytic tools provide new ways to analyze the data and automatically detect patterns. These techniques and technology-based tools are called data mining (Figure 2-6).

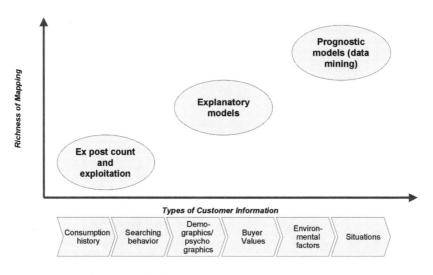

Figure 2-6. Sophistication of data mining.

Sophistication of data mining depends on the data to be included in the modeling process. Dependent on the data included, three steps can be distinguished that enhance the richness of data mining techniques.

3.4.1. Documentation of Historical Consumption Behavior

❑ *Consumption History:* The actual history of which products or services a customer purchased before is the basic knowledge about the customer. It needs to be distinguished, whether to know the history in purchasing own offers or other companies' offers.

❑ *Searching Behavior:* The consumer has an individual behavior how he searches for information, services, and products. Focusing on known channels and sites can do this. Decisions for a new vehicle, for example, can include a sophisticated comparison of different brands, models, retailers, and financing options. The financing options can be taken into account as a parameter for the selection of the car or as a secondary decision after the vehicle has already been ordered.

❑ *Decision Behavior.* Again, this is very specific to the individual customer. Some consumers just rely on their own judgment; others are more dependent on recommendations by accepted experts or friends.

Observing and documenting these data is the first step in understanding the customer. Although it is relatively easy to document the history related to own products and services, the observation of the customer's history with competitors is much more advanced and sometimes almost impossible. Many companies make use of indirect techniques. For example, airlines try to observe whether a customer carries a competitor's frequent flyer tag on his bag.

3.4.2. Explanations for Consumption Behavior

In order to explain a customer's consumption behavior, it is necessary to understand the consumption's environment. The environment is comprised of general buyer value patterns and specific situations. Individual buyer value patterns are fairly stable over time. They can be determined by general motivation, psycho-graphic characteristics, or the customer's social environment (Sinus, 2000). In accordance with involvement theories mentioned above, the specific situation of the consumption event nevertheless is the dominant factor for the consumption behavior. For example, an airline customer who is explicitly comfort-oriented does not care too much about this general buyer value if he is just about to miss his flight.

Explanatory models describe how buyer value patterns and specific situations influence behavior (cause–effect models).

3.4.3. Indicators for the Future Occurrence of Behavioral Root Causes

The knowledge of cause-and-effect mechanisms itself is a necessary but insufficient asset to treat a customer effectively. Indicators to identify the occurrence of the described causes are the necessary third step. In the minority of cases, the influencing factors (explanations for consumption behavior) can be observed directly. Most of the time, only indirect indicators can help to trigger the right treatment.

Based on the described evolution of data mining, prognostic models for individual customers can be developed. Then, customized market activities can be implemented with a high likelihood of achieving the best possible fulfillment of customer needs.

4. Industry Case Studies

The following three industry case studies shall now be matched against the theoretical background presented in the models described above.

4.1. Automotive Industry

The automotive industry is facing several hurdles with regard to Customer Knowledge Management. These hurdles are mainly driven by the characteristics that are very specific to the industry.

First of all, contact between the OEM (Original Equipment Manufacturer) and the customer is very rare. On average, the customer buys a new car every three years. Between that time there are almost no regular or foreseeable contacts. The relationship is very much focused on the car itself—a relationship to the brand. Whatever contact there is is mostly related to a negative perception or experience, such as vehicle maintenance, repairs, or complaints. All these contacts normally do not lead to a perceived value-add for the customer, but just to restoring the former status of the vehicle. Additionally, the relationship is mostly owned by the dealership and not by the OEM itself. This means that unless the OEM owns the sales network or unless there is at least a contractually established data interchange, the OEM might not even know the names of its customers.

The situation is even more critical since new competitors make special use of new technologies and try to enter elements of the vehicle sales- and after-sales value chain. Three types of new competitors can be distinguished:
1. *Business Specialists* focus on profitable elements of the automotive value chain. Pit Stop, for example, offers cheap repair and maintenance services, cherry picking on high margin services, and fast moving parts. This allows them to avoid the cost-intensive burden of a

full-range service provider but also allows them to gather information about the customer that never gets to the attention of the OEM.

2. *Information Integrators* focus on the information interface between the customer and the OEM, dealer, or other service providers. Therefore, they are able to avoid capital and the fixed-cost intensive elements of the value chain. Microsoft CarPoint in the United States, for example, allows their customers to search for new cars across all participating brands and dealerships. CarPoint is the Internet portal for vehicle queries of its customers and therefore is able to own a tremendous amount of customer data independent of the selected brand at the end of the buying process. Depending on the future Block Exemption legislation in Europe, this phenomenon will also gain even more importance in Europe.

3. *Business Integrators* try to cover a huge variety of value chain elements with mutual synergies. The German rental car company Sixt, for example, is trying to manage the entire lifecycle of the car and the customer. Sixt is covering elements like new car sales, car rentals, finance and leasing, used car sales, mobility, and fleet management. CarAbo, one of Sixt's service offerings, allows the customer to lease a car for a specified timeframe. But the customer is not dependent on this one car. For example, he can leave his leased BMW 5 Series at Frankfurt Airport and get another 5 Series at Berlin Airport on the same leasing contract. This, of course, allows the customer to make maximum use of all means of transportation and to increase his mobility flexibility. In this case, the customer is even able to avoid buying a car at a dealership, and Sixt is the owner of the customer and all data occurring during the lifecycle.

Today, automotive OEMs react to these challenges by establishing a direct dialog line to their customers. In the early 1990s production-oriented concepts like lean production were still a major focus in the automotive industry, but in the late 1990s the OEMs discovered the customer phenomenon. Initiatives around the Customer Relationship Management idea emerged quickly around the globe. Ford and Mercedes-Benz, for example, have set up large-scale call centers that allow the customer to get in contact with the OEM on issues like road-side assistance, complaints, and product or general inquiries. OEMs like BMW USA offer extensive product configuration tools on the Internet. Volkswagen already in the early 1990s established a bonus program that enforces the submission of service events data from the dealership to the central sales and marketing department.

Additionally, OEMs try to establish a continuous emotional dialog through membership clubs, such as BMW's Internet-based 7 Series Owners Cycle. Similarly, Mercedes-Benz interacts with its customers and prospects in the Mercedes Club, a club that aims at offering lifestyle-oriented products, holidays, and events, at the same time gathering extensive customer information.

Data management has also become a priority issue in the automotive industry. In the United States, for example, Lexus is connecting its dealers via satellite in order to establish an exhaustive shared-data platform, while many European OEMs are still facing contractual issues with their dealerships, who often fear losing ownership of the customer.

Nevertheless, with regard to Customer Knowledge Management, there is still room for improvement in the automotive industry. Customer knowledge is not yet extensively used for the identification of critical situations and the so-called moments of truth. For example, not many OEMs are yet using the leverage of financial services for their CKM activities, such as using leasing contracts to identify the right time to contact a customer for a new car. Additionally, most OEMs are still focusing on the individual customer. Creating knowledge about the customer's extended household, for example, enables the OEM to offer vehicles specific to the household cycle: a small car for the teenager going off to college, a mini-van or sports utility vehicle for the newly married, or other offers based on the intelligent interpretation of various event combinations.

4.2. Airline Industry

The airline industry is—by comparison to the automotive industry—in a much better position to generate customer data, mainly because the primary offering has service characteristics. The customer actually is present when the "product" is produced, which means that the product perception is very much dependent on a relationship experience. Especially for frequent flyers, the relationship event takes place regularly, often even several times per week, and without any artificial enforcement to generate customer contacts.

This fact becomes even more important in the spotlight of the competitive environment in the airline industry. In the perception of the customer, flight services have become a commodity. Flight schedules of different airlines normally offer several alternatives for specific legs, although in Europe many domestic flights are still operating in a monopoly market. On the other hand, several "no-frills" airlines—like Ryanair in Europe or Southwest Airlines in North America—are continuously emerging. These airlines operate with significant cost advantages of up to 59 percent compared to premium airlines (Ryanair, 2001). From the customer perspective, these airlines have gained an excellent reputation. For example, 86 percent of European business travelers who have traveled in 1999 with a no-frills airline stated that they were satisfied or very satisfied with the offering, and 68 percent of these business travelers intended to travel with no-frills airlines again (IATA, 1999).

This is remarkable, especially since business travelers normally are the most profitable customers and not very price sensitive. On the other hand, premium airlines have always been innovators in creating loyalty schemes and bonus programs. These programs allow documenting participating customers' travel histories, as customers have a very strong incentive to identify themselves in a consumption situation relevant to mileage awards. The tremendous power of these first-mover loyalty schemes has enabled airlines to extend the spectrum of services eligible for mileage awards significantly. Today, customers can earn airline miles with hotel stays, credit card transactions, phone calls, car rentals, new car test drives, and many other services not directly linked to a flight booking.

In terms of direct cost, these partnering efforts are neutral or even directly profitable for airlines; they additionally generate masses of data covering their customers' wide-ranging consumption behavior. Extensive customer profiles have become a reality. This has enabled airlines to create sophisticated, nonanonymous customer segmentations that go far beyond purely flight-related segmentations.

To create flight miles as a new "accepted currency" is a significant advantage for airline mileage programs, compared to other pure rebate loyalty programs like the Payback program in Germany. Although 500 bonus miles have a very high perceived value for the customer, they represent much lower actual cost for the airline. This perception gap is a tremendous advantage compared to a relatively small loyalty rebate of, say 1 percent, which directly impacts the absolute net profit margin.

Many airlines already operationalize customer knowledge in various ways. They offer special services to their top customers, such as airline lounges, preferred seat reservations, and easier check-in procedures. Alitalia has implemented a self-service kiosk that displays offers customized to customers' specific interests. Delta Airlines has assigned individual call center agents to their top customers in order to build a lively and consistent one-to-one relationship with them. Continental has set up an Internet-based process to inform customers about changes in flight status automatically.

It can be assumed that future CRM initiatives will specifically concentrate on individualizing the top customer relationships in terms of the most important business traveler needs: seamless travel and time savings. This is a promising way to create competitive advantages, especially against no-frills airlines. To be successful, airlines need to make use of online dynamic knowledge about customer needs depending on specific situations, particularly in critical situations such as flight delays, connecting flights, overnight flights with follow-on business meetings, or lost baggage. These situations need to be matched with the customers' individual buyer values and specific needs to create data-driven (and automated) customized solutions for the top customers.

4.3. Credit Card Industry: American Express

The American Express Company provides charge and credit cards, traveler's cheques, banking services, financial planning, brokerage services, mutual funds, insurance, and other investment products. The company is one of the world's largest travel agencies and issuers of traveler's checks, and it offers travel and related consulting services to individuals and corporations around the globe. Worldwide, American Express has issued over

50 million credit cards and in 2000, the company generated consolidated net revenues of approximately U.S. $22 billion.

The example of American Express shows how already today, historical customer data can be analyzed and used for efficient Customer Relationship Management.

American Express aims at building an intensive and long-lasting relationship with its customers with mutual benefits for them and for American Express and its allied partners. The company's philosophy is based on the conviction that direct customer contact is crucial to achieve this goal. This philosophy is in contrast to other large credit card companies like Visa or Master Card, which mainly rely on their issuing partners.

American Express extensively uses technology to evaluate and operationalize customer data. This has led to a large variety of different cards offered to specific segments. Besides the basic American Express Card, there are the Blue, Gold, Platinum, Centurion, Credit, and Golf cards. These cards differ in terms of characteristics and demands of the specific target customers. The American Express Golf Card, for example, offers green fee discounts, special golf events, and even hole-in-one insurance (!).

As mentioned above, American Express is able to analyze customer data on behavioral patterns across all types of consumption paid for with the Amex Card. Through this process, it is possible to identify travel patterns, preferred products, or channels. Attached to their monthly account overview, American Express sends a selection of individualized offers based on each customer's consumption history. The longer the relationship lasts and the higher the portion of buying transactions processed with the Amex Card, the more appropriate and specific the offers can become. Additionally, American Express is able to use the experiences of other customers with similar characteristics to apply other customers' lifecycle evolvement on forecast models.

Nevertheless, all these data show an historic perspective on the customer. Stand alone, the credit card business offers limited potential to apply historic knowledge to future consumption situations. But the other core businesses of American Express open up the opportunities for potential applications. The company can offer specific types of insurance for customers entering the family stage in the lifecycle. Also the travel business offers a wide range of opportunities, such as offering special hotel or event arrangements based on the customer's specific interests. Overall, American Express keeps an important strategic advantage by occupying the full vertical credit card value chain. Therefore, American Express is able to gather worldwide a broad range of customer data across many areas of everyday transactions. For the future, the company is in an excellent position to customize the spectrum of services and offers for individual customers. In order to become even more relevant for the customer, they have to focus on the moments of truth by identifying when, where, and how a specific offer has the greatest impact on a customer's behavior. Limitations, of course, might occur due to privacy legislation restrictions, especially in Europe.

5. Summary of Key Learnings

The key learnings are discussed in terms of the key question. In general, leaders in each of the industries discussed spend a huge effort on using customer knowledge for the enhancement of their customer relationship management capabilities. Nevertheless, with regard to the described models in this chapter, most companies do not make full use of the shown mechanisms and dependencies.

The three elements of the key question can be stated as follows:

1. *What information is needed in order to generate relevant insight into the customers' consumption behavior?* This is the most crucial element of the question and requires a clear understanding of general consumer behavior patterns, and also very specific knowledge of customer needs for the products or services offered by the respective company. Many companies are still driven by data that occurs "incidentally" or based on current data availability, rather than by a concrete conceptual map that is set up as a greenfield profile, which would be ideal for understanding the customer's behavior in specific situations. Figure 2-7 shows the fundamental data dimensions needed to understand the customer.

The characteristics of the four dimensions shown in the figure are the very specific typologies of respective products and services consumption processes.

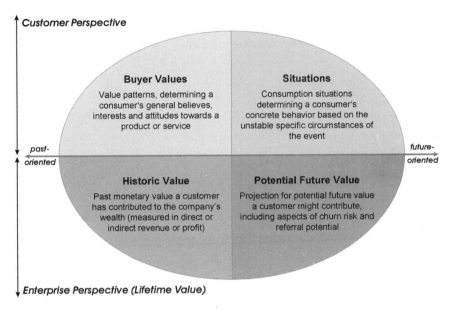

Figure 2-7. Data dimensions for effective CKM.

2. *What are the right sources, processes, and mechanisms for gathering the specified information?* This can be answered only after a thorough process of defining the right data as described above. Gathering information about the past-oriented dimension from the enterprise perspective is definitely the easiest part. Even identifying general buyer values for the specific product or service is fairly simple, although flagging which customer carries which buyer values is already much more complex and usually demands working through a questionnaire with every customer. Of course, this makes sense only for high-value customers where benefit and cost build a positive ratio.

The future-oriented dimensions are the most neglected ones so far. From the enterprise perspective, aspects like today's share of wallet, complaint history, or common patterns in general lifecycle models can help to predict potential future value. This is closely linked to the customer perspective that has to identify the right timing and right information for specific situations in which data is needed in customer contact processes. This is probably the area that is not yet fulfilled efficiently and sufficiently in the industries described.

3. *How can the gained customer insight be made operational and implemented into sales and customer relationship processes?* Only if the first and the second element of the key question are answered sufficiently can the third element be implemented easily. That is the part of Customer Knowledge Management that can make best usage of technology in order to trigger activities automatically. Companies in the airline industry and American Express are especially rushing to implement or enhance state-of-the-art solutions.

As a conclusion, three hypotheses are offered as an outlook on the future emergence of Customer Knowledge Management in the context of the eConomy:

❑ *The fundamental business rules for Customer Knowledge Management have not changed through the Internet.* Sales and Marketing have always been focused on generating demand, which from the outset has meant identifying target customers and sending rational and emotional messages to these customers through the appropriate communication channel. Advertising has already been focused on specialty channels (e.g. MTV, Eurosport) in order to target the right customers. Events have been created around brands in order to involve targets that multiply the image effect in their peer groups. New technologies are "only" a tool that make this process much more sophisticated and efficient (Porter, 2001).

❑ *Internet and database technologies are crucial enablers for Customer Knowledge Management.* In the "monopoly" era of mass channels, the customization of content specific to target customers had been fairly limited and expensive. This has changed in the Internet era. Now, new technologies allow automatic gathering, processing, and usage of customer data. The Internet allows the sophisticated segmentation of customers and their treatment according to the detailed characteristics of the respective segments. The "segment of one" is becoming reachable also for companies with frequent low-revenue customer transactions.

❑ *Only those companies that will be able to understand and operationalize complex cause–effect mechanisms in customer behavior will use the potentials of new technologies effectively.* Only the market offerings of these companies will be perceived as relevant by their customers in situations specific to the customer's current environment.

Chapter 3

Managing Customer Knowledge in Electronic Commerce

Thomas H. Davenport
Accenture, Boston
and
Sirkka L. Jarvenpaa
University of Texas, Austin, Texas

1. Introduction

In order to successfully compete in e-commerce, companies must develop a new portfolio of operational capabilities (Fahey et al., 2000). One of those capabilities is better managing the knowledge flow to and from customers (Davenport, Harris, and Kohli, 2001). This capability requires a company to capture, distribute, and apply customer knowledge more effectively in its product, market, and customer activities. For a seller, customer knowledge allows customization of offerings and communications (i.e., knowledge-intensive products and services), segmentation, analysis of customer behavior from Web site transactions, redesign of Web sites in

An earlier version of this chapter appeared in V. Mahajan and Y. Wind (Eds.), *Digital Marketing* (New York: Wiley, 2001).

response to customer usage patterns, product feedback, and influence on the customers' evaluation standards to accord with the site's offerings. A company might be able to obtain customer knowledge more efficiently on the Internet than through another channel, such as a human sales representative.

Good customer knowledge management can increase a company's advantage over other companies—closing off competition. On the Internet, where traditional industry and technology-based sources of competitive advantage are nonexistent or fleeting, competitive advantage is tied to continuous innovation and customer focus (Davenport, Harris, and Kohli, 2001). Customer knowledge is one of the strongest sources of new innovations in general (Sanchez and Elola, 1991) and particularly so in the highly dynamic Internet environment. Customer knowledge is also the basis of a customer-focused organization (Kohli and Jaworski, 1990), which strives for market orientation, high service quality, and customer relationship management. Positive company performance has been associated with customer focus in traditional businesses (Jaworski and Kohli, 1993; Rust et al, 1995). A similar relationship is widely assumed to hold for Internet businesses: Customer focus has been the rallying ground for the more successful companies, such as Amazon.com:

> Our vision is to use this platform to build Earth's most customer centric company, a place where people can come to find anything and everything they might want to buy online.... We'll listen to customers, invent on their behalf, and personalize the store for each of them, all while working hard to contribute to earn their trust.
>
> (Amazon.com 1999 Annual Report: Letter to Shareholders)

Well-managed customer knowledge should allow a company to deliver many benefits to its customers, including more refined searchers, more depth and interactivity at a time, more tailored editorial content, a better fit of product and service offerings with needs, a better ability to use those offerings effectively, more accurate evaluations, and overall more customer satisfaction. For example, Trilogy Software, a provider of

Web-based product configuration software, offers unique catalogs for each of their customer organizations' employees based on their buying authority. Merchants can use information about customers' buying patterns, articulated preferences, and/or demographics systems to predict other products that the customer might want to purchase. This knowledge can be used to present appropriate advertising or incentives tailored to the customers' tastes, with the aim of increasing their purchases and their satisfaction.

2. What Is Customer Knowledge?

Here we define customer knowledge pragmatically as the higher-value forms of explicit or tacit information about the customer that can reside either in an individual employee or a collective organization (Davenport and Prusak, 1998). This customer knowledge embeds human learning, experience, insight, interpretation, and synthesis. For customer information to be transformed into knowledge, it must be acquired by someone who can give it meaning and context, and used within the specific time span of its relevance and currency. A merchant who provides information such as troubleshooting tips or testimonials is offering information.

To transfer knowledge, customers must be able to tell how a specific product meets their needs, and how the product will provide benefits in a specific situation. Likewise, a customer who provides data on demographics, required product characteristics, and the like is only providing information. On the other hand, companies can use that information along with other sources to determine the customer's motivations, their attitudes, their future intentions, and so on, which would constitute customer knowledge. To recap, our distinction between data/information and knowledge conveys that the source of value does not arise from possessing the information resource, but from acting on it in a context of a specific meaning at a specific time relevant to a customer. Throughout the remainder of this chapter, we use the term "customer knowledge" as synonymous with the opportunity for a company to transform digital information into knowledge that is of value to a customer.

The mining of customer information is highly dependent upon what information is available. Customer data can be mined from the particular customer's past behavior, or from more general profiles developed through various statistical filtering techniques applied to customer data. Whereas the first option (i.e., content-based filtering) can be implemented by using data only from the customer to whom the recommendation is to be made, the other option (i.e., collaborative filtering) requires that information about observed customer behavior or volunteered preferences be pooled, and comparisons made among a sample of customers (Pazzani, 1999).

Turning data and information to and from customers into knowledge requires focus and investment of knowledge processes and skills (Davenport et al, 2001). Any Web site can gather transaction data; only a few companies thus far have sorted, categorized, synthesized, and recontextualized it in order to create new meaning, make decisions, and take actions based on it. Few companies share the information they have with their customers in a value-adding fashion. Any site can broadcast product documentation, but to turn that information into knowledge requires interventions of customization, currency, pruning, structuring, and relating that to the specific customer at the specific time and space.

To recap, e-commerce presents expanded opportunities for management of customer knowledge, but so far this opportunity has been significantly underutilized. Many companies offer considerable information about themselves, and their products and services on Web sites, for example, without extracting any customer information that could be synthesized into deeper customer knowledge (Forrester Research, 1999). Next, we discuss some of the benefits from managing customer knowledge in e-commerce.

3. The Promise of E-Commerce Lies in Customer Knowledge Management

Developing customer knowledge management capabilities helps a company take advantage of the unique capabilities of the e-commerce channel, namely convenience, interactivity, addressability/segmentation, and transparency. Customer knowledge management is also critical for companies in countering some of the problems they face as they embark on e-commerce: commodification, channel conflict, and dis/reintermediation (see Figure 3-1). Hence, much of the touted promises of e-commerce are dependent on good customer knowledge management.

3.1. Convenience

New modes of direct retailing are traditionally first patronized more by high income, better educated, and younger shoppers than by low income, less educated and older shoppers (e.g., Eastlick, 1993). This particular profile of shoppers places a higher value on convenience and is less price-conscious (Reynolds, 1974; Peterson et al., 1989).

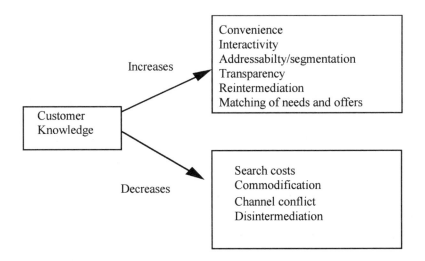

Figure 3-1. Customer Knowledge Management in e-commerce

To increase the convenience of the shopping experience, the seller must have knowledge of the customer. Many stores have created search engines tailored to their stores, but to meet the highest level of expectations for convenience, the store's search engine needs to be tailored to the customer and linked to personalized cross-site search engines (e.g., "my Yahoo"). Convenience is also increased by providing personalized lists for a quick reorder of previously purchased goods, and search engines that provide more accurate matches to customers' queries. The caveat is that unless well designed, the knowledge capture can be perceived as too effortful or intrusive by customers who might have turned to the digital channel to save time—and to avoid revealing their identities, habits, preferences, needs, and evaluations in the first place.

3.2. Interactivity

Interactivity is touted as one of the greatest advantages of digital channels in general and the Internet in particular (Alba et al., 1997; Peterson et al., 1997). The Web is asserted to provide an immediate response similar to face-to-face communications, but without the constraints of such synchronous communications. Interactivity assumes a two-way communication that is not just dynamic but also personalized. Interactivity is the key function offered by vendors of e-commerce software (e.g., Broadvision and Vignette) that purport to address knowledge. Similarly, in their model of communication-based marketing, Duncan and Moriarty (1998) describe interactivity as "personal customized communication" (p. 8). To personalize the communication, the sending party needs to have some knowledge of the receiving party's situation, goals, or previous interaction patterns (Hof and Green, 1998).

3.3. Addressability/Segmentation

The Internet has expanded the opportunities for addressable (Blattberg and Deighton, 1991), micro-segmented, and one-on-one marketing relationships (Peppers and Rogers, 1997). Addressability and micro-segmentation mean that offerings should be targeted directly to individual customers. *Addressability* is the ability to identify a specific customer with whom a business interacts. *Segmentation* is the tailoring of offerings and messages based on that identification. Unlike traditional marketing environments in which vendors cannot know what product or service knowledge a customer consumes, in e-commerce we can know at least what Web pages a customer clicks onto.

Marketers can also learn from where a customer arrived at a site, and to where he or she goes upon leaving. Sophisticated Web sites use knowledge of previous customer interactions to determine what product or service offerings to display or highlight. However, recent research suggests that companies may not fully understand under what conditions customers want their e-commerce interactions to be personalized, and hence should be conservative in pursuing personalization. In one survey, for example, 42 percent of respondents said they saw no value in personalization. When the same sample was asked to choose between a grocery site making its own personalized recommendations and one that offered customization based on a customer's expressed preferences, only 6 percent chose personalization based on the site's intelligence (Nunes and Kambil, 2001).

3.4. Transparency of Knowledge Extraction

Web technologies allow the transparent capture of fine details of customer transactions and browsing patterns without the customers' awareness. However, customers are likely to allow sellers to take advantage of this transparency only when a trusted long-term relationship exists between the seller and the customer. Because of recent regulatory actions in Europe, if the data flows involve citizens from European Union countries, companies will have to restrict the nature of information they can collect on customers and use for commercial purposes without the customers' explicit consent to cooperate (Smith, 2001). A comprehensive privacy law has also been passed in Canada that requires customer consent for gathering personal information.

So far, U.S. regulations have been sectoral: the Gramm-Leach-Bliley Act regulates financial information and the Health Insurance Portability and Accountability Act regulates health information. In other industries in the United States, companies are expected to self-regulate themselves and the slowly emerging norm is that sellers inform their customer what information and when the information is collected about them, disclose how it will be used, allow access to personal information for verification purposes, disclose safeguards for protecting customer information, and give customers a choice of either opting-in or opting-out of information collection (Department of Commerce, 1998).

3.5. Commodification

Commodification in the digital channel is usually beneficial to customers, but can be a challenge to vendors. The channel allows the widest group of buyers to be informed on current prices with the largest selection of similar offerings by merchants. One potential outcome is that it becomes remarkably easy for customers to shop on the basis of price, reducing previously differentiated products to commodities. Particularly when customers are seeking goods whose characteristics are widely understood (e.g., books, CDs, automobiles, etc.), it is a straightforward matter to find the lowest price on an item through a few clicks of the mouse. Some Web-based price comparison services (see, e.g., www.jango.com and www.mysimon.com) take a customer's request for a price on an item, send it to multiple vendors, and come back to the user within seconds with the lowest price. Services are not immune from this sort of price-based comparison; the insurance quote services www.quick-note.com and www.insweb.com, for example, allow easy comparison of term life insurance policies.

One of the only remedies available to fully transparent price comparison is the use of knowledge to differentiate products offered at a particular site. The differentiation might involve transforming a commodity product to a knowledge-intensive product or service. Musicmaker (www.musicmaker.com), for example, allows a customer to choose artists and songs to create personalized CDs.

Differentiation might also involve augmenting the purchase process with knowledge. A user might search for books on Amazon.com, for example, because of its extensive book reviews and recommendations, even when books are available for slightly less elsewhere. Amazon's customer knowledge and information (e.g., recommendations of books based on past purchases, capturing mailing addresses of customers for the previous sale) make it easier for customers to purchase particular books, and its product knowledge helps them to choose the right book in the first place. It is possible, of course, for customers to get a free ride by consuming Amazon's knowledge and then buying the book elsewhere, but Amazon makes it easier to do the entire transaction on its site.

One experimental study on Internet-based wine shopping found that customers who were provided with product and consumption-related information were significantly less price sensitive than those customers who were not provided with such information (Lynch and Ariely, 1998). Degeratu and colleagues (1999) studied how price response in an online subscription grocery service differed from price response in traditional grocery stores. They found lower price sensitivity for several product categories in a relatively commodified industry. Similarly, Shankar and colleagues (1999) found in their study of online and offline customers of the hospitality industry that the Internet did not necessarily increase customer price sensitivity and price competition as long as the sellers offered information-rich Web sites that effectively transferred product knowledge to customers. Hence, in markets where the traditional marketing mix elements are becoming commodified, sellers can use customer knowledge to reduce the importance of price and strengthen their customer relationship by delivering convenience and interactivity.

3.6. Channel Conflict

For most organizations, e-commerce is one of several different distribution channels. Selling over the Web may compete with a direct sales force, distributors and resellers, or catalog and telephone sales, or it may complement these other channels (Peterson et al., 1997). Proliferation of undifferentiated channels may confuse customers, and new electronic channels may antagonize those who work with existing channels. One approach to reduce channel proliferation and conflict is to view that the electronic channel augments the other existing channels by cultivating knowledge-intensive relationships between the company and its customers. It may be difficult or uneconomical for sales representatives, for example, to collect large amounts of knowledge from customers or furnish substantial amounts of knowledge to customers.

The electronic channel never gets tired of transferring knowledge to customers, never furnishes undesired knowledge, and even allows company personnel to keep track of what knowledge the customer peruses. It may be much more efficient to remove sales personnel from the flow of knowledge: they can be a bottleneck for complex, technical sales processes. In several industries in which vendors are not yet comfortable with using digital channels to take orders (e.g., automobiles), the Web channel's primary role is one of transmitting product knowledge tailored to a customer. Of course, designating the electronic channel as the primary medium for knowledge-intensive activities with customers will not resolve all channel conflict problems, but it may be a start toward clarifying channel objectives and differences.

3.7. Disintermediation/Reintermediation

E-commerce has been discussed as a driver of disintermediation; because electronic channels are directly accessible to many customers, the potential exists for producers to bypass intermediaries and connect directly to their customers, and in the process lower transaction costs (e.g., Benjamin and Wigand, 1995). According to the transaction cost model (Williamson, 1975), intermediaries add costs to the value chain, which are then reflected in higher final prices to customers. Benjamin and Wigand (1995) illustrate how the retail price in the high-quality shirt market would be reduced by almost 62 percent if wholesalers and retailers were eliminated. Analysis of the grocery industry reveals similar benefits if the many intermediaries were eliminated (Rifkin, 1997).

While some industries (e.g., air travel) have seen disintermediation through electronic channels (Christiaanse, 1994), other industries (books, music, industrial products, automobiles) have seen the emergence of new electronic intermediaries. Intermediaries can also experience a loss of business from producers through electronic disintermediation if they do not maintain the desirability of existing business arrangements (Kambil and van Heck, 1998).

Knowledge management provides some of the richest opportunities for reintermediation in e-commerce (Bakos, 1997; Peterson et al., 1997; Kannan et al., 1998). Many cybermediaries will arise for the purpose of gathering, interpreting, and combining customer knowledge to sellers (Sarkar et al., 1998). These predictions are seconded by Kannan and colleagues (1998), who postulate the rapid rise of marketing information intermediaries—which provide value by researching customer needs, acquiring the relevant information products, managing intellectual properties and copyrights, authenticating information servers, and complementing, processing and adding value to information products. Bakos (1998) similarly describes the rise of electronic intermediaries that provide functions, such as matching of buyers and sellers, providing product information to buyers and marketing information to sellers, aggregating and integrating goods and components from multiple producer sites, providing trust relationships, and ensuring the integrity of markets.

In sum, intermediary channel structures can be created or maintained if they add value. Because intermediaries typically have more direct access to customers, customer knowledge can be gathered (Hagel and Rayport, 1997) and used to personalize marketing communications as well as product and service offerings. And because distribution intermediaries often distribute more than one producer's products, they can include customer-accessible comparisons of products on their Internet or extranet sites. Examples of such intermediaries are directories, search services, online malls with automated ordering services and order consolidation, virtual resellers, and rating services (Peterson et al., 1997). Of course, producers can use some of the same approaches to provide more value than intermediaries; the dynamics of channel relationships may be largely based on whether direct or indirect channels provide the greater level of knowledge intensity.

4. Challenges to Customer Knowledge Management and Some Recommendations for Overcoming Them

Although e-commerce can be used to cultivate more knowledge-intensive relationships, this is not always easy to bring about. Several barriers must be overcome before knowledge can successfully be gathered, analyzed, distributed, and reused between buyers and sellers in electronic environments. Some of these may be more problematic than others for specific types of products or services. Table 3-1 summarizes the challenges.

Suppliers' Viewpoint	Customers' Viewpoint
• Pricing knowledge	• Value or payoff to the customer
• Ensuring fair exchange value to customers	• Fairness of the process
• Data integration and maintenance issues	• Negative disclosure
• Sense-making abilities	• Trust
• Sharing and innovation culture in the organization	
• Negative knowledge disclosure	
• Trust	

Table 3-1. Challenges.

The barriers revolve around four conditions that are frequently cited as critical for knowledge creation, transfer, or use (e.g., Nonaka and Takeuchi, 1995; Menon and Varadarajan, 1992; Frenzen and Nakamoto, 1993; Kim and Mauborgne, 1998; Nahapiet and Ghoshal, 1998; Moorman et al., 1992; Szulanski, 1996). The conditions are:

1. The parties must be able to anticipate the benefits of the information disclosure and processing to be greater than the costs.
2. The knowledge sharing process must be fair.
3. The technical, human, and organizational capabilities to access, combine, and utilize the knowledge must exist.
4. Social and technical mechanisms must exist for safeguarding customer knowledge.

4.1. Value to Customers

It is usually the case that sellers find it easier to anticipate the value from managing customer knowledge than buyers disclosing the information that leads to that knowledge. Hence, for buyers to feel that it is worthwhile for them to disclose information, they must be provided with incentives. Customers are assumed to place economic value on the information that is generated through transacting, communicating, and collaborating with them and are willing to release this information if they can profit by doing so (e.g., compensation, gifts, coupons, rebates, special offers). Airlines' frequent flyer programs are a prime example of customers' "economic calculus" at play. Customers' perceptions of the value of their contributions to this calculus have been predicted to be especially high in e-commerce because of the tremendous value of personal customer information to sellers (Hagel and Rayport, 1997).

The "economic calculus" arguments assume that at some level, the customer can estimate the value of information before it is shared. However, this explanation has its limitations: The value of information and particularly of knowledge can be often determined for either party only after it has been shared and acted upon. Moreover, there is evidence that people will accept outcomes that are not in their economic favor and commit personal sacrifices in terms of personal time and effort (Rumelt et al., 1991). On the Internet, many electronic communities are a prime example of individual behavior driven in search of social and community benefits rather than short-term economic benefits (Wellman et al., 1996).

But, whether it is about economic or social benefits, the reciprocity principle suggests that sellers must ensure that customers get something in return for sharing information. Currently there are two basic incentive approaches offered in return for personal information on the Internet (Kannan et al., 1998)—although variations of these are rapidly proliferating. The first approach, a *pay-for-performance model*, builds on the "economic calculus" principle. The model asks members to provide demographic and product/service information and they are paid in cash or bonus points for interacting with advertisements and providing product information. The second, a *community model*, provides free services such as e-mail access, chat groups, news, weather, magazines, and other services that provide a community experience in return for customers providing demographic and product/service preferences. The communities expose customers passively to advertisements and new products and seek their comments (Kannan et al., 1998). Epinions.com is one such service.

From the seller perspective, Kannan and colleagues (1998) argue for the superiority of the community model. The community model fosters more loyalty because a community of friends is at stake, and the pay-for-performance model leads to more switching as customers pursue more favorable incentives. From the buyer perspective, the community model is also superior for its free services (Kannan et al., 1998).

4.2. Cost to Sellers

For customers, the out-of-pocket cost of sharing information is usually less of an issue than for sellers because at stake are easily available information or knowledge about the customer's identity, situation, or preferences. For sellers, the cost of providing something worth exchanging can take at least two different forms.

First and most commonly, the seller offers knowledge in return for knowledge, but that knowledge can be expensive in multiple respects. A knowledge base about products and services, for example, is usually expensive to create and to maintain. Content management is a labor-intensive activity (Meyer and Zack, 1996). Even when customers and channel partners are providing content (as is the case with reader reviews and publisher-provided book descriptions on Amazon.com), it still may take considerable effort to structure, format, prune, and police the contributed knowledge. Giving away product and service knowledge to customers may also mean unavoidably giving it to competitors as well—another form of cost. Finally, giving away knowledge online may reduce sales of knowledge-based products in other media. Most newspapers, for example, also have free Web sites, and they often hold back important news items for their paying print customers.

Sellers through digital channels can also give away actual products or services in return for customer information; giving away information products is a common means of demonstrating value (Shapiro and Varian, 1999). In most cases, this will take the form of smaller or less sophisticated versions of the real product or service for sale. In the computer game industry, for example, it is common for vendors to give away versions of games that have been "hobbled" in some fashion: how long they may be played, how many levels on which they can be played, and so on. Books listed on the *New York Times* best seller Web page often give away the first chapter online.

The risk here, of course, is that customers receive sufficient content to satisfy their desire, and then do not buy the larger product or service. In fact, sharing knowledge with the customer hardly ever makes economic sense in the short term. Sharing is best considered as an investment to strengthen the relationship with a customer. Sellers should therefore reframe the cost of knowledge sharing as the investment to strengthen long-term brand value in the relationship.

4.3. Fair Disclosure to Customer

Although customer knowledge management practices are targeted to provide value to customers, they also raise concerns of privacy to customers. "Personal information is information identifiable to an individual" and "Privacy is the ability of the individual to control the terms under which personal information is acquired and used" (Culnan and Armstrong, 1998).

Most of the concern about privacy comes from customers who are wary of vendors using the data or information they supply in an exploitive manner (Hoffman and Novak, 1997). Several high profile cases have occurred where information about customers has been gathered without their knowledge or without full disclosure of the data collection's purpose—resulting in an outcry of customer complaints (e.g., Real Networks, DoubleClick). In surveys of customers involving database marketing (Godwin, 1991; Culnan, 1995), it is clear that they do not want to sacrifice their privacy to sellers. The August 2000 *National Consumer Survey* suggested that:

- ❏ 88 percent of consumers say privacy policies that guarantee privacy encourage them to register on a Web site and provide personal information.
- ❏ 87 percent say such policies encourage them to purchase products or services online.

❑ 74 percent say such policies encourage them to use the Internet more in general.

Privacy policies articulate the *extent* to which a company wants to collect and use personal information and the *manner* in which a company collects, uses, and protects data, as well as the choices offered to consumers to exercise rights in their personal information. The Federal Trade Commission's "fair information practices" provide the baseline for constructing such policies. They address the key components that should be covered in any corporate privacy policy:

❑ *Notice/Awareness:* a Web site is required to provide consumers notice of their information practices, such as what information they collect and how they use it. Notice addresses whether the company allows third-party use or sale of the personal information. The disclosures need to be stated clearly and be easily readable by all customers from different demographic backgrounds.

❑ *Choice/Consent:* Web sites are required to offer consumers choices as to how that information is used beyond the use for which the information was provided (e.g., to consummate a transaction). Choice addresses opt-in versus opt-out and whether cookies are used or not used on the site.

❑ *Access/Participation:* Web sites are required to offer consumers reasonable access to that information and an opportunity to correct inaccuracies. Access requires excellent database management and Web log management from a Web site.

❑ *Security/Integrity:* Web sites are required to take reasonable steps to protect the security and integrity of that information. Security entails data encryption outside the corporate firewall.

Many companies such as Dell have explicitly addressed these four fair information practices on their Web sites. Particularly, a new seller on the Internet must carefully construct its privacy policies to maximize comfort to a customer.

4.4. Knowledge Utilization

Another barrier to successful knowledge management is the seller's difficulty in utilizing the knowledge contributions made by customers. The information that is typically supplied by customers, whether voluntary or through clicks on Web pages, is in primitive form. To turn this data into knowledge requires several important human, technical, and organizational components (Davenport et al., 2001):

❏ People who understand the data, the business objectives of data analysis, and the analytical tools (e.g., statistical) to add meaning to the data

❏ A stable data environment combining transaction data and demographic information about customers

❏ The software and hardware environment in which to store and analyze the data

❏ An organization with a culture that promotes the active exchange of ideas and increased communication and knowledge flows

The technical requirements for turning Web transaction data into knowledge are often met, but in many cases the human and organizational requirements are lacking. Companies may not plan or budget for human analytical and sense-making capabilities because they believe that technology alone can do the work. Similarly, the availability of technology is often assumed to automatically induce an organizational climate that promotes information and knowledge sharing (Davenport, 1997). In fact, creating the organizational and human capabilities is likely to be more difficult than creating the technological capabilities. Sellers should therefore begin now to invest proactively in human and organizational capabilities of knowledge use from e-commerce, not just in technological capabilities.

4.5. Negative Knowledge Disclosure

A specific problematic area in e-commerce concerns one aspect of the nature of information, that is, the disclosure of negative information or knowledge. The most likely scenario of this type is when a customer posts negative information about a vendor in a discussion group or on a personal Web site. This is a frequent problem, for example, on customer service Web sites (Sterne, 1996), where customers may criticize vendors for poor service or product quality. One well-known example is negative reviews by customers of books sold over Amazon.com. Sterne argues that it is important for vendors not to censor negative comments because openness for negative comments builds consumer trust in the seller's objectivity, though this is surely a deterrent to some vendors considering such forums with customers. Another challenge may be internal; negative information may be discounted or ignored regardless of its quality. Sellers must develop an approach to negative information disclosure and be careful that it does not get out of hand.

5. An Agenda for Practice

Little of what constitutes knowledge management today in e-commerce has been undertaken with a clear understanding of its implications and permutations. Instead, companies engaged in electronic commerce are experimenting with multiple approaches to the issue, and attempting to learn from their initial experiences. We encourage companies to experiment and carefully measure how their customer knowledge activities lead to greater customer loyalty, higher purchase levels, higher satisfaction rates, and so forth. We have only seen the tip of the iceberg on how good customer knowledge management can affect customer relationships.

A key domain for experimentation is the area of consumer/ customer attitudes and behavior for information sharing. As yet we know little about the conditions where customers will furnish customer knowledge, their sensitivities to what companies do with the knowledge, and how much they are willing to invest in a relationship based on deep knowledge about them. Since the entire field of e-commerce has largely been driven not by what consumers desire but by what technology makes possible, there is a large gap in our understanding of Internet-based consumer behavior.

Over the past one or two years, many software vendors have begun to offer tools that supply customized knowledge to customers on demand. This technical capability can be used to differentiate products and services, to improve customer service, or even to enhance revenues through the selling of knowledge. Few companies have yet to make use of such software in their e-commerce initiatives.

Entirely apart from new technical capabilities for customer knowledge management, as stated above, a major opportunity lies in taking better advantage of the customer data and information—already being captured in electronic commerce environments—that is not currently being analyzed or otherwise turned into knowledge. The largely human ability to analyze data, make decisions, and act on customer data has been de-emphasized relative to new analytical approaches (e.g., neural networks and data mining) and automated approaches to customer-specific marketing (e.g., collaborative filtering). We believe that many companies could profit substantially from building up their general capability for turning customer data into customer knowledge.

6. Conclusion

The Web provides new opportunities for knowledge-intensive customer–supplier relationships. The Web not only enables faster and more accurate product customization to the individual, but also higher levels of personalization in communications between the seller and merchant. Outside of the Internet, knowledge-intensive relationships have been labeled as synonymous to the value of customer relationships (Evans and Wurster, 1997), as the determining source of brand acceptance and loyalty (McKenna, 1995), as the only way to ensure that a new product "on Internet time" is not obsolete by the time it is introduced (Iansiti and Mac Cormack, 1997), and as the way to turn your satisfied customers into completely satisfied customers who do not defect (Jones and Sasser, 1995; Pine et al., 1995). We can only echo these benefits to e-commerce.

But developing effective customer knowledge management practices in e-commerce is not without challenges. Vendors will have to develop strategies for knowledge development, content management over time, and approaches to knowledge-based community building. Customers will have to develop their own norms about when to share their own knowledge with vendors, and how to use a vendor's knowledge effectively in their own situations. Both parties and the larger society will have to develop new approaches to what constitutes a fair knowledge exchange, and how violators of fair policy should be treated.

Chapter 4

KNOWLEDGE MANAGEMENT: THE SOURCE OF INNOVATION?

Dr. Svenja Falk
Accenture, Frankfurt, Germany

1. Introduction

In 2000 alone, more than one hundred books were published on Knowledge Management. Countless dissertations and papers have been written on this topic, based on the premise that knowledge has become the most valuable resource in an economy based on intangible assets. Furthermore, the emerging global market demands an accelerating speed in innovation, which is identified as the main source of real competitive advantage. Empirical findings from various studies supported the argument that poor management of intellectual commodities could lead to a

Special thanks to Caroline Jacobs for helping me have four rather than one sentence on one page, to Michael M. Mackey for patiently explaining the Mackey-Glass equation, and to Rolf Henkel for his truly innovative thoughts.

loss of revenues and market share. Highly regarded analysts have calculated that over half of employees' skills become outdated in three to five years. IDC has stated that U.S. *Fortune 500* companies today lose $12 billion annually due to inefficient Knowledge Management; this will reach $31 billion by 2003 (IDC, 2000).

For the past two decades companies have been exploring the question of how to preserve and develop the competitive assets originating from their human capital, which they only own for a limited—and decreasing—amount of time. Many companies tried to institutionalize the creation of new ideas in specific departments, as well as documenting almost every byte of knowledge and information through tools and processes provided by Knowledge Management. The assumption was that the faster ideas translate into business value, the greater the competitive advantage that can be preserved. In markets evolving from transnational to global, this resulted in a strong focus on innovation, considered to be originating directly from knowledge creation. Therefore, the delivery of the right knowledge to the right place for the right person needed to be supported by a process and an organizational entity to ensure competitive advantage. To facilitate innovation, "Knowledge Management" became the well-known secret weapon for coping with the challenges associated with the transformation from the industrial to the knowledge economy.

Professional services firms like management consultancies were the first to recognize the importance of managing their knowledge assets. The major consultancies, which are typically global organizations selling mainly strategy and organizational expertise, made strategic decisions in the 1980s to invest in Knowledge Management. At that time, Knowledge Management was commonly understood to be the collection and storage of documents using the technological infrastructure provided by groupware like Lotus Notes. Since then, however, far more sophisticated Knowledge Management organizations have become widespread. Elaborate processes for the capture, storage, and distribution of knowledge by professionals with clearly defined roles and responsibilities have been developed and supported by rapid/major technological advancements. According to analysts Ovum, companies today spend $4 billion on Knowledge Management services and are expected to spend $10.5

billion by 2004 (Ovum, 2000). However, the return on the high investments into knowledge organizations and infrastructure is increasingly
questioned. The notion that knowledge creation is a prerequisite for
innovation is well accepted, but there are increasing doubts about
whether there is a clear correlation between the existence of dedicated
knowledge management organizations as we know them today and higher margins, greater market share, or more patents.

2. What Do Knowledge Organizations Look Like Today?

Companies mainly use one of two approaches to capturing and sharing
knowledge: a codification or a personalization strategy (Hansen et al.,
1999). The codification strategy tends to be used by companies offering
more or less standardized products, which therefore focus on capturing
as much knowledge as possible on a specific topic to truly bring the right
document to the right person. Companies that offer their clients personalized and innovative solutions tend to follow the personalization strategy, which focuses on bringing the right people together. Whichever strategy is adopted, knowledge organizations contain the same components
to a more or less elaborate extent, whether we talk about Accenture's
"Knowledge Xchange," Ernst & Young's "Kweb," or Lotus' "People,
Places, Things" (Duder, 2000). The main objective is always both virtually and physically to link individuals to documents, or individuals to each
other or to create communities. Aligned to the strategy of the enterprise,
all Knowledge Management organizations share the intention to integrate business processes and culture as well as the organization with the
technology at hand. From a technical point of view, they are all built on
groupware-based knowledge repositories in their intranets, and they have
document management systems of varying sophistication, expert directories and workflow, and virtual teaming applications.

2.1. Case Study: Accenture

Accenture started thinking about building a knowledge infrastructure in
the 1980s and began implementing a Lotus Notes–based Knowledge
Management system in 1992 (Falk, 2000). The knowledge infrastructure

was used intensively right from the beginning, as employees began putting everything that they subjectively considered being of value into the databases. This led to information overflow and to duplication and redundancies within the information stored. Therefore, the architecture as well as the design was globally standardized and the process for contribution of documents formalized. Today, the Knowledge Xchange system allows approximately 70,000 consulting and other professionals globally to use and share project methodologies, frameworks, and approaches.

Accenture's strategy is to identify, capture, and deploy best practice project content in sales cycles and current engagements. The focus is on re-using as much knowledge as possible, based on the assumption that problems are more or less similar. The content is collected at the close of a project using the same technology with which it is accessed. The repositories are organized around the organizational structure of the consulting practice. Project Teams, Communities of Practice, or locally based initiatives launch databases whenever they intend to facilitate information sharing or need storage. Therefore, more than 3,600 databases exist within the Knowledge Xchange system. Out of those, around seventy are used intensively on a global scale, while the others service particular groups of people.

Nearly 250 knowledge managers are responsible for reviewing the content contributed to these databases and selecting examples of best practices with the support of subject matter experts. From the vast ocean of information the best pieces are synthesized and stored in homepages built around topic areas. Discussion databases provide a forum to discuss problems in real time; expert directories help identify the firm's experts; repositories for methodology provide materials to help with training and skills enhancement.

The replication function provided by Lotus Notes allows mobile consultants to access the freshest content from each of the 150 offices worldwide while working at a client's site, in a hotel room, or at home. The value that this infrastructure brings includes increased speed at client engagements as well as increased innovation. Accenture has adopted a codification strategy with the goal of bringing documents to people in a very short time.

2.2. Case Study: McKinsey

McKinsey launched a Knowledge Management project in 1987 to meet the challenges resulting from the accelerating growth of the company and the increasing competition in strategic consulting (Bartlett, 2000). They started building repositories for deliverables from client work, populated and maintained by a practice coordinator, who acted as an "intelligent switch" between the employees and the databases. The Firm Practice Information System (FPIS) contained information on client engagements, while the Practice Development Network (PDNet) was the central resource for documents containing the core knowledge of individual consultants. The Knowledge Resource Directory (KRD) listed the firm's experts in practice areas and identified the core documents for specific topics. In contrast to the experience at Accenture, McKinsey staff were slow to adopt these database solutions. The main problem was that anything that appeared to be a standardized solution or a proprietary concept was never going to be accepted by the McKinsey consultants, who pride themselves on providing unique solutions specifically tailored to clients' differing needs. Consequently, the repository-based "discover-codify-disseminate" model was changed into an "engage-explore-apply-share" approach, which focused on the facilitation of collective learning and team building around subject areas.

Whereas Accenture's consultants welcomed the intranet-based knowledge-sharing approach, regarding the time spent searching targeted databases for the right expert, document, or framework as critical to avoid reinventing the wheel, McKinsey's consultants perceived the time spent in this pursuit as time that could be better spent thinking creatively about the problem in hand. With this approach, dedicated knowledge management professionals are more likely to be part of the human resource department, specializing in bringing people to people. The value from this personalization strategy is seen as helping to foster team building and integration within the company. Furthermore, face-to-face interaction with the person with the right skills and knowledge is considered to be the best source of valuable, innovative solutions to clients' problems.

2.3. Codification or Personalization?

Companies using the codification strategy are facing the problem of information overflow and the increasing difficulty of structuring the vast collections of documents. On the other hand, those adopting only the personalization strategy cannot cope with the challenge of speed in the "new economy." Bringing together people with the right skills to address business problems in the global economy—ideally in real time—is very time consuming as well as cost intensive. However, whatever the approach is, the main challenge remains translating the significant efforts involved in effective knowledge management into sustained competitiveness and innovation. Furthermore, the growing ranks of self-enabled employees do not seem to appreciate Knowledge Management organizations in their existing form (see Alfs, Chapter 9, in this book).

3. Journeys into the Anatomy of Innovation

"Science is rooted in conversations," wrote Werner Heisenberg, one of the twentieth century's great physicists. Scientists' dialogues can be based on the same premises for a very long time, can be painful, boring, going around in circles, or containing redundancies often hidden by the number of footnotes added to a text. Advancements can be slow and scientific problems can sometimes seem to be solved, finished, exhausted. The notion that everything has already been discovered and there is nothing left to investigate pops up time and again in all scientific fields (Horgan, 1997). Until, all of a sudden, somebody comes up with an idea, an approach, or just a simple question that challenges existing paradigms in a compelling way. In the early 1900s, for example, students were advised not to study physics because everything of interest had already been explored in detail. Twenty years later quantum mechanics and the theory of relativity revolutionized the way physics problems were addressed.

Innovation creates new perspectives or uncovers new questions that need to be answered. Innovators spark new and emphatic discussions about their thoughts, triggering the creation of new knowledge rewriting the previously accepted wisdom.

The same is obviously true for innovation in business, although here the complexity of the system creates a different dynamic. In the business world, where the creation of new products or services has become crucial, the outcomes of innovation can be measured: Key performance indicators (KPIs)—such as the number of patents or new products per year or the percentage of revenues from new products—are compelling reasons for companies to invest in managing their intellectual capital to more efficiently create value. Hewlett-Packard, for example, developed more than 75 percent of the equipment it sold in 2000 during the preceding three years. According to a study by the Product Development & Management Association, sales of new products were expected to account for 37 percent of total sales globally in 2000 (PDMA, 2000).

However, innovation is a much broader term in business than in science because it does not focus on one specific question to be solved and touches every part of the organizational structure. Companies are increasingly addressing this challenge by opening departments for innovation management to ensure that all organizational entities are keeping up with the pace of innovation cycles. This group defines and formalizes the nature and speed of innovation required and the objective—which is ultimately competitive advantage, through bringing products to market faster in the most cost-effective way. Innovation management basically aims to translate the creation of knowledge into business output. Despite some proven wins, managing innovation remains a challenge. A study on innovation management among German and British manufacturing companies based on the performance data of nearly 200 companies, as well as qualitative interviews with more than eighty managers, showed that companies that tried to accelerate the pace of innovation were likely to get caught out, as increasing the number of projects in research and development did not create increased output—in fact, it had the opposite effect (Goffin/Pfeiffer, 2000).

Clearly, it is difficult to trigger the creation of innovation. Whether in academic think tanks, research and development departments, or incubators, the ideal circumstances for generating predictable outputs simply do not exist. What can we say about the intentions of both scientists and business people who can claim for them having created a truly new approach?

3.1. In Science

In 1977, Michael C. Mackey and Leon Glass proposed a new type of differential equation in an effort to model the dynamics of white blood cell production in the human body. Since biological processes are composed of complicated, interacting production cycles, a sudden change of one variable is generally only visible in the dynamics of the system after a certain time delay. Therefore Mackey and Glass introduced a time delay as a new prime component of their equation. This seemingly small change in the equation caused a dramatic change in the dynamic behavior: Complicated dynamic trajectories and even chaos can be obtained as solutions of the Mackey-Glass equation. In the end, the dynamic turned out to be a more complicated system than the equation assumed, and the problem addressed was never solved fully.

Over time, the equation lost the connection with the original research subject, namely white blood cell production. Nowadays it is widely used as a prototypical system for chaotic dynamics and as a test tool for time series prediction. The Mackey-Glass equation became very well known both within and outside the scientific community and has been successfully applied to a number of analytical problems. Therefore, although the problem originally addressed by the two scientists from McGill University in Montreal was never fully solved, their innovation actually became a powerful analytical tool for approaching various scientific questions outside of their original sphere.

3.2. In Business

In 1969 the Japanese calculator manufacturer Busicom asked Intel to design a set of chips for a family of programmable calculators. The original design required a twelve-chip solution, but at that time Intel did not have the manpower to design a twelve-chip set. So Intel Design Engineer Ted Hoff opted for a bold step: Instead of twelve separate special-purpose chips, Intel would design a single, general-purpose logic chip. Although initially skeptical, Busicom agreed to this and awarded Intel a $60,000 contract. The project was completed successfully after nine months, and the chip was delivered to Busicom.

At some point however, Intel obviously realized that they had developed a truly revolutionary piece of hardware. Whereas previously integrated circuits used in household appliances or industrial applications had to be specially developed and manufactured for every new application, the new general purpose Intel chip could simply be reprogrammed to fit a specific purpose. Eventually, Intel offered Busicom the chips for a lower than agreed price, in return for securing the rights to the design. Busicom agreed, and Intel conducted a major marketing campaign to raise awareness and gain acceptance of their new product for generic engineering applications. The following year, Busicom went bankrupt, but the new chip was soon found in everything from machines to traffic lights. It was even used in the *Pioneer 10* spacecraft, which was launched in 1972 and is still exploring the outer regions of the solar system. Within a few years, the microprocessor, as the new chip was now called, was also being manufactured in *similar designs* by other companies.

By the mid-1970s, hobbyists and small start-up companies realized that microprocessors could be used to build "home computers," small-scale replicas of the huge mainframe computer systems employed at that time. Pioneers in this field were Commodore, Radio Shack, and Apple Computers.

These early home computers were not based on Intel chips, but on other designs. This changed in 1981, when IBM, which until then had been building only mainframes, stepped into the home computer market. Despite the fact that other chip manufacturers offered more advanced microprocessor chips, IBM opted to use the Intel-8086(8) chip for their "personal computer"—probably because they owned the production rights.

Because IBM used an open architecture and refrained from using special chips like the small computer manufacturers in the market, other companies were able to produce personal computer clones as well as component parts. The first movers, still using their proprietary chips, were losing market share (with the exception of the Apple Macintosh). This resulted in a de-facto standardization of the IBM PC with "an Intel inside." Market explosion followed standardization, and the rest is history.

So a new piece of hardware, originally "invented" as a way to secure a contract that was otherwise impossible to fulfill, became through historic twists and quite unpredictable circumstances the cornerstone of the most interesting market since the 1970s, and also the basis for an economic revolution with as yet unknown consequences for society as a whole.

4. Key Learnings

These two case studies from science and business show how difficult it might be to group knowledge organizations around people's intentions of being innovative. How can we know that they are really addressing a problem that requires innovative thought? How can we be sure that the right people address certain issues? How do we ensure that the approach of addressing a scientific or a business problem is really the right one? The answer is simple: There is no way to do so and therefore no real business case exists to establish an institutionalized organizational entity around the intention of being an innovator.

Creating an environment for solving complex scientific problems or finding a new innovative approach to a business model can kill innovation right away. Numerous more or less pejorative remarks have been made about scientific think tanks, and millions of dollars have been spent unsuccessfully on incubators and the like. Therefore, it seems extremely unlikely that people can come together in whatever environment with the express intention of being innovative.

Knowledge Management is a very powerful tool for harvesting, storing, and accessing company knowledge, which might trigger the right thought at the right time. Also, conversations at selected locations might sometimes help to bring a number of diffuse ideas together in a powerful new way. Anyhow, three things need to be considered:

❑ The half-life of Knowledge is decreasing.
❑ The Knowledge worker is a self-enabled user of information.
❑ Innovation does not follow on the heels of information technology.

Innovation comes into existence through conversations, fights, uncertainty, and doubt, and it can also simply be the powerful result of the wrong idea at the right time, or vice versa. Furthermore, creativity is not simply an instantaneous "eureka" experience, but is the—both actual and imagined—process of addressing the ideas of others.

Therefore:

1. Don't overdo the institutionalization of arenas for innovation within the firm; employees or scientists will themselves find the right place to innovate. Rather, allow people to take time out to build up their skills, and to work or learn in a different environment for a period of time to ensure they are developing a different perspective on various business problems.

2. Don't expect your Knowledge Management organization to be the source of innovation. Rather, make sure that dedicated content experts are available to help get the best from a sophisticated document management system. Make the system user-friendly and value-adding: Knowledge workers will not use nor advocate the use of a system that is illogical or difficult to use.

3. Don't expect innovation to be the result of fantastic ideas out of the blue. Rather, focus on generating new insights from research-based analysis to better understand markets, services, and products.

4. Don't only rely on the pockets of excellence within your firm. Rather, build alliances with partners that allow the "stranger's perspective" on what your company is trying to achieve.

Chapter 5

MAKING SENSE OF THE eCONOMY

Entrepreneurial Strategic Thinking and Acting as Theory Building and Theory Testing under Ambiguity

Dr. Simon Grand
Institute for Management, University of
St. Gallen, Switzerland

1. Introduction

1.1. Technological Innovation, Strategy Formation, and Entrepreneurial Strategizing

Technological innovation and the emergence of new businesses are ambiguous by nature: New market opportunities are created, while established industries are challenged (Dosi, 1982; Dosi, Teece, and Chytry, 1998); new core competencies have to be built, while existing core competencies turn into core rigidities (Henderson and Clark, 1990; Leonard-Barton, 1992; Teece, Pisano, and Shuen, 1997); disruptive technologies emerge, while the dominant knowledge architecture is questioned (Christensen, 1995). Strategy formation in these circumstances is thus subject to multiple kinds of uncertainties, ambiguities, and complexities.

73

While the large incumbent companies can rely on their strategy process-es to come to appropriate strategic responses, entrepreneurial new ven-tures must first and foremost build up strategizing capabilities in order to respond to such environmental challenges.

Established strategy processes allow incumbent firms to deal with uncertain and ambiguous situations in a structured way (Utterback, 1994; Dosi, Teece, and Chytry 1998; Cohen and Levinthal, 1990; Levinthal 1995). These processes delineate the appropriate procedures to define and evaluate strategic options, according to the competencies, worldviews, and value systems of the company (for an overview, see Pettigrew, 1992; Van de Ven, 1992; Eisenhardt and Zbaracki, 1991; Chakravarthy and Doz, 1992). At the same time, they limit the range of possible responses (Foster, 1986; Andersen and Tushman, 1986; Henderson and Clark 1990; Bower and Christensen, 1995; Christensen, 1995), imposing past strategic com-mitments, organizational rigidities, and path-dependencies (see also Leonard-Barton. 1992). Entrepreneurial new ventures on the other hand do not dispose of such established processes and routines. This provides them with a high degree of flexibility, while at the same time making it difficult to make structured and explicit strategic decisions.

1.2. Rational Decision Making and Strategy Process Research

Strategy formation is by its very nature subject to multiple kinds of uncertainties, ambiguities, and complexities (Szulanski and Doz, 1995). Yet, strategy formation is predominantly understood by strategy research as being the outcome of a more or less limited rational decision-making process (for an overview, see Eisenhardt and Zbaracki, 1992; March, 1994; Rumelt, Schendel, and Teece, 1994). This is problematic to the extent that rationality fails to be specified in uncertain and ambiguous situations (Knight, 1921; Alchian, 1950; March, 1994), because the means necessary for evaluating a priori whether the reasoning behind a decision or an action is valid are lacking (Gomez and Jones, 2001).

Therefore, the rationalist approaches are paralleled by an impressive body of work in strategy process research (overview by Pettigrew, 1992; Chakravarthy and Doz, 1992; Eisenhardt and Zbaracki, 1992), challeng-ing such simplified conceptualizations (Allison, 1971; Mintzberg, 1994).

In this perspective, strategy is emergent (Mintzberg, 1978; Quinn, 1980; Mintzberg and Waters, 1985), forming patterns of decisions and actions distributed across multiple organizational levels (cf. Mintzberg and McHugh, 1985), only partially shaped by managerial intentions. They insist on the interpretative character of strategic orientation (Ginsberg, 1994; Ocasio, 1997) as well as the structural embeddedness of strategic decisions (Granovetter, 1992; Barnett and Burgelman, 1996).

While the first approach overstates the objective value of deliberate thinking and rational planning (Eisenhardt and Zbaracki, 1992; Mintzberg, 1994), the second under-emphasizes the coherence of rational strategic actions emerging within most companies, despite the impact of cognitive limitations, power constellations, and context-specific biases (Ginsberg, 1994). As a consequence, various contributions argue for understanding these different perspectives as alternative analytical lenses with their specific focus (Burrell and Morgan, 1979; Schoemaker, 1993), finally combined in the mundane managerial practice. Although such theoretical pluralism seems highly laudable and analytically fruitful, it leads to ambiguous descriptions and conflicting predictions (Grand, 1997). This is especially problematic in situations of uncertainty and ambiguity, characteristic of companies facing disruptive technologies (Christensen, 1995), fast changing environments (Bourgeois and Eisenhardt, 1988), emergent industries (Roos and von Krogh, 1994), and contradicting competitive situations (Stone and Brush, 1996). However, these circumstances, typical for innovative and entrepreneurial situations, are of increasing interest to strategy research.

1.3. Strategy Formation as Dynamic Capability

Recent contributions in the tradition of the resource-based view share this conclusion, extending the existing frameworks toward an explicit consideration of dynamic markets (Teece, Pisano, and Shuen, 1997). The rationale is that the resource-based view does not adequately explain how and why certain firms gain competitive advantages in situations of uncertainty and ambiguity, due to rapid and unpredictable change (Eisenhardt and Martin, 2000). Dynamic capabilities (Teece, Pisano, and Shuen, 1997) are the managerial, organizational, and strategic competencies to acquire, shed, integrate, and recombine resources to create new value-creating strategies (Pisano, 1994; Grant, 1996; Eisenhardt and Martin, 2000).

This definition of dynamic capabilities corresponds to our understanding of the strategy process:

> ...dynamic capabilities as the firm's processes that use resources—specifically the processes to integrate, reconfigure, gain and release resources—to match and even create market change.
>
> (Eisenhardt and Martin, 2000)

They lead to new resource configurations as markets emerge, collide, split, and evolve [similar concepts in the scientific literature are 'combinative capabilities' (see Kogut and Zander, 1992), 'capabilities' (see Amit and Schoemaker, 1993), and 'architectural competencies' (see Henderson and Cockburn, 1994].

Despite the significance of the approach, it has been challenged for being conceptually vague and tautological (Williamson, 1999), focused on intangible and hard to observe concepts (Grant, 1996; Spender, 1996), inattentive to the underlying mechanisms by which resources and competencies are actually built (as exceptions see Henderson, 1994; McGrath, MacMillan, and Venkataraman, 1995; Zollo and Winter, 1999), and unclear about the ways in which it contributes to competitive advantage (Cockburn, Henderson, and Stern, 2000). An in-depth understanding of the emergence, development, and routinization of entrepreneurial strategizing will thus contribute to a more tangible analysis of dynamic capabilities (Eisenhardt and Martin, 2000).

As a consequence, the present chapter argues for a theoretical perspective that focuses on the ways in which rational decision making and embedded strategy processes are co-existing in organizational settings (Szulanski and Doz, 1995), as well as on how they result in the formation of strategic capabilities. Organizational realities and strategic issues are seen as inherently uncertain and ambiguous, due to contradicting interpretations and conflicting interests within and between competing companies (Spender, 1989; 1996). Strategy research needs to understand how strategy processes deal with these uncertainties and ambiguities in order to promote valuable strategic initiatives and form successful strategic activities.

1.4. Strategy Formation as Theory Building and Theory Testing

In this line of thought, it is interesting to observe that strategy and innovation research draw various conceptual parallels with the new studies of science, exploiting the similarity between an iterative, problem solving oriented view of strategizing and an evolutionary perspective of scientific theory building and testing. Strategizing is understood as an organizational process of theory building and theory testing.

The research interest of the new studies of science consists of better understanding of how scientific theories are actually built in mundane research practices and scientific discourses (Elkana, 1986; Lynch, 1993; Galison, 1997; Latour, 1987; 1998; Knorr Cetina, 1999). In this line of argument, they deal with theoretical issues that are of relevance to strategy research: the creation and transfer of revolutionary new knowledge through established discursive processes and institutional settings; the interpretation and sensemaking processes taking place in the face of new, surprising, ambiguous insights and data; and the translation of local experiences and specific observations in the laboratory into explicit scientific arguments and discourses in the scientific community.

Based on these contributions, strategy formation under uncertainty and ambiguity can be re-interpreted as an organizational sensemaking, theory building, and theory testing process. We exploit the similarity between an iterative, problem solving oriented view of the strategy process, focusing on the interplay between rationalization in managerial discourses and strategic initiatives through situated activities, and an evolutionary perspective of scientific theory building and testing as the interplay between scientific discourses and local research activities (for similar ideas, see Weick, 1989; 1995; Szulanski and Doz, 1995).

1.5. Structure of the Argument

First, the chapter discusses how strategy research defines uncertainty and ambiguity, as well as why rational decision making fails in situations of uncertainty and ambiguity. We analyze some premises of the predominant contributions in strategy process research. The chapter argues that the conceptual dichotomy between strategic thinking and acting, underlying almost all approaches in the field, becomes increasingly problematic under these conditions.

Second, the chapter transcends this dichotomy by analyzing rationality in strategy formation as the result of ex-post rationalization (Weick, 1995), explication, and justification practices (von Krogh and Grand, 1998). Strategic actions are not dependent on rational decisions alone, but refer to the question of whether management is able to rationalize patterns of strategic action as being reasonable to relevant others (Gioia and Chittipetti, 1991; Gomez and Jones, 2001). This is consistent with the more recent conceptualization of theory building as a discursive process in the studies of science (Foucault, 1971; Latour, 1987; Galison, 1997). Furhermore, it corresponds to the insights of strategy process research (Pettigrew, 1992; Chakravarthy and Doz, 1992; Mintzberg, 1994) that managers spend considerable time communicating, explaining, and justifying the course of action of the firm (Mintzberg, 1973; 1978).

Third, we must admit that a major part of the ongoing activities and initiatives within the process of strategy formation are not explicable. They are never discussed because they are taken for granted (Meyer and Rowan, 1977). Any appropriate understanding of strategy formation thus has to consider the mundane practices of managerial discourses and strategic action, in order to understand how they are shifting the strategic orientation of the company (Bower, 1970; Burgelman, 1983a; 1983b; Noda and Bower, 1996). This is consistent with both the intuition of the dynamic capability view (Nelson,1994; 1995; Teece, Pisano, and Shuen, 1997) that the explicit strategy is only the surface of the managerial routines guiding the firm, as well as with insights from the new studies of science on the mundane practices of scientific research (Latour and Woolgar, 1979; Pickering, 1995; Galison, 1997).

2. Strategy Process Research, Strategic Thinking, and Strategic Acting

2.1. Strategic Decision Making under Uncertainty and Ambiguity

Strategy research is characterized by the ongoing controversy between heroic rational decision-making frameworks based on economic theory, and different streams of critique. While the first invokes the image of strategy as a course of action consciously deliberated by top management as well as an analytical exercise of rational decision making (Chandler, 1962; Andrews, 1971; Ansoff, 1965; Porter, 1980), the second challenges such simplified conceptualizations, insisting on the emergent, distributed, interpretative, mundane character of strategizing (Allison, 1971; Mintzberg, 1978; Quinn, 1980; Mintzberg and Waters, 1985; Mintzberg, 1994). Given our interest in strategizing under uncertainty and ambiguity, it is thereby highly problematic that models of rational decision making fail to be specified in uncertain and ambiguous situations (Knight, 1921; Alchian, 1950; Kahnemann, Slovic, and Tversky, 1979; March, 1994). Under these conditions, rational action lacks the means necessary for evaluating *a priori* whether the reasoning behind a decision or an action is valid (Gioia and Chittipetti, 1991; Gomez and Jones, 2001).

Thereby, uncertainty and ambiguity are defined as follows: *Uncertainty* refers to imprecision in estimates of future consequences conditional on present actions. Under uncertainty, the world is imperfectly understood, and strategy has to be formed with incomplete knowledge. *Ambiguity* refers to decision making in situations where alternative states are hazily defined or where they have multiple meanings simultaneously opposing interpretations (March, 1994). Under ambiguity, strategy is formed in the face of contradicting but justified and founded alternatives. Models of strategic planning and rational choice are forced to reduce such uncertainty and ambiguity to some structured decidable set of alternatives, turning the real-world complexity into a well-defined model situation.

In strategy processes, uncertainty and ambiguity exist first and foremost with respect to the relevant environment (Szulanski and Doz, 1995). It is not an object discoverable before the events (Penrose, 1959), but rather the result of permanent strategic interactions between various firms. Second, uncertainty about the capabilities of the organization are key. An organization often will discover the reach of its capabilities only ex post facto (Williamson, 1975). While the dynamic capability perspective in strategy (Barney, 1991; Teece, Pisano, and Shuen, 1997) argues that this leads to inimitability, it also implies causal ambiguity to management. Third, there is never a comparable situation in the past that allows to unambiguously learn from past experiences (Knight 1921; March, Sproull, and Tamuz, 1991). What we value as being an important experience depends on our actual situation (Weick, 1995).

Strategy research can be characterized by a fundamental separation between contributions conceptualizing real-world strategy as local deviations from rational decision making in the line of rational decision making models, and contributions explicitly addressing uncertainty and ambiguity, assuming significant degrees of incalculability (Spender, 1993). The first turns uncertainty into a special case for a rationalistic framework, in which strategy formation has to deal with the interpretation of probabilistic information (March, 1994). Only the second insists on the fundamental fact that uncertainty and ambiguity make the rational decision-making model conceptually inappropriate.

2.2. The Conceptual Dichotomy of Thinking and Acting

In this second line of thought, it is crucial to understand the mechanisms shaping strategy formation in the face of internal and external uncertainty and ambiguity (see Stone and Brush, 1996). However, strategy research so far suffers from a conceptual bias, which makes this explicit analysis of strategy formation under ambiguity difficult (Grand, von Krogh, and Pettigrew, 1999): the analytical separation of strategic thinking and strategic acting. However, to overcome this dichotomy is a precondition for strategy research to advance in analyzing the procedures structuring and determining strategy formation in the face of internal as well as external uncertainty and ambiguity.

The separation of thinking and acting originates in the basic architecture of organization theory (March and Simon, 1958; see also Burrell and Morgan, 1979; Astley and Van de Ven, 1983) and in strategic management (Chandler, 1962; Andrews, 1987). The predominant positions in strategic management invoke the image of strategy as a course of action consciously deliberated by top management (Chandler, 1962; Andrews, 1971), based on analytical exercises undertaken by corporate strategists (Ansoff, 1965; 1971; Porter, 1980; Ackoff, 1983). Adequate strategic thinking finds its [self-evident] realization in corresponding actions and strategic moves, manifested in the patterns of corporate resource allocation and major strategic changes (Steiner, 1979; Mintzberg, 1994). Implementation relies on information-based routines and formal procedures managers use to maintain or alter organizational activities (Simons, 1995). Empirical research investigates patterns of strategic behavior, assuming that they are the self-evident realization of strategic thinking.

Such a conceptual separation is of high analytical value for a focused understanding of strategic thinking or strategic acting. However, under uncertainty and ambiguity, the coherent interplay of deliberate strategies and emerging strategic initiatives stops to be self-evident (Pettigrew, 1985; Grand, von Krogh, and Pettigrew, 1999). As a consequence, instead of assuming their rationality, consonance, and consistency (Rumelt, 1997) or of referring to their overall configuration (Miller, 1986; 1996; Miller and Friesen 1984; Mintzberg, 1994), it is crucial to understand the mechanisms structuring, determining, and coordinating strategic thinking and strategic acting in the face of internal as well as external uncertainty and ambiguity.

Strategy process research provides theoretical approaches that discuss the procedures shaping the interplay of thinking and acting, however, without transcending the underlying dichotomy. Thereby, strategy turns into an ongoing process of successive steps, initiatives, and issues (Lindblom, 1968; March and Olsen, 1976):

❑ *Agenda Setting*: Strategy research describes how strategic agendas emerge from local initiatives of front and middle managers, shaped by concrete challenges, problems, and experiences, as well as how they gain attention in top management discourses (Dutton, 1988; Dutton and Ashford, 1993). In this bottom-up process, important ideas and strategic initiatives originate in the experiences and skills of people at the bottom of the hierarchy (Pinchot, 1985). These internal entrepreneurs compete for the scarce resources and limited managerial attention. Strategy formation is seen as a situated strategic thinking process dispersed within the organization (Bartlett and Ghoshal, 1993).

❑ *Logical Incrementalism*: Strategy formation is re-interpreted as logical incrementalism (Quinn, 1980). Strategic planning is seen as an incomplete model for describing how organizations develop their strategies. The real strategy evolves as internal decisions and external events flow together to create a new, widely shared consensus for action among key members of the top management team, by intertwining formulation and implementation of strategies (Mintzberg and Waters, 1985; Mintzberg, 1994). The role of top management turns into setting a structural and strategic context that allows an appropriate co-evolution of situated thinking and acting (Quinn, 1980).

❑ *Evolutionary Perspective*: Logical incrementalism shares major arguments with an evolutionary theory (Nelson and Winter, 1982; Nelson, 1994; Barnett and Burgelman, 1996). Companies are not governed by global strategic rationality, and no single consistent framework guides major choices and changes. They emerge from the cumulative interaction among basic action systems and routines. Routines are patterns of activity that underpin the smooth functioning of companies beyond their explicit analysis at the top-management level. Major shifts of strategic behavior emerge when established routines contradict with novel situations, leading to local learning and changes (Barnett and Burgelman 1996). Since these routines are interlinked, change in one set will impact on others, creating cascading, unplanned effects on situated strategic actions.

❑ *Resource Allocation*: In this line of thought, the strategic resource allocation [Bower-Burgelman] model (Bower, 1970; Burgelman, 1983a and b; Noda and Bower, 1996) is a prominent attempt to relate an in-depth understanding of explicit strategic thinking to the analysis of organizational processes and strategic action. The model relies on four sub-processes (Noda and Bower, 1996): two interlocking bottom-up

processes of definition and impetus, relating the discussion of strategic moves with the socio-political processes of promoting their
appropriateness (see Dutton, 1988; Dutton and Dukerich, 1991, for
similar arguments); and two overlying organizational processes of
structural (in parallel to Ghoshal and Bartlett, 1994) and strategic context determination, forming the settings in which decisions and
actions are made, and thus shaping the development of strategic initiatives.

Given our interest in understanding the interplay of strategic thinking and acting under uncertainty and ambiguity, it is essential to understand how entrepreneurial initiatives, the brokering activities of middle
management, and the context setting of top management interrelate in
established firms (Ghoshal and Bartlett, 1994; Noda and Bower, 1996).
Another key issue is to understand how these various processes are covered in entrepreneurial new ventures: iterations of strategic actions,
resource allocation activities, and local searches create patterns of escala-
tion or de-escalation of the strategic commitment based on experiences
that confirm or disconfirm the premises of the initial actions and their
credibility. In the case of successful first steps, continuous incremental
learning leads to a coordinated shift in resource allocation on the one
hand, as well as in their explanation of and justification for the investments on the other hand.

Early initiatives and experiences are thus key for entrepreneurial
new ventures in providing the experiences necessary to further elaborate
the arguments necessary to explain and justify new ideas and strategic
moves. Thereby, acting is crucial for the elaboration and specification of
a possible strategic reorientation, which finally becomes evident and
explicit in the strategic thinking of top management (Weick, 1995). The
first assertions, unspecific ideas, and initial attempts become the strategic
premises that structure subsequent strategic thinking and acting (Cyert
and March, 1963; Levitt and March, 1988). They are the resources and
mental references for strategic orientation, argumentation, and explanation of new initiatives. They are incremental to the extent that they structure the local search of managers for specific problems and issues
(Szulanski and Doz, 1995; Weick, 1995). They relate to strategic inten-

tions to the extent that planning-dependent evaluation processes generate incentives and provide feedback on the success of certain ideas.

Although the contributions discussed allow the conceptualization of the interplay between strategic thinking and strategic acting, they do not explain how coherent strategic discourses and consistent strategic behavior of companies emerge over time.

2.3. Strategizing Practice Beyond Strategic Thinking and Acting

This is at the heart of the dominant [general management] logic concept. *Dominant logic* is defined as consisting of the cognitive schemes developed through experience and appropriated through past justification processes in order to determine the ways an organization approaches its core business as well as any new and as yet inencountered situation (Prahalad and Bettis, 1986).

The concept of dominant logic draws on key concepts like "Denkkollektiv" (Fleck, 1935), "paradigm" (Kuhn, 1970), or "episteme" (Foucault, 1966), originally developed in the context of the studies of science, referring to the worldviews shared by a specific group of relevant people, and structuring their basic perceptions, reflections, arguments, and activities. In a business context, a dominant logic or paradigm answers questions like:

- ❑ What are the assumptions we make on our business?
- ❑ What are the success criteria we look for when evaluating projects and activities?
- ❑ What are the "success stories" that guide our reasoning?

The way in which a firm answers these questions has a decisive effect on major decisions, resource allocation, and strategic investments (see Prahalad and Bettis, 1986; Grant, 1988; Bettis and Prahalad, 1995; von Krogh and Roos, 1996; Grand, von Krogh, and Pettigrew, 1999).

The dominant logic of a firm defines its mindset as well as the corresponding key activities. It is the amalgam of all the different ideas and interests, activities, and experiences shared by a collection of past and present key individuals in a specific institutional context. These individuals can be seen as forming the dominant coalition (Cyert and March, 1963), having a significant influence on the way a company is managed and how resources are allocated. In the strategy formation process, a dominant logic becomes the interpretative resource for coping with uncertain and ambiguous situations. It emerges from the multiple interpretation and sensemaking of current and past experiences in specific contexts, situations, and competitive constellations. It provides the frame in which managers focus attention (Ocasio, 1997), simplify ambiguous situations (Schwenk, 1984; 1986), categorize new events, assess their consequences, consider appropriate actions, and do so rapidly and efficiently.

It is these shared strategic heuristics, based on predominant schemata and institutional procedures of argumentation and justification, manifested in specific arguments and discursive patterns, that shape strategic decisions within a company or industry, often without being present in the explicit, conscious reflections of the people involved. Very often managers are not aware of the extent to which they are guided by organizational routines as well as the extent to which they rely on such implicit theories when making major strategic decisions

Contrary to certain attempts to conceptualize such dominant logic as organizational filters or lenses (see Prahalad and Bettis, 1986; Bettis and Prahalad, 1995), we argue that they must rather be understood as resources for social practices and discourses (Bourdieu, 1972; 1980). Mental models bundled as dominant logic allow people to interpret and evaluate complex, uncertain, and ambiguous situations (Weick, 1995), to grasp the intentions of others, to achieve intersubjective understandings, coordinated actions, judging and further developing ideas and tasks. Managers actualize these interpretative resources and arguments in their mundane practice, while at the same time reproducing and routinizing these patterns of argumentation and action (Garfinkel, 1967; Garfinkel and Sacks, 1970).

2.4. Entrepreneurial Strategizing Practice and Scientific Practice

Although the concept of dominant [general management] logic provides important insights into the interdependencies of strategic thinking and acting as well as their coherence, it remains unclear under what conditions and how an established dominant logic is to be challenged or transformed; how and why alternative ways of coherent strategic thinking and acting among companies emerge; and why and how a dominant logic is able to actually shape managerial decisions and actions.

In order to develop a coherent theoretical approach to analyze strategizing practice under uncertainty and ambiguity, the chapter suggests looking at strategy formation as an iterative problem-solving process. This view of strategy formation exhibits striking similarities with an evolutionary view of scientific research and its core activities of theory building and theory testing (Szulanski and Doz, 1995; Weick, 1995): Instead of conceiving of strategy formation as purely ex ante rational decision making, it might be conceptualized as the result of ex post facto rationalization, explanation, and justification (Weick, 1995), interpreted as a theory building process (Weick, 1989); in parallel, a major part of the relevant ongoing activities are not explicable and never discussed because they are taken for granted (Meyer and Rowan, 1977; Nelson and Winter, 1982), similar to research practice.

3. Strategy Formation as Theory Building and Theory Testing

3.1. Ready Made Science and Science in Action

In the new studies of science investigating how theories are built in mundane research practices and scientific discourses (Lynch, 1993; Galison, 1997; Latour, 1998; Knorr Cetina, 1999), theory building is conceived of as a process of structuring uncertain and ambiguous situations. While traditional philosophies of science interpret theory building as a process of rational reflection, theory formulation, and subsequent testing (similar to traditional concepts of strategy formation), it becomes more and more evident that this way of describing theory building is more of an ex post facto rationalization than the actual description of the process itself (Elkana, 1986; Galison, 1997):

> We will have to learn to live with two contradictory voices talking at one, one about science in the making, the other about

> ready made science. The latter produces sentences like "Just do this ... just do that ..."'; the former says "Enough is never enough."
>
> (Latour, 1987, p. 13)

It is an essential difference to study science in action and not ready made science. The same is true for strategy formation. While a rational decision-making approach provides a coherent picture of strategy ex post facto, strategizing in action means for managers to deal with internal and external uncertainties and ambiguities in an iterative problem-solving process (Weick, 1989; Szulanski and Doz, 1995; Szulanski and Amin, 1999). As a consequence, we assume theories [strategies] to develop in an ongoing critical dialogue between the established understanding of the appropriate strategy [theoretical], and various concurrent perspectives, experiences, and initiatives, relating different frames and horizons of meaning in different ways (Elkana, 1986; Galison, 1997).

Processes of justification and rationalization are thus key, turning local initiatives, first ideas, and managerial experiences [research activities] into relevant perspectives and acceptable arguments beyond individual activities (see also Dutton, 1988; Dutton and Ashford, 1993; Dutton and Dukerich, 1991; Dutton and Jackson, 1987). While strategic initiatives might be evident to people directly involved in the process, any communication beyond this local situation implies explanation, argumentation, and justification (see also Ocasio, 1997).

3.2. Justification in Scientific Discourses

To understand strategy formation [theory building] thus means to study how rationalization and justification relates new ideas, innovative contributions, and local initiatives with the predominant structures of managerial [scientific] discourses. We distinguish three perspectives on strategy, identifying three major qualities in the rationalization process of theoretical propositions and contributions (Elkana, 1986): corpus of knowledge as the implicit theories and understandings of the organization (the content of the established views); images of knowledge as the appropriate processes of rationalization (the epistemological basis and evaluation criteria for new and existing ideas); and ideological values as the overall status of managerial discourses on strategy within the organizational and socio-cultural context (cultural, institutional, and political aspects) (see especially von Krogh and Grand, 1999):

❑ *Corpus of Knowledge*: At any point in time, one can determine some dominant strategic orientation. It integrates the currently accepted, reproduced, and shared ideas of existing solutions, open problems, relevant frames, and implicit theories that structure and dominate arguments and discussions, representing the shared understanding of important issues. This corresponds to what science studies understand by "paradigms" (Fleck, 1935; Kuhn, 1962; 1970) and "episteme" (Foucault, 1966; 1971), including the contents of what is explicitly known.

In the context of strategy formation, the corpus of knowledge includes the delineation of business boundaries (what is our business about?); implicit theories about the key success factors in the business (technological progress, product innovation, procedural efficiency?); and referential success stories that serve as benchmarks of the industry (leading organizations in the world? why are they successful?). Together, these different arguments, implicit models, and underlying narratives form the patterns and arguments dominating most managerial speaking and acting.

❑ *Images of Knowledge*: This corpus is related to the images of knowledge that specify the appropriate argumentative structures that legitimize and rationalize strategic initiatives. Images of knowledge range from logical deduction ("It is reasonable to do it like this") to explanations in terms of tradition ("We have always done it like that"), authority ("Top management or the specialists decide"), analogies ("It is just like that case we had ..."), as well as novelty ("We really should try something new"). These images of knowledge are concerned with the unquestioned epistemological assumptions.

In the context of strategy formation, these images of knowledge include processes and arguments that are accepted as demonstrating the soundness and cogency of an argument. Do managers have to explain their strategies in terms of financial return, or rather of technological trends? Are the customers key, or does the strategy focus on the shareholders? Should discussions dwell upon past success, or upon future returns? To choose the appropriate explanation for strategic initiatives is key for succeeding in a top management meeting, and for being considered in resource-allocation decisions.

❑ *Ideological Values*: Finally, the role of justification in managerial discourses has to be defined in terms of the overall values of the company. They express the fundamental value system of the company and its social and institutional context, determining the basic business philosophy as well as the vision of the organization. With respect to the images of knowledge, the ideological values decide to what extent arguments and managerial discourses are relevant at all, and what the basic reference points of the organization should be (success, vision, ethics, and/or culture).

Theory building and strategy formation relate local initiatives, new ideas, and basic issues to these discourse structures. Strategy is thereby a theory insofar as it constitutes an ordered set of assertions and propositions about a consistent organizational behavior to hold true through a range of environmental circumstances (Boltanski and Thévénot, 1991). Like scientific theories, successful strategies highlight the important relationships and connections that structure the competitive landscape of the company, as well as attempt to anticipate and predict the unfolding of a phenomenon (Szulanski and Doz, 1995).

Rationality in strategy formation can thus be re-interpreted as being the result of ex post rationalization (Weick, 1995), explication, and justification practices (von Krogh and Grand, 1998). Strategic actions are not that much dependent on rational decisions alone, but refer to the question of whether the management is able to rationalize patterns of strategic action as being reasonable to relevant others (Gioia and Chittipetti, 1991; Gomez and Jones, 2001). This is consistent with the insights of strategy process research (Pettigrew, 1992; Chakravarthy and

Doz, 1992; Mintzberg, 1994) into the fact that managers invest considerable time resources for communicating, explaining, refining, and justifying the actual course of action of the company (Mintzberg, 1973; 1978).

3.3. Narratives in Managerial Discourses

However, it remains unclear how these managerial [scientific] discourses relate to other mundane practices involved in strategy formation [theory building]. In addition, it remains to be discussed how these discourses relate to the reality of managerial action. In order to further elaborate on these questions, we must admit that strategy must be seen as a specific type of theory: an action theory (Argyris and Schön, 1978). Strategy as an action theory refers to managerial and organizational activities, describing their interplay as well as their impact on firm behavior and success. While scientific theorizing basically [although not entirely] argues in terms of well-developed concepts, models, and propositions, managerial discourses also include stories, metaphors (Ricoeur, 1975), images, and narratives as important parts of any managerial rhetoric (Tsoukas, 1989). [Actually, this is increasingly seen as holding also for scientific arguments; see Elkana, 1986, Bruner, 1991, in general; and McCloskey, 1986, in the context of economic theory.] While arguments convince of their conceptual appropriateness, stories work with their life-likeness.

In the perspective of cognitive psychology, the two modes of thought can be characterized as follows (Bruner, 1986, p. 11 ff.): The argumentative or paradigmatic mode of thought employs categorizations and conceptualizations, as well as the operations by which categories are established, instantiated, idealized, and related one to the other to form a system. Its domain is defined not only by observable statements, but also by the set of possible worlds that can be logically generated and tested; that is, it is driven by hypotheses and conceptualizations. The narrative mode of thought on the other hand is built upon a concern for the specific local situations and personal encounters that characterize organizational activities (Bruner, 1986; see also McCloskey, 1986). Stories must construct two landscapes simultaneously. "One is the landscape of action, where the constituents are the arguments of action; agent, intention or goal, situation, instrument, something corresponding to a 'story grammar.' The other…is the landscape of consciousness: what those involved in the action know, think, or feel, or do not know, think, or feel" (Bruner, 1986, p. 14).

While the conceptual mode of thought that dominates scientific discourses [although not entirely] intends to be as general and precise as possible, the narrative mode of thought is ambiguous, situational, and context dependent. Managers use narratives and stories in order to make sense of their actual strategic situations, past and present experiences, as well as to articulate their implicit knowledge and ideas on strategic issues (Bruner, 1990; Weick, 1995). From the perspective of the discussed rational decision-making model, these insights must be understood as deviations from an ideal analytical strategy formation [theory building] process (see also Galison, 1997). In our perspective, it is an alternative, appropriate way of dealing with uncertain and ambiguous situations, allowing arguments and concepts in organizational discourses to be related to the everyday mundane practices, as well as acting them out, making events and shaping major choices and changes (Weick, 1995).

In this perspective, theory [strategy] is more likely to correspond to organizational reality when this reality is represented more accurately and in greater detail, both in the form of concepts as well as narratives (Weick, 1989; Szulanski and Doz, 1995), thus allowing the implicitly relevant knowledge to be made explicit, the consideration of a greater number of heterogeneous alternative solutions, as well as the application of more criteria to evaluate elaborated propositions (Weick, 1989; Szulanski and Amin, 1999). In situations of uncertainty and ambiguity, the quality of the explanations, rationalizations, and justifications within managerial and scientific discourses increases with the heterogeneity of the arguments, conceptual approaches, narrative modes, and objections they deal with (Elkana, 1986; Galison, 1997; Latour, 1998).

3.4. Managerial Discourses and Mundane Practices

Although this holds for the discursive elaboration of uncertain and ambiguous situations, it does not fully describe situations of successful managerial [scientific] practice. We have to assume that major portions of the ongoing activities and initiatives within strategy formation are not explicable, since they rely on the self-evident foundation that determines what has never to be discussed but is taken for granted (Nelson and Winter, 1982). For a significant part, strategy emerges in the mundane practices of managerial and organizational activities (Wittgenstein, 1953; Suchman, 1987).

The discursive elaboration of uncertain and ambiguous situations leads toward an increasing heterogeneity of potentially relevant but contradictory arguments, stories, and narratives, as well as ambiguous justifications (Elkana, 1986; Galison, 1997; Latour, 1998), but it does not automatically lead to successful managerial practice. In order to put an end to inhibiting rounds of cross-justification and never-ending discursive evaluation, it is necessary to suspend beliefs considered as justified de facto. Individuals accept these beliefs because they remove the necessity of repeatedly calling on others in order to time and again validate actions and initiatives (Schelling, 1960; Lewis, 1969). The attempt to explicate and justify decisions and actions faces an equally strong attempt to the self-evident acceptance of major strategic concepts or issues.

Indeed the fact that beliefs are not expressed is essential because it is a necessary condition for individual calculation and action to take place (see also Bourdieu, 1972; 1980; 1994; Bourdieu and Wacquant, 1992). This does not imply that mundane managerial practices are less rational, but rather that they are not rationalized and explicated (Gomez and Jones, 2001). Managerial practice [theory building] relies on self-evident patterns of activities that guarantee a certain stability (Lynch, 1993; Weick, 1995, based on Garfinkel, 1967; Garfinkel and Sacks 1970; see also Bruner, 1990).

One way of conceptualizing these mundane strategizing practices [of telling a story about them] is to make an analogy with improvisation in jazz (Meyer, Frost, and Weick, 1998; Weick, 1998). Instead of focusing on actual activities as the realization of justified strategic moves and rationalized strategic decisions, improvisation is characterized by local trial-and-error activities as well as the development of concepts and interpretations (Weick, 1979; Nelson, 1995). We emphasize improvisation instead of experimentation, since it includes "reworking pre-composed material and designs in relation to unanticipated ideas conceived, shaped, and transformed under the special conditions of performance, thereby adding unique feature to every creation" (Berliner, 1994, cited in Weick, 1998).

4. Making Sense of the eConomy

The theoretical separation of strategic thinking and acting emerges partly from the academic tradition in organization theory [subjectivism versus objectivism] and strategic management [formulation versus implementation], and partly from the phenomenon under study. Until recently, the companies mainly observed were operating in stable environmental situations, and when researchers observed uncertainty, ambiguity, and fundamental change, it was treated as an extraordinary response to changing environmental and organizational demands, new technologies or market conditions, rather than being a part of the very process of handling uncertainty and ambiguity faced by the firm.

If uncertainty and ambiguity are extraordinary, the analytical separation between thinking and acting makes sense; if they are inherent in the attempts of the company to survive in its environment, as it holds for entrepreneurial strategizing in the economy, a new theory is called for that focuses on managerial discourses and mundane practices. At the heart of such a theory are three constructs: 1) ambiguity as an inherent characteristic of a strategy formation process; 2) mundane strategic practice as situated strategic thinking and acting; and 3) discourses among the various communities involved in strategy formation, as well as the ongoing interaction among them. Given these key dimensions, we specify some of the operating principles to be covered by such a theory:

❑ *Entrepreneurial Strategizing Under Ambiguity:* Ambiguity is ordinary, emerging from the tension between routinized behavior and new thinking, existing patterns of thought and improvisation. New arguments do not convince of the benefits and the allocation of resources to alter routines. Improvisation and experimentation to come to terms with changing tasks at hand provide the seeds of new routines, while thinking remains unchanged. Existing arguments cannot explain the benefits of the resources allocated to improvisation. In this sense, ambiguity is the engine that drives innovation and change, and innovation and ambiguity are more ordinary than extraordinary, especially in the actual sensemaking processes around the eConomy.

Ambiguity is situational and local, and any attempt to resolve ambiguity through simplistic concepts will lead to new sources of ambiguity. Much of the current debate on the eConomy focuses on the search for simple strategies for both new and established companies, strategies that are easy to communicate and fast to implement. However simple these strategies appear, any strategic initiative needs to be re-thought and re-routinized locally. Ambiguity is indeed in the situation, and has to be resolved in the situation in which it appears. This holds both for strategy formation in innovative and thus entrepreneurial situations, and for theory building in scientific research.

Any attempt to simplify strategic thinking and acting [theory building and theory testing] becomes an exercise in strategic overdetermination. This overdetermination makes the very process by which it was created indeterminate. Companies cannot resolve ambiguity by choosing one reality over the other, nor by preferring strategic thinking in the form of a deliberate strategy pursued by top management, nor by preferring the existing routines and patterns of resource allocation to wishful strategic thinking. The interplay between strategic practice and rationalizing strategic initiatives is key.

❑ *Mundane Strategizing Practices*: Because ambiguity is situational and local, thinking and acting blend into local mundane practice, and serve to sustain mundane practices over time. As uncertainty and ambiguity increase, local practices change within the boundaries set by the cognitive, spatial, temporal, and resource limitations of the local communities internal and external to the firm. People cope with uncertainty and ambiguity through their ongoing mundane practices. The cardinal differences between them are the boundaries that constitute these practices, basically delineated by the disposal over relevant financial, cognitive, and people resources.

Since ambiguity is related to particular forms of mundane practices, every community is associated with its specific thinking patterns, resource allocation activities, and shared routines. This is a serious issue facing any theory and practice of strategy. The present chapter introduces a series of building blocks developed in the new studies of science that provide a conceptual and narrative base to start thinking about these issues, looking at strategy formation as iterative problem solving, retrospective storytelling, organizational knowledge creation, and discursive sensemaking process, thus profiting from the striking similarities with an evolutionary view of scientific theory building and theory testing.

❑ *Managerial Discourses*: Managerial discourses as interactions among various key people and their communities are framed by the dominant logic, discursive setting, and established knowledge base, reducing uncertainty and ambiguity for certain people, communities, and companies, while enhancing uncertainty and ambiguity for others, within as well as outside these entrepreneurial new ventures. The various people involved shift ambiguity, focusing on certain issues, while leaving other issues open for further discussion and elaboration; they emphasize certain aspects of the organizational corpus and images of knowledge, while neglecting other aspects. Strategizing is situational in the sense that it sustains local practices over time, but it also creates a contest for possible strategic thinking and acting, and the need for communities to interact and coordinate their discourses, in order to make sense of the internal and external uncertainty and ambiguity.

Part 2

KNOWLEDGE MANAGEMENT

AND THE COMMUNITY

PERSPECTIVE

Chapter 6

UNLEASHING THE POWER OF NETWORKS FOR KNOWLEDGE MANAGEMENT

Putting Knowledge Networks into Action

Andreas Seufert
Andrea Back
Georg von Krogh
University of St. Gallen, Switzerland

Most important, in an age of rapidly proliferating knowledge, the central domain is a social network that absorbs, creates, transforms, buys, sells, and communicates knowledge. Its stronghold is the knowledge embedded in a dense web of social, economic, contractual, and administrative relationships.
—Badaracco, 1991, pp. 13–14

The authors are very grateful for the support from our colleagues in the "KnowledgeSource" at the University of St. Gallen, especially the core team of the Competence Center Knowledge Networks, E. Enkel, M. Köhne, J. Raimann, S. Vassiliadis, and Y. Wicki.

The theoretical challenge is to understand the knowledge of the firm as leading to a set of capabilities that enhance the chances for growth and survival.

—Kogut and Zander, 1992, p. 384

1. Knowledge as a Strategic Resource

Increasing competitive pressure, the constantly accelerating transformation of the economy, and a stronger focus on value added have initiated the search for sustainable sources of competitive advantage. In this context, "knowledge has become the most crucial component in the struggle for competitiveness" (Richter and Vettel, 1995, p. 37). As a result of searching for sources of competitive advantage, two prominent views have emerged. The first—the industry-structure view—associated with Porter (1980) suggests that supernormal returns are primarily a function of a company's membership in an industry with favorable structural characteristics (e.g., relative bargaining power, barriers to entry). The second view—the resource-based view of the company—argues that differential company performance is fundamentally due to the company's heterogeneity rather than industry structure (Barney, 1991; Wernerfeld, 1984). Firms that are able to accumulate resources and capabilities that are rare, valuable, not substitutable, and difficult to imitate will achieve a competitive advantage over competing companies.

The resource-based view generally addresses performance differences among companies using asymmetries in knowledge, associated with competencies or capabilities (Peteraf, 1993; Prahalad and Hamel, 1990; Winter, 1995). Many authors describe knowledge as the single most important source of sustainable competitive advantage, and thus also as a source for generating value in the modern company. Therefore, a knowledge-based view can be seen as the essence of the resource-based view (Winter, 1988; Conner and Prahalad, 1996; Grant, 1996). In this respect, the knowledge-based view was developed further, since knowledge is being regarded as the most important strategic resource. Therefore the challenge of Knowledge Management is to advance the knowledge work processes such as "localizing and capturing," "transferring," and "creating" through tangible activities.

2. The Challenge: Managing Knowledge in Network Structures

2.1. Managing Knowledge

2.1.1. Characteristics of Knowledge

Many contributions in the field of "resource-based/knowledge-based view" have categorized organizational resources and described their influence on the creation of sustainable competitive advantage. In this chapter, however, the use of knowledge for problem solving and decision making is at the center of attention. Knowledge is hence seen as "information combined with experience, context, interpretation, and reflection. It is a high-value form of information that is ready to apply to decisions and actions" (Davenport et al., 1998, p. 43; and more elaborately in Davenport and Prusak, 1998).

Regarding the type of knowledge, one can differentiate between implicit and explicit knowledge, whereas these types can be conceptualized as two ends of a spectrum (Leonard and Sensiper, 1998, p. 113). *Explicit knowledge* can be transported, respectively coded in formal systematic language (Nonaka and Takeuchi, 1995, p. 59). It can also be represented, distributed, and stored in books, documents, or databases (disembodied knowledge). Contrary to that, *implicit knowledge* is very hard to formalize and communicate. This implicit knowledge, which is heavily rooted in personal experiences, subjective perceptions, values, and emotions (embodied knowledge), is very difficult to share with others. Implicit knowledge has two main dimensions: technical and cognitive. Whereas the technical dimension is comprised of skills and capabilities—often called "know-how"—the cognitive dimension is made up of our mental models—defined by our beliefs, values, and convictions—with which we perceive our environment (Nonaka and Takeuchi, 1995, p. 60). Regarding the level at which knowledge is present, four levels can be distinguished: the individual, the group, the organizational, and the inter-organizational level.

2.1.2. Managing the Knowledge Flow

Knowledge is never idle. It flows continuously from activity to activity, from person to person, and from task to task. Although these processes are often strongly linked to each other, and influence each other as well, it was proven helpful to create generic categories of these knowledge processes. First, it is possible to divide knowledge management into logical phases of evolution through these categories. Second, these categories help management identify knowledge barriers and develop knowledge-enhancing measures. The knowledge processes can be classified into four categories:

1. Localizing and capturing
2. Sharing and transferring
3. Creating
4. Applying

The focus of *localizing and capturing* knowledge lies on finding and charting already existing knowledge in the company. This is a big challenge, especially for companies that have a widely dispersed knowledge base. In these companies, it is quite often the case that business units encounter problems that have already been solved in another part of the company, yet they do not know that, and are thus forced to reinvent the wheel. Consequently, professional knowledge management must create clarity in the existing knowledge base of the company. Many companies have developed "Knowledge Maps" and "Yellow Pages," which dramatically reduce search costs.

Knowledge *sharing and transferring* refers to the leveraging of existing knowledge in groups, teams, divisions and business units, in order to generate value for the company. Explicit knowledge can often be easily transferred through electronic media or other forms of documents such as manuals and handbooks. But knowledge can also exist in stories, actions, metaphors, analogies, behaviors, or visions. Sharing this implicit knowledge is more difficult, since the direct interaction of the people inside the organization is crucial (Brown and Duguid, 1991; Leonard and Sensiper, 1998).

The process of *knowledge creation* is concerned with the development of new explicit or implicit knowledge by groups or individuals, which does not already exist in the company. New knowledge can be created either through the expansion of already existing implicit or explicit knowledge, or through a new method of combining these forms of knowledge.

And lastly, applying knowledge comprises the application and usage of the knowledge in actual business situations, such as decision making or problem solving.

2.2. Increasing Importance of Networks

2.2.1. Characteristics of Networks

The network concept has been used in many different forms (Nohria, 1992).

According to a frequently quoted definition, a network can be seen as "a specific set of linkages among a defined set of actors, with the additional property that the characteristics of these linkages as a whole may be used to interpret the social behavior of the actors involved" (Mitchell, 1969, p. 2). Consequently, the term "network" can be interpreted as a social relationship among actors. Actors in a social network can be persons, groups, but also collectives of organizations, communities, or even societies.

The relationships that evolve among actors can be categorized according to contents (e.g., products or services, information, emotions), form (e.g., duration and closeness of the relationship), and intensity (e.g., communication-frequency), whereas the form and intensity of the relationships establish the network structure (Alba, 1982, pp. 42–43). Besides formalized networks, literature stresses the importance of informal networks as results of and prerequisites for decision-making processes in organizations, and the importance of the interconnection of organization-wide actions. Since the boundaries of networks are difficult to determine, we may speak of blurred boundaries, which are socially constructed by the network members. Using this perspective, we shift the focus from the consideration and protection of the boundaries of a company to the management of and care for relationships. Reich, (1991,

p. 81) depicts a company as "...a facade, behind which teems an array of decentralized groups and subgroups continuously contracting with similar diffuse working units all over the world."

Networks may result through internalization, implying an intensification of cooperation, or externalization, in the form of a limited functional outsourcing achieved by loosening hierarchical coordination mechanisms. With regard to different functional areas, both internalization and externalization, which entail more than just modifications of divisions of labor, can be pursued in parallel within an enterprise. Moreover, they can occur not only horizontally, that is, on the same level, but also vertically with regard to actors on different levels of the value chain, such as suppliers or customers. Given the constant rethinking of the network, the activities and rotations within a network are thus core processes within a network (Seufert et al., 1999b).

2.2.2. Networks as an Omnipresent Phenomenon

Today, hardly any industry remains unaffected by the evolution of network-like relationships within and among companies (Fleisch, 2000). Some examples may help to illustrate the increasing importance of networks in the modern economy.

❑ *In manufacturing industries*, the automotive industry is a representative example of the evolution toward the networked organization. In the course of the reduction of manufacturing depth and breadth, more and more parts and components from stand-alone suppliers are being linked into a system of industrial partnerships (Lodge and Walton, 1989). One should think of the networking that takes place between manufacturers and subcontractors, between manufacturers and trade organizations, and even among manufacturers themselves.

❑ Even if the *biotechnology industry* is still in its infancy, there are a great number of networked organizations to be found here. "The locus of innovation should be thought of as a network of inter-organizational relations. Biotechnology is probably an extreme case of this tendency" (Arora and Gambarella, 1990, p. 374). Weisenfeld and Chakrabari (1990) found that this general assumption was concompanyed in an investigation of the technology and marketing strategies of ninety-six American and seventeen German biotechnology companies.

❑ Taking the systemic character of most hardware and software products and the market structure into account, there is almost no industry in which there are more strategic alliances and networks already established than in the *electronics industry*. The telecommunications industry, for example, is very similar to the international co-operative relationships found in the automotive industry (Pisano et al., 1988).

❑ *Retail trade* began many years ago to outsource even its most basic original functions (e.g., transportation, rack-care, shop-in-the-shop principle), and to cooperate instead with companies that supply them with these services. The entire spectrum of vertical distribution systems—from agency contracts to appointed retailer systems on up to franchises—can be seen as a form of close coordination among cooperating business networks.

2.3. Integrating Network and Knowledge Management Perspectives

Concerning the integration of networking and knowledge management, we believe two aspects to be crucial. First, knowledge management should comprise a holistic view of knowledge, meaning the integration of explicit and tacit knowledge. Furthermore, knowledge management should take a holistic view on where and how knowledge is being created and transferred.

Knowledge is often thought of as an objective commodity, which is transferable independently of person and context. On the basis of this mental model, people often try to solve problems by improving the information flow with the intensive use of modern technologies, such as intranet-based yellow pages, knowledge maps, or information warehouses. The potential of innovative technologies is undisputed. However, what is required is an integrated approach, which includes both explicit and tacit knowledge. For this reason, we are convinced that in order to make effective use of knowledge, networks must be built in which the knowledge and experience of employees are available.

Although working, learning, and innovation complement each other, they are still considered independently in many companies as a result of their disparate mental models (Brown and Duguid, 1991). Working is traditionally seen as the production and delivery of products or services. As attention is focused on the efficiency with which the task is fulfilled, "working" is frequently resistant to modifications. Learning is regarded explicitly as the absorption of new knowledge. Given the potential associated with learning, it is, unfortunately, often not being used adequately to increase the company's ability to innovate. On the one hand, these processes simply focus on individual employees' acquisition of knowledge instead of inducing them to learn how to learn, and how to inter-link areas of knowledge; on the other hand, they obstruct the transfer of new knowledge into working-skills (Seufert and Seufert, 1999). Finally, innovation is often associated with revolutionary proposals developed, for example, in the research laboratory. This form of innovation admittedly constitutes an important part of change in general, but is just one extreme within a continuum of innovations. They can also take the form of mere renewals and improvements in daily business, for example, process improvements.

Focusing on explicit knowledge only, as well as taking too narrow a view of work, learning, and innovation areas, involves the danger of erecting various barriers: functional and hierarchical; barriers to customers, suppliers, and cooperative partners; and mental barriers that impede the generation, transfer, and application of new knowledge. These not only hinder the short-term flow of knowledge, but also in the long term prove detrimental to a company's innovation and learning capability.

Knowledge Networking may deliver a conceptual framework for rethinking the knowledge-management model. In this case, knowledge barriers should be overcome by "networking," and knowledge islands should be cross-linked in order to stimulate the evolution, dissemination, and application of knowledge. The integration of networking into knowledge management yields great benefits. The openness and richness of networks are believed to foster a fertile environment for the creation of entirely new knowledge, while also accelerating the innovation rate (Powell et al., 1996).

3. The Model: A Framework for Managing Knowledge in Network Structures

3.1. Characteristics of Knowledge Networks

3.1.1. Key Elements of Knowledge Networks

We use the term "Knowledge Network" to signify a number of people and resources and the relationships among them, which are assembled in order to accumulate and use knowledge primarily by means of knowledge creation and transfer processes, for the purpose of creating value. This network is backed up and transformed by information and communication technology. As this network of knowledge-resources is continuously being augmented by knowledge gained from learning situations, a Knowledge Network should be regarded as a dynamic structure rather than as a static institution.

Actors and/or members in a social network can be persons, groups, but also collectives of organizations, communities, or even societies. The employees' minds, and the files they manage, carry a share of the company's intellectual capital. Members of Knowledge Networks take on different roles. From an organizational perspective, customers, suppliers, competitors, or government organizations, as well as employees, have distinct functions within a network. Additionally, members within the network can contribute actively or passively, or even carry out the purpose of a true knowledge manager. The type of membership within the network can be very task-orientated or output-orientated. While some members may identify strongly with the network and show a high level of care, others may be less attached to the Knowledge Network and therefore less committed to it. Also, the type of membership can vary substantially from one's position within the network. A member can be at the core of the network or more at the perimeter, and may take on the role of the knowledge activist (Von Krogh et al., 1997) or a knowledge sponsor.

In order to enhance the connectivity of the members through interaction within the network, we have to closely examine the relationships. The characteristics of these relationships are the "platforms" for knowledge exchange. Relationships within networks can vary in duration, intensity, as well as the frequency of the interactions. This naturally implies the personal involvement, commitment, and care behind the relationship. The way members of Knowledge Networks communicate is also about how they use communication tools, and the media richness of the relationship describes distinct characteristics of the relationship. The connectivity of a Knowledge Network also depends on the size of the network. Centralization, formalization, posture, or geographical scope of the Knowledge Network influence the way knowledge is exchanged. Entry barriers, participation possibilities, and ownership can limit the flow of knowledge. Moreover, the integration of business, the origin of the network, and the ownership play a distinct role.

As stated above, knowledge can vary: it can be tacit or explicit, social or individual. Even though individual knowledge plays an important role within Knowledge Networks, we argue that social knowledge (the common, shared knowledge) is per se more prevalent. The expansion of tacit and explicit knowledge within a Knowledge Network is one of the major distinctions in our categorization of Knowledge Networks.

3.1.2. Knowledge Networks and Other Network-Like Structures

Since formal groups/networks (e.g., project teams, task forces) and informal networks (e.g., communities of interest or communities of practice) transfer, share, create, and apply knowledge among actors within a web of relationships, they can be conceptualized as Knowledge Networks. As shown in Figure 6-1, these Knowledge Networks can have different appearances.

A community of practice is a group of people who are, to a large extent, involved in similar work in a common craft. The exchange of experiences holds the community together. They are an integral part of our daily lives. Human beings are constantly engaged in the pursuit of enterprises of all kinds, and in their daily work they have interaction with others, carry out similar tasks, or undergo similar experiences. The community thus develops in the course of its ongoing routines. The personal interests and engagement of participants allows for a high-care relationship within the community by letting individuals share their intuition, judgment, and common sense with other colleagues. Self-developed roles

Organizational Form	Purpose	Membership	Cohesion	Lifetime
Communities of practice	To develop members' capabilities; to build and exchange knowledge	Member who select themselves	Passion, commitment, and identification with the group's expertise	As long as there is interest in maintaining the group
Formal work groups	To deliver a product or service	Everyone who reports to the group's manager	Job requirements and common goals	Until the next reorganization
Informal networks	To collect and pass on business information	Friends and business acquaintances	Mutual needs	As long as people have a reason to connect
Formal networks	To accomplish a specified task in focus of knowledge	Employees assigned by network manager	Job requirements and common goals	Until the next reorganization/ until the task is fulfilled

Figure 6-1. Types of network-like structures (following Wenger and Snyder, 2000).

and a sense of a joint enterprise nurture a shared repertoire of collaboration. These characteristics, supported by a sense of friendship and loyalty, establish cohesion among community members through mutual engagement, therefore binding members together into a social identity.

Formal groups/networks represent a group of people having a specific issue or a problem to solve in order to achieve a specific goal. The participation of members in this network takes place by virtue of their experience and of their abilities or interests with respect to knowledge. As a rule, the building of formal networks is not driven by the members themselves, but by management. This kind of Knowledge Network does have a high formalization degree, and usually exists permanently. This common goal provides cohesion for the group's identity and fosters commitment. Whereas in a community, people share a common knowledge base, members of teams are more conscientiously selected from diverse fields and crafts, to intentionally produce a creative abrasion and intellectual conflict among their diverse viewpoints (Leonard-Barton, 1995). It is temporary and ends mostly with the accomplishment of the task.

Informal networks might be considered a loose confederation comprised of people who share a common interest, and who are willing to share the information they have regarding their interest. Contact among members may be sporadic, due to the lack of cohesion and shared purpose, other than for the purpose of sharing information. Members of such communities know what the interests of the other members are. The absence of an implied practice and the relatively low involvement of group members do not foster high–care relationships.

3.2. Components of the Framework

3.2.1. Underlying Rationale

According to the notion of the duality of structure conceptualized in Giddens's Structuration theory, the structural properties of social systems are both medium *and* outcome of the practices they recursively organize (Giddens, 1984, p. 25). Building on these fundamentals, Knowledge Networks can be understood as a coming together of institutional frameworks (i.e., structures) and modalities or aids, where actors engage in social interactions and in which they conceptualize interaction processes. Based on this understanding the referential model of Knowledge Networks encompasses the following components: processes/relations among the actors; tools/resources that are available to the actors; and sur-

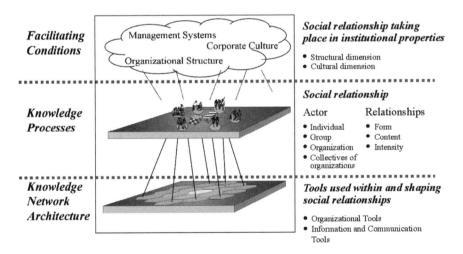

Figure 6-2. Components of the Knowledge Networks reference model.

rounding facilitation conditions, such as control mechanisms, operating procedures, norms and rules, and communication patterns (Seufert et al., 1999a, pp. 185–186).

3.2.2. Facilitating Conditions

Facilitating conditions define the environment, meaning the structural and cultural dimensions, within which the network's knowledge processes take place (von Krogh et al., 2000). They define either the supporting or restricting environmental variables, such as organizational structure, management systems, or cultural aspects (i.e., norms and values or the communication culture). Facilitating conditions can be clustered into several categories. Figure 6-3 provides an overview.

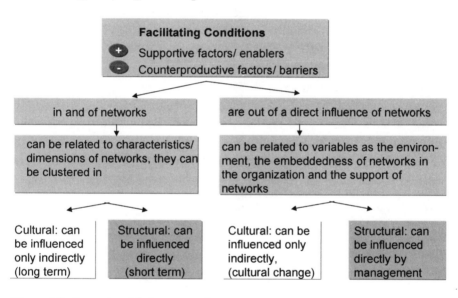

Figure 6-3. Categories of facilitating conditions.

We distinguish between supportive factors/enablers and counterproductive factors/barriers. Whereas supportive factors can be regarded as conditions, which do have a positive effect on network activities, counterproductive factors might be considered as hindering the network's success. Second, facilitating conditions do exist within networks—that is, they are manageable for the Knowledge Network members—and in the network environment, and are therefore related to variables that embed the network into the organization. Finally, cultural as well as structural facilitating conditions can be distinguished. Whereas structural aspects can be influenced directly and therefore have relatively short-term effects, cultural issues are manageable indirectly and do show results only on a long-term basis.

3.2.3. Knowledge Work Processes

As stated earlier, research has shown that there are four generic knowledge processes that can be distinguished: locate/capture, share/transfer, create, and apply. The bottom line for all categories is the application of existing or newly gained knowledge to create value and therefore for the organization itself. In our model of Knowledge Work Processes (Figure 6-4), the application of knowledge takes the center role to indicate that knowledge should not be managed per se, but rather should be tightly connected to business drivers.

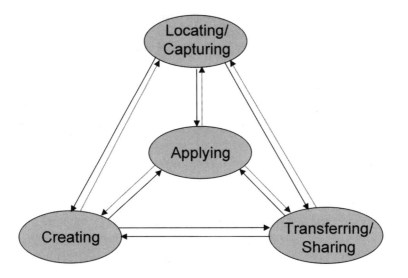

Figure 6-4. Knowledge process categories.

Within these categories, different focuses may be identified. In locating and capturing knowledge the focus lies mainly on the content, whereas in creating new knowledge the focus lies on the process of building new knowledge. These generic knowledge processes can be regarded as the nuclei of every interaction and communication process on an individual and/or group level. For example, in order for implicit knowledge to be exchanged, it first needs to be identified, so that it can be internalized.

3.2.4. Tools

Knowledge network architecture comprises the tool set used within social relationships. These tools include organizational tools, as well as information and communication tools used to enable and improve knowledge processes and Knowledge Network building. This architecture is not merely a collection of modular tools. In the form of "solution frameworks," it is rather an architectural design that is a combination of ICT and organizational tools and methods, supporting the underlying knowledge transformation process. From a technology standpoint, significant potential is found by strongly integrating group-/team-centered approaches and solutions within the area of management support. On the one hand, these can be seen through the reciprocal usage of already existing procedures and mechanisms, and on the other hand, they can be seen in scaleable models that support the mutual transition from a rather person-oriented to more computer-oriented knowledge processing. The potential effectiveness of these tools depends directly on the knowledge processes, or—in other words—how Knowledge Networks can be perceived, poised against the backdrop of structuration theory, as dynamic configurations, continuously expanding and changing through social interactions and learning processes.

3.3. Dimensions of the Framework

The components of the reference model can be perceived from different perspectives. We distinguish between a static and dynamic perspective, as well as between a micro and macro perspective (Figure 6-5).

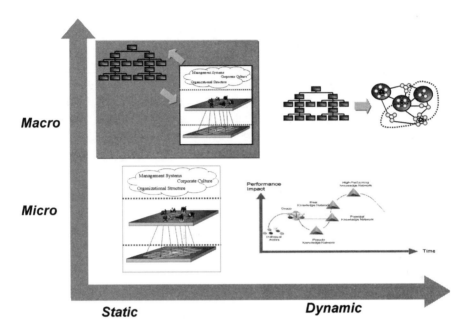

Figure 6-5. Dimensions of the reference model.

3.3.1. Micro Perspective

Referring to the earlier network definition, Knowledge Networks may then be understood as social networks among knowledge actors, in order to allow the creation and transfer of knowledge on an individual, group, organization, and inter-hierarchical level. Using a *static perspective*, the fit within and among the different components is crucial. This means on the one hand that measures within each layer (e.g., activities within the facilitating conditions) should support the same objective so as to avoid any confusion. Using a dynamic perspective, where network building and design are significant, this can be conceptualized using a life-cycle model. Since networks are flexible and the objectives of a Knowledge Network might change over time, a *dynamic perspective* of the reference model should not only encompass the building of a network per se, but rather the adaptation to internal changes or changes in the surrounding network. Therefore, it is essential to enable the networking between individual knowledge types (explicit and implicit), and the networking among different levels (e.g. individual, group, organization) and areas of knowledge (e.g., customer knowledge, R&D knowledge).

3.3.2. Macro Perspective

In our understanding, Knowledge Networks are not a new kind of organizational structure, rather they are an additional cross-divisional, dynamic layer within an organization. In this regard, the macro perspective on Knowledge Networks needs—from a *static perspective*—to take into account the interdependence of Knowledge Networks, as well as their role within their existing organizational units. In order to develop high-performing Knowledge Networks, they must be synchronized by facilitating conditions, which we divide into structural (e.g., organizational structure, management systems) and cultural (e.g., corporate culture, organizational behavior) dimensions.

One can think of the organizational unit as an organ receiver, the Knowledge Network as a life-saving organ that is to be transplanted, and the facilitating conditions as the actions taken to prevent the organ's rejection by the body. Considering Knowledge Networks from a long-term rather than a short-term *dynamic perspective*, one might hypothesize a positive relationship between Knowledge Networks and organizational development. As a consequence of Knowledge Networking, companies will have the opportunity to develop themselves into truly networked organizations. From a macro dynamic perspective, and using the structuration approach as a basis, one should bear in mind that the potentials of Knowledge Networks lie not only in the efficient implementation of knowledge management concepts. Rather, they have a significant influence in shaping the surrounding conditions within which the processes—therefore, the Knowledge Network itself—take place.

4. The Blueprint for Implementation

4.1. Deriving Knowledge Network Reference Types

As stated earlier, the generic knowledge processes—locating/capturing, sharing/transferring, creating, and applying—can be regarded as the nuclei of every interaction and communication process. Following

Nonaka (1991), these processes can be conceptualized as dynamic transformation processes between explicit and tacit knowledge.

Socialization comprises the exchange of tacit knowledge among individuals in order to convey personal knowledge and experience. Joint experiences result in new, shared implicit knowledge, such as common values or technical skills. *Externalization* describes the conversion of implicit knowledge into explicit knowledge. Since implicit knowledge is difficult to express, the conversion process is often supported by the use of metaphors, analogies, as well as visualization aids. The transformation of explicit knowledge into more complex and more systematized explicit knowledge represents the *combination* stage. This systematization and refinement increases the practical value of existing knowledge, increases its transferability, and makes new knowledge available on an organization-wide basis. *Internalization* comprises the conversion of organization-wide, explicit knowledge into the implicit knowledge of the individual.

Referring to Nonaka, we therefore conceptualized four Knowledge Network reference types, each addressing one of the described dynamic knowledge transformation processes. These Knowledge Network refer-

Figure 6-6. Characteristics of Knowledge Network reference types.

ence types can be used to identify "ideal" forms and arrangements in order to contribute to specific business goals. In order to describe the different Knowledge Network reference types, we use specific Knowledge Network characteristics. These characteristics have been selected based on their suitability to distinguish the Knowledge Network reference types from one another. Figure 6-6 gives an overview of the relevant characteristics.

What is of great importance is that these characteristics can be influenced by the application of appropriate tools. In doing so, they affect the facilitating conditions for the underlying knowledge processes and therefore can help to achieve a high-performing Knowledge Network. We now describe the four Knowledge Network reference types in more detail.

4.2. Knowledge Network Reference Type: "Experiencing Network"

4.2.1. Overview

Knowledge Network reference type "experiencing network" mainly pursues the knowledge process of transforming implicit knowledge from one knowledge body to implicit knowledge of another knowledge body. It primarily supports the members to exchange their knowledge, best practices, and solutions through common experiences. In business, this Knowledge Network reference type has the objective to enable people to interact with other members within the company. In this Knowledge Network, social knowledge and impressions from inside and outside the company are collected and distributed, for example, directly with customers or through interaction with internal/external experts. On an individual level, people sharing their experiences with suppliers, customers, and with competitors, for example, accumulate implicit knowledge regarding sales. An "experiencing network" ideally can be described as shown in Figure 6-7.

The degree of these characteristics can be derived from the underlying knowledge process of transforming implicit knowledge into implicit knowledge and the ensuing requirements. Personal relationships

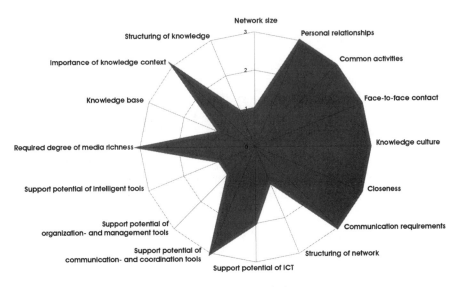

Figure 6-7. Characteristics of an "experiencing network."

are of great importance for this network reference type, since they are most efficient for the transfer of implicit or tacit knowledge (Hansen et al., 1999). Narrow personal relationships are needed on the one hand for creating a climate of trust, which is necessary for sharing knowledge, and on the other hand for the actual exchange of implicit knowledge, which in this network type takes place more directly through personal interaction.

As a consequence of narrow relationships, the network size, which is another important network characteristic, has to be rather small. Other characteristics—such as common activities, face-to-face contact, knowledge culture, closeness, knowledge context, communication requirements, degree of media richness, and support potential of communication and coordination tools—are very important and highly distinctive for an "experiencing network," since these characteristics may support the sharing of tacit knowledge among individuals.

4.2.2. Facilitating Conditions

In order to achieve a high Knowledge Network performance, appropriate facilitating conditions inside and outside the network have to be in place. In case of configuring the facilitating conditions for the "experiencing network," the knowledge operational task of transforming implicit knowledge into implicit knowledge has to be considered. According to Nonaka, the exchange of implicit or tacit knowledge takes place "through joint activities—such as spending time together, and living in the same environment" (Nonaka et al., 1998). Therefore, the direct interaction of individuals within personal relationships is crucial for the sharing of tacit knowledge. As our research has shown, shared experiences and activities, stimulated by meetings among individuals, as well as the typical values of a "high-care knowledge culture" (e.g., shared trust basis, empathy, and openness), are also of great importance. Other major facilitating conditions are communication aspects. Ideally, there must be a high degree of face-to-face contact, and an intensive communication among the network members, which includes long-term interaction and a low degree of lingual and cultural differences. Geographical and social closeness are also required in order to enable sharing experiences as well as context-bound knowledge.

4.2.3. Tools

With regard to facilitating conditions, the use of tools must be aligned to the needs of this network reference type. The appropriate organizational and ICT tools must be employed and designed in order to support the specific characteristics of "experiencing networks."

In practice, the process of acquiring knowledge is largely supported through direct interaction with suppliers, customers, and so forth. Another key task is disseminating implicit knowledge and sharing personal knowledge (ideas, etc.) directly (Figure 6-8).

Tools can generally be used in order to support or influence knowledge work processes as well as network building processes. Furthermore,

Figure 6-8. Key tasks of an "experiencing network."

the characteristics of a Knowledge Network, and the structural and cultural facilitating conditions inside and outside the Knowledge Network, are both influenced by tools. Since intensive communication among the network members is crucial, communication tools are the most important tool class. Regarding organizational tools, knowledge forums, knowledge workshops, meeting and moderation tools, conversation and negotiation techniques, active listening, and also language tools (dialogue, story telling, metaphors, controlled vocabulary, organizational thesaurus) might be used in order to support communication. Also, many ICT tools can be rather helpful. Virtual communities demonstrate that establishing personal relationships, trust, and sharing experiences and implicit knowledge are to some degree also possible. Therefore, ICT communication tools (especially synchronous technologies and tools with a high degree of media richness) are mostly relevant for this network type. Figure 6-9 gives an overview of relevant organizational and ICT tools to support the knowledge reference type "experiencing network."

4.2.4. Example: Seven Eleven Japan

In regards to efficiency, Seven Eleven Japan (Nonaka et al., 1998) is widely seen to be one of the globally dominating retail companies. Inside Japan, the company enjoys the highest return on revenue in the retail sector. One of the decisive factors for this is its ability to capitalize on market knowledge. Seven Eleven Japan is organized as a franchising system with 7,000 outlets. These Seven Eleven outlets sell over 3,000 different products, with foodstuffs accounting for about 77 percent. Seventy percent of these products are switched each year. Seven Eleven, being the franchiser, sells knowledge to the outlets, which they use as the basis of their sales policy. In order to be able to offer this service, Seven Eleven has developed a comprehensive knowledge management concept.

> Since the customer is often only implicitly aware of these needs, meaning that the needs are only subconsciously present, and that they are difficult to articulate, Seven Eleven attempts to use Knowledge Networks to promote an experience-exchange that brings forth new knowledge.

Communication and coordination tools:

> Knowledge forums, knowledge workshops
>
> Coffee corners/talk rooms
>
> Meeting and moderation tools, conversation and negotiation techniques
>
> Active listening
>
> Language tools (dialog, story telling, common language, metaphors, organizational thesaurus)

Organization tools and management tools:

> Management tools
>
> Conflict management tools
>
> Presentation techniques
>
> HMR tools (e.g., job rotation, job enrichment, mentoring/coaching, training and education)
>
> Knowledge vision/goals

Organizational structure tools

> Group work
>
> Roles and responsibilities (e.g., knowledge activists, community/ network roles)

Organizational culture tools

> Change agent
>
> Corporate culture change programs
>
> Organizational development tools

Figure 6-9. Organizational and ICT tools for an "experiencing network."

One of the greatest central elements is the knowledge regarding the needs of the customers, and the implementation into new products and services. For this purpose, direct customer contact is sought at the various locations, and this implicit customer knowledge is then shared among the employees of the different Seven Eleven outlets. This knowledge, in turn, is shared at regular meetings with the store consultants of Seven

Eleven. These consultants then exchange their experiences in weekly consultant meetings at headquarters. Seven Eleven can attribute its high effectiveness of this procedure to transforming often only implicitly available customer knowledge. Despite the relatively high effort—exchanging implicit knowledge through personal experience-exchange, rather than through information systems—the company's efforts have proven to be worthwhile, considering its profitability and its innovation ability (70 percent product exchange per year).

4.3. Knowledge Network Reference Type: "Materializing Network"

4.3.1. Overview

The Knowledge Network reference type "materializing network" comprises the knowledge process of transforming implicit knowledge into explicit knowledge (Figure 6-10). It primarily serves to motivate and stimulate people possessing implicit knowledge to externalize their experiences and thoughts. In this type of Knowledge Network, individuals having a particular knowledge must be identified and motivated to make this knowledge accessible in an explicit form to others, for example, in corporate knowledge bases.

An appropriate knowledge culture that provides values such as care, trust, and openness is extremely important in this network type. Without such values, network members won't be willing and able to make their tacit knowledge explicit. Communication requirements for "materializing networks" are high, since tacit knowledge must be articulated and then translated into readily understandable forms. Consequently, the support potentials for communication and coordination tools are rather high. Since the knowledge that has been made explicit within "materializing networks" will quite often be stored using a knowledge base, the usage of a knowledge base is very significant. This network reference type should be well structured, since the process of translating knowledge into an understandable form can be subdivided into different roles (i.e., knowledge authors, reviewers, etc.). Personal relationships, face-to-face-contact, and geographical and social closeness are important to establish trust. "Common activities" are not as important here as they are in "expe-

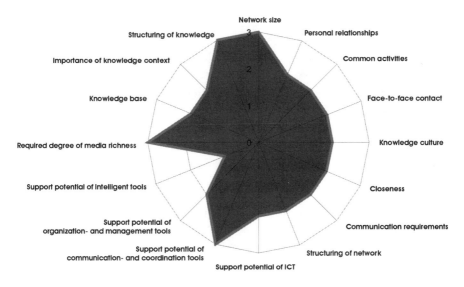

Figure 6-10. Characteristics of a "materializing network."

riencing networks," since the knowledge does not have to be embodied by the network members. The required degree of media richness is medium. Quite often, text-based media are sufficient and even more efficient for storing and transferring the knowledge. The knowledge itself should be structured to some extent to make its transfer easier. It also should not be absolutely bound to a specific context since otherwise difficulties in transferring it may result.

4.3.2. Facilitating Conditions

Dialogue and discussion are key for this network reference type. Also, the selection of employees with an appropriate mix of specific knowledge and skills is crucial. The major facilitating conditions for this Knowledge Network reference type are trust within the network, a high degree of communication, and shared values and interests among the network members. This can be done, for example, through communication rules or through the composition of project teams, usage of appropriate tools such as creativity and visualization, and so forth. When designing the facilitating conditions for this network reference type, one must keep in mind two tasks that need to be supported: the articulating of implicit knowledge and its translation into a form that is easy to understand. The task of articulating knowledge is very dialogue-intensive and therefore, opportunities for dialogue with colleagues, suppliers, customers, and so on, must exist. Translating the knowledge into an understandable format is less communication-intensive, but requires other facilitating conditions such as clear-cut network roles, sufficient time to structure the knowledge and to put it into a knowledge base, and so on.

4.3.3. Tools

Organizational and ICT tools in "materializing networks" primarily have to support the process of transforming implicit knowledge into explicit knowledge. This process can be subdivided into two parts, as illustrated in Figure 6-11.

Figure 6-11. Key tasks of a "materializing network."

First, implicit knowledge has to be identified and then articulated. The process of articulating knowledge is communication-intensive. Therefore, the whole class of organizational as well as ICT communication tools is crucial. Second, the articulated knowledge has to be translated into an appropriate form. In order to manage the process of bringing the knowledge into a well-structured and understandable format, organization and management tools such as knowledge maps, clear-cut roles and responsibilities, should exist. Since this process can be intentionally well structured, the utilization of workflow management tools could be effective. Intelligent tools, such as skill mining tools to identify experts for certain content areas, may also be incorporated. Figure 6-12 gives an overview of relevant organizational and ICT tools to support the knowledge reference type "materializing network."

Organizational Tools	ICT Tools
Communication and coordination tools: Knowledge forums, knowledge workshops Coffee corners/talk rooms Meeting and moderation tools, Conversation and negotiation techniques Active listening Language tools (dialog, story telling, common language, metaphors, controlled vocabulary, organizational thesaurus and dictionary)	**Communication and coordination tools:** Messaging/E-mail Workflow management Group decision support systems Real/non real-time conferencing systems Community tools, CSCW suites
Organization and management tools: Management tools Knowledge maps Visualization tools Knowledge vision/goals Organizational structure tools Roles and responsibilities (e.g., knowledge authors, reviewers, content manager) Knowledge units	**Organization and management tools:** Visualization tools Creativity tools **Intelligent tools:** Skill mining Categorization/clustering (e.g., semantic networks, knowledge ontologies)
Organizational culture tools: Change agent Corporate culture change programs Organizational development tools	**Integration and database tools:** Knowledge management suites Data warehousing

Figure 6-12. Organizational and ICT tools for a "materializing network."

4.3.4. Example: Sharp

Sharp (Nonaka and Takeuchi, 1995) was founded by the inventor and craftsman Tokuji Hayakawa in 1912 as a small metals company. Hayakawa was rather ingenious, and he motivated his employees to act creatively with statements such as: "Do not imitate, do something that others want to imitate." Since its founding days, Sharp has become known to continually bring forth new products—ranging from a belt buckle that self-adjusts and the Sharp pencil of the early years to the liquid crystal televisions and electronic notebooks of today. Each division can submit urgent projects of this kind, which are then evaluated by the general technology conference (participants are the president, the heads of competency areas, and the lab managers). Projects that are received positively are given a maximum project time of eighteen months during which they have nearly unlimited access to the resources of the entire company, helping to ensure high-quality developments within short time spans.

> Continued search for creativity and originality has led Sharp to structure its R&D according to a hypertext model. Part of this organizational model are so-called Urgent Project Teams, which are responsible for strategic development projects.

In order to speedily access core knowledge present in the different divisions, cross-functional teams are usually formed. This could, in certain cases, result in divisions losing their star employees for the duration of the project. The Urgent Project Teams work together with a special Corporate Design Group, facilitating the knowledge exchange among specialists of different disciplines. These designer groups aid the externalization of implicit knowledge, for example, through visualizing concepts in the form of imagery. This, in turn, serves the Urgent Project Teams as input for the development of first prototypes, which finally can be used to materialize abstract concepts and be utilized, for example, as a basis for discussions in meetings.

4.4. Knowledge Network Reference: "Systematizing Network"

4.4.1. Overview

The Knowledge Network reference type "systematizing network" mainly deals with transforming explicit knowledge into explicit knowledge. In this type of Knowledge Network, existing explicit knowledge is being systemized and refined in organizational handbooks, yellow pages, newsletters, and training materials, in order to be reused more efficiently. The characteristics of a "systematizing network" are illustrated in Figure 6-13.

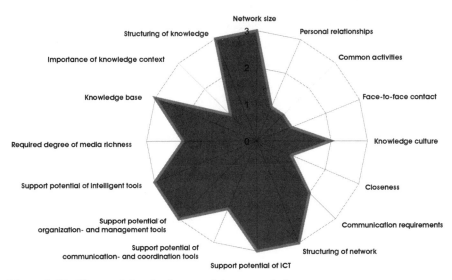

Figure 6-13. Characteristics of a "systematizing network."

To structure and systematize explicit knowledge, all ICT tool classes can be employed to a high degree. A characteristic of the knowledge itself is that the knowledge can be well structured (structuring knowledge is a main goal of this network reference type). Other characteristics, such as personal relationships, common activities, face-to-face contact, as well as geographical and social closeness, are less important since knowledge is not tightly coupled to personal relationships. Due to these characteristics and possibilities of ICT communication tools, the network size and its geographical dispersal can be rather large. A high-care knowledge culture, which provides values such as trust and openness, is not as important for this reference type as it is for the other network types.

4.4.2. Facilitating Conditions

When establishing the facilitating conditions, the knowledge process of transforming explicit knowledge into explicit knowledge defines the requirements that must be met. A basic condition is a knowledge culture that ensures that no information hiding takes place or that hiding of explicit knowledge is at least minimized. Further, explicit knowledge should be accessible within the company without any restrictions. The knowledge culture and related values must be very "ICT-friendly," since the widespread usage of ICT tools is crucial for this network type.

Also, a high degree of consciousness about the possibilities and limitations of ICT tools to transform explicit knowledge is required. This includes reflection on systematizing and structuring of knowledge, including measures to design the related knowledge work processes (capturing/locating, sharing/transferring, creating knowledge) and to adequately integrate them. As our research has shown, other major facilitating conditions for this network reference type are clear-cut roles and a high degree of formalization. Clear-cut roles help to manage the different processes of systematizing knowledge. Roles such as the "knowledge gatherer" (who scouts for external knowledge) or the "knowledge analyst" (who interprets client needs, etc.) may be established. The high degree of structure and formalization also helps to manage its size, which can be quite large.

4.4.3. Tools

To support a "systematizing network," a large range of tools should be utilized. This is particularly true for ICT tools. In practice, systematizing knowledge relies on three processes (Figure 6-14). First, capturing and integrating new explicit knowledge is essential. This may involve collecting externalized knowledge from inside or outside the company and then combining such knowledge. Second, the dissemination of explicit knowledge is based on the process of directly transferring this form of knowledge, for example, through meetings, presentations, or ICT tools. Third, editing or processing explicit knowledge will make it more usable.

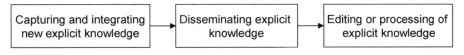

Figure 6-14. Key tasks of a "systematizing network."

The use of intelligent tools—in particular "intelligent agents," which are able to act to a certain degree autonomously—might lead to a broader understanding of Knowledge Networks, in which software systems not only play a role as tools, but also function as autonomous actors beside human representatives (see, e.g., Schmid and Stanoevska-Slabeva, 1998). Figure 6-15 gives an overview of relevant organizational and ICT tools for "systematizing networks."

Organizational Tools	ICT Tools

Communication and coordination tools:
  Knowledge forums, knowledge workshops
  Meeting and moderation tools
  Language tools (common language, metaphors, controlled vocabulary, organizational thesaurus and dictionary)
 	
Organization and management tools:
Management tools
  Visualization tools (e.g., knowledge maps)
  Rewards and incentives
  Knowledge vision/goals
Organizational structure tools
  Roles and responsibilities (e.g., knowledge gatherer, knowledge analyst, knowledge author, knowledge reviewer, content manager)
  Knowledge units
Organizational culture tools
	Communication and coordination tools:
	  Document management/archiving
	  Workflow management
	  Messaging/E-mail
	  Calendaring/scheduling
	  Real-time conferencing systems (Audio/video conferencing, chat, whiteboard, application sharing)
	  Non real-time conferencing systems
	  Group editing/group document handling
	  Community tools, CSCW suites, Collaborative filtering
	
	Organizational and management tools:
	  Decision support systems
	  Management/executive support systems, business intelligence
	  Visualization tools
	  Creativity tools

(continues)

Organizational Tools *(con't)*	ICT Tools *(con't)*
Corporate culture change programs Organizational development tools Change agent	**Intelligent tools:** Intelligent agents Data/text mining Categorization/clustering tools Problem solving tools (neural networks, case-based-reasoning systems) **Integration and database tools:** Knowledge management suites Enterprise portals Data warehousing

Figure 6-15. Organizational and ICT tools for a "systematizing network."

4.4.4. Example: Accenture

With over 70.000 employees, 137 locations in 46 countries, and revenues of more than $10 billion in 2000, Accenture is recognized as the world's largest and most successful management consulting firm. Because of this "one firm" concept ("act as one firm and speak with one voice"), actions that supported the access and distribution of uniform standards and procedures gained central importance early on. As part of this concept, large parts of this knowledge were stored in its Knowledge Management System Knowledge Xchange. Basic statistical information is in databases called Jobs, Engagements, and Projects. A list of all Accenture professionals and their skills is in the Skills, People, and Assignments database.

> Knowledge capital is our most valuable asset and it drives our organization. It's what we sell, and what we must continue to protect and perfect. Our people should diligently find new ways to share and reuse information and deploy it around the world.

Further specific knowledge bases included core methodologies, industry–specific knowledge (visions, major business processes, best practices), discussion databases on various topics, and repositories of or pointers to external information of various types, including technology research and customized news alerts on business topics. This should shorten the learning curve for other employees. Next to the identification of relevant knowledge, a combination of media and didactical capabilities is particularly important, so as to prepare knowledge in a way that best facilitates learning for others. For this purpose, a team with various experts was assembled. Experienced consultants take part as Knowledge Managers, identifying relevant knowledge.

Further, the firm's communities of practice play a central role in Accenture's Knowledge Management. They are more and more shifting from knowledge sharing, that is, receiving knowledge from innovative engagements in the field and putting it into a repository for global distribution, to knowledge creation. For instance, they proactively identify leading engagements in a particular core area. Then Accenture brings representatives from each engagement together to figure out the underlying issues and guidelines. The result that is put into the Knowledge Xchange system is synthesized, enriched, validated knowledge. In some areas where the new service offerings are needed, Accenture periodically invests several man-months or even years to re-invent a service offering. The firm pulls together community of practice leaders, diagnoses its own approaches and those of its competitors, and creates a leading-edge approach to delivering the service.

4.5. Knowledge Network Reference Type: "Learning Network"

4.5.1. Overview

The Knowledge Network reference type "learning network" comprises mainly the knowledge process of transforming explicit knowledge ("know what") into implicit knowledge ("know how"). It supports the learning, embodiment, and application of existing explicit knowledge. As a result, new implicit knowledge is created. A "learning network" can be described by the characteristics shown in Figure 6-16.

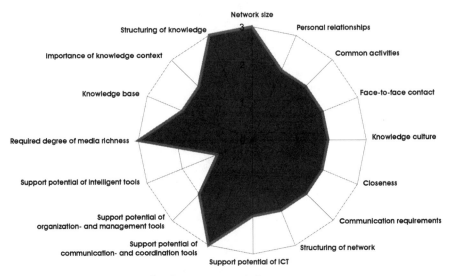

Figure 6-16. Characteristics of a "learning network."

Most characteristics seem to be of medium distinction within this Knowledge Network reference type. An explanation is that this Knowledge Network reference type has to deal with explicit knowledge and related knowledge processes, as well as with implicit knowledge. First, explicit knowledge has to be identified and understood in its context. Second, there is a process of embodying the explicit knowledge by using simulations, learning-by-doing processes, and so forth. Actually, from a dynamic point of view, the characteristics might vary considerably, since at different stages of transforming explicit knowledge into implicit knowledge, different characteristics are becoming more important. For example, personal relationships, face-to-face-contacts, geographical and social closeness, communication requirements, and common activities are, to a certain degree, not as relevant in the stage of identifying and understanding knowledge. Thereby, one might think about the possibilities of local, personal, individualized, and self-directed learning. However, these characteristics are becoming more important in the stage of embodying the knowledge in action and practice, through trainings, mentoring, and so on.

Another reason for various characteristics of learning networks is that there exist several forms of learning networks with different designs and approaches. Frequently, phases of ICT-supported learning have to alternate with more traditional forms of learning, such as teamwork, training sessions, or discussions. Still there exist many possibilities to utilize ICT tools (e.g., simulation systems, learning platforms).

Different media also may compensate to a certain degree for personal relationships that rely on physical proximity. The knowledge itself in "learning networks" is not tightly bound to context, because it exists in an explicit form. The transmission of context-bound knowledge might be improved through additional use of context information, tools with a high degree of media richness, and accompanying practical exercises and tutorials. Also, knowledge in "learning networks" should be well structured (e.g., in learning modules) to improve learning processes within this Knowledge Network reference type. The Knowledge Network itself does not necessarily need a high degree of structure. The process of providing a "learning network" with explicit knowledge (i.e., content delivery) can thereby be well structured, whereas embodying knowledge must also consider individual preferences.

4.5.2. Facilitating Conditions

Central to this type of network is the experimenting and experiencing with new knowledge, as well as continuing the application and practice of already obtained knowledge. Learning by doing, experimentation, the trial-and-error process, experiencing and learning on the job, informal communications, and the simulation of existing problems—all are typical processes. Therefore, in order to support these processes, the structural and cultural conditions should enable practice-oriented and continuous learning, exercise and practice of new knowledge, learning from experience, and so forth. The knowledge culture in "learning networks" should provide values, such as tolerance of failures, enjoying experiments, and so on. Providing enough time for learning and reflection, as well as helping one another, are also important values within such a "learning culture." Further action-oriented processes to apply knowledge should be supported.

4.5.3. Tools

Tools in "learning networks" primarily need to support the transformation of explicit knowledge into implicit knowledge. Therefore, two (sub)processes must be supported (Figure 6-17). First, explicit knowledge must be made available in a suitable form (e.g., well structured, easy to read and understand). A discipline that is specialized in dealing with structuring knowledge for effective learning is for instance instructional design (Seufert and Seufert, 1999). Second, the explicit knowledge has to be embodied through action and practice.

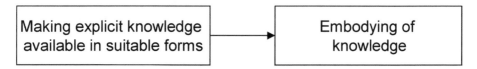

Figure 6-17. Key tasks of a "learning network."

Meetings and moderation tools, visualization tools (e.g., different types of knowledge maps), as well as corresponding roles, support the process of making explicit knowledge available in an adequate form. Within ICT exists a large range of tools to provide access to explicit knowledge for the purpose of learning (Seufert et. al., 2001), such as visualization tools, audio and video streaming, and community tools. The second process—the embodying of explicit knowledge, whereby communication plays an important role—may also be supported with organizational and ICT tools. Organizational tools consist of various communication tools and organization and management tools (i.e., coaching, mentoring, simulation, scenario learning, and groupwork). ICT tools that support this process cover the entire tool class of synchronous and asynchronous communication tools, for instance, simulation or modeling tools. Figure 6-18 provides an overview of organizational and ICT tools to support "learning networks."

Organizational Tools	ICT Tools
Communication and coordination tools:	**Communication and coordination tools:**
Knowledge forums, knowledge workshops	Messaging/E-mail
Meeting and moderation tools	Real-time conferencing systems (audio/video conferencing, chat, whiteboard, application sharing)
Language tools (common language, metaphors, controlled vocabulary, organizational thesaurus and dictionary)	Non real-time conferencing systems
	Learning technologies and learning systems for training, such as CBT, WBT
Organization and management tools:	Community tools, CSCW suites
Management tools	**Organizational and management tools:**
Visualization tools (e.g., presentation techniques, knowledge maps)	Personal Information management
Scenario learning, planning tools (e.g., scenario techniques), simulation	Scheduling/calendaring
HMR tools (e.g., mentoring, coaching, training and education)	**Integration and database tools:**
Learning tools (e.g., learning lessons, learning journeys)	Knowledge management suites
Feedback, rewards and incentives	Enterprise portals
Knowledge vision/goals	
Organizational structure tools:	
Roles and responsibilities (e.g., network moderator, media expert, trainer, coach)	
Group work	
Organizational culture tools:	
Corporate culture change programs	
Organizational development tools	

Figure 6-18. Organizational and ICT tools for a "learning network."

4.5.4. Example: Buckman

Buckman Laboratories (Bulab) was founded in 1945 as a specialty chemicals corporation. The fundamental business competence was its unique ability to provide solutions for controlling the growth of microorganisms. Today, Buckman's 1,300 employees generate an annual revenue of around $300 million, serving customers in over 100 countries by providing help in the use and application of advanced technology in the area of specialty chemicals. Since the intense customer orientation requires individual solutions, an average of 86 percent of Buckman's employees work at client sites. As a response to the extensive innovation dynamics in the area of specialty chemicals, which cause a constant creation and exchange of new knowledge, the Bulab Learning Center was founded.

> The 1996 founding of the Bulab Learning Center represents an important evolutionary milestone for Buckman in its quest to increasingly abandon its traditional and isolated training units and to search for new approaches.

The Bulab Learning Center is a virtual online-net of learning that makes globally coordinated training and global, multilingual knowledge standards available to the company's employees. Buckman Lab sees this center as a learning and knowledge management tool, which is offered to its employees in their usual work environment. The Learning Center makes training and learning available, giving each employee the responsibility and freedom to design their own personal and career development. Self-governed learning hereby provides the employees with the opportunity to call upon "learning units on demand" when and wherever they are needed, prompting a continuous performance increase in practice. Working together in a virtual learning environment allows employees to improve their communication and teamwork abilities, which can only be taught with great difficulty when using traditional teaching methods, but which are essential for a globally active company, as Buckman essentially is. To feed this competitive advantage, Buckman has transferred the responsibility for personal development to its employees.

Chapter 7

COMMUNITIES OF STRATEGIC PRACTICE

How Managers Create and Share Intuition in Strategic Processes in Turbulent Environments

Markus Venzin
SDA Bocconi, Milan, Italy

1. Introduction

Why is strategy implementation so hard to achieve? Why do so many strategy projects fail? Why are strategy statements often meaningless to employees? How do management teams develop knowledge about the future? How do individuals share strategic knowledge across the organization? The answer is—we don't know exactly. Hamel (1998) urges researchers and consultants to search for preconditions for strategic innovation: "What we need is a deep theory of strategy creation" (p. 10). He claims that—against the general opinion—strategy creation is harder to achieve than strategy implementation, particularly if a company is in search of revolutionary ideas.

Looking at the media sector, the task of strategy creation seems to

be even more difficult, given the elevated uncertainty. The media industry is being revolutionized by (digital) technology, globalization, and
changing customer preferences. As a result new industry dynamics and
industry players with distinct strategic resources and capabilities are
emerging. The field of multimedia applications has become the latest
hunting ground of large, entrepreneurial corporations coming from:

1. The "old" media sector (e.g., Viacom, Walt Disney, Bertelsmann, News
   Corp., Seagram, Time Warner)
2. Computer and consumer electronics (e.g., Sony, IBM, Microsoft)
3. Telecommunications (e.g., Deutsche Telekom, BT, AT&T, MCI
   WorldCom)
4. Online services (e.g., eBay, Amazon, Yahoo, AOL)

Those media companies are forced to make huge, risky bets on the
future while attempting to preempt upcoming opportunities by building
powerful and innovative strategic market positions.

Yet, is it legitimate to ask on what basis such strategic bets are made?
Put differently, how do media companies plan their future development
in the face of a turbulent and uncertain environment? Particularly on the
corporate level of media conglomerates, the complexity of strategic decisions seems to force top-management teams to make educated guesses
rather than analytical plans. Formal strategic planning processes seem to
lack flexibility and speed. But can companies simply leave strategy making to visionary and powerful CEOs?

We claim that even in turbulent times, companies need a system to
capture the innovative and very often intuitive ideas of talented people
both in and outside their organization. Relying only on the "gut feeling"
of the CEO, trial and error, or just simply pure luck may lead to a successful strategy once, but it is most unlikely that a second superior strategy will be crafted once the current one is outdated. Firms therefore
need to understand the fundamental principles underlying successful
strategies. There is, however, little recorded evidence of companies being
able to successfully link personal intuition from various places in the
company to the formal strategy processes.

2. Strategizing Under Conditions of Uncertainty

The dynamics of change have thickened the haze of uncertainty, and believing in traditional strategic forecasting tools may become increasingly hazardous (Courtney et al., 1997). As a consequence, it seems to be difficult to sustain conversations on a strategic (long-term) level (Roos and von Krogh, 1996, pp. 90–92), and instead of searching for foresight, some researchers suggest focusing on the problem of how to live without it (McDermott, 1996, p. 194).

This situation of "absence of strategy" (Inkpen and Choudhury, 1995) might be an attempt by top-management teams to increase flexibility and innovation. Research in complexity theory (Stacey, 1995) suggests "organizing" rather than "planning." The focal point within strategic management might therefore move from long-term planning to supporting flexible organizational forms and practices (Beinhocker, 1999; Schreyögg, 1999), or pure experimentation with new business models (Leonard-Barton, 1995). The corporate planning diffused during the 1960s and 1970s consisted mostly of "scientific" decision-making techniques, including cost–benefit analysis, discounted cash flow appraisal, linear programming, econometric forecasting, and macroeconomic demand management (Grant, 1998, p. 17). Most of those planning techniques seem to take a reactive approach to external changes and provide limited results when coping with increased uncertainty.

The goal of this chapter is to consider how companies extend and recreate (remodel?) two separate strategy processes—the formal strategic planning process that commits organizational resources to performance targets and the informal entrepreneurial processes through which new ideas emerge and strategic innovations are born in order to cope with uncertainties and make the most of entrepreneurship, creativity, and intuition. The guiding research question to be explored is the following:

How do firms facilitate creative strategic thinking and foster the development of innovative wealth-creating strategies in the face of uncertainty?

We focus on the interplay between formal planning and informal strategic conversations. We also explore the ways in which companies integrate innovative ideas into their regular and systematized strategic planning processes and thereby increase their "strategic metabolism," that is, the quality of strategic thinking in terms of generation of strategic innovations. The myth of the "mogul leadership"-style, attributed to most media companies, is of particular interest. For example, to what extent do strong personalities with extensive decision power like Rupert Murdoch of News Corp., Disney's Michael Eisner, or Viacom's Sumner Redstone govern the destiny of media companies based on their intuition or "gut feelings"? How far down the hierarchy is decision-making power shifted, making the strategy process more participative, transparent, and explicit to the rest of the organization?

This chapter aims at uncovering some of the complex rule structures that lead to strategic decisions in fast moving industries. The role of intuition in decision making has been intensively discussed in the strategic management and cognition literature. It is mostly argued that intuition may increase the speed and quality of decision making, especially in situations characterized by high uncertainty. It is, however, not well researched how intuition grows in an executive and how individual intuition can be transferred or even shared among executives. As shown in Figure 7-1, we first discuss the levels and types of uncertainty the media industry is currently facing (the project will focus on past strategic decisions whenever current strategic issues are too sensitive to be explored). Second, we discuss the impact of uncertainty on the strategic processes. Strategy processes are defined as a process of organizational learning involving intuition, interpretation, integration, and institutionalization of strategic ideas. And finally, we discuss the impact of strategy processes on the development of a strategic position.

3. Strategy Processes Research

Issues concerning the development of sound strategies have recently moved up the agenda of strategy research (Lechner and Müller-Stewens, 1999; Schreyögg, 1999). In a fluctuating and competitive environment,

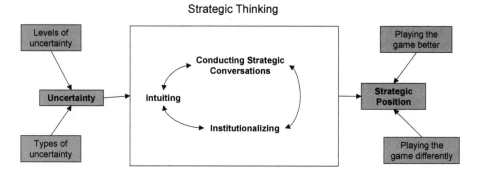

Figure 7-1. Strategic thinking under uncertainty.

strategy formation abilities are more likely to be a source of competitive advantage than clever strategic positioning (Whittington, 1999). Decreased sustainability of competitive advantage due to weakened barriers against imitation and substitution has given rise to a phenomenon labelled "hypercompetition" (D´Aveni, 1994): Companies need to destroy their competitive advantages themselves before their competitors do it; strategies can only be short term by nature; logical strategic behavior leads to predictable actions and should be avoided; the ability to identify and develop surprising sources of competitive advantage is the only sustainable competence in hypercompetitive markets. To survive in a hypercompetitive environment, companies may need to develop superior strategic capabilities.

Gary Hamel (1998) recognizes that management theory has advanced substantially on the *content* dimension of strategy. However, knowledge of the *conduct* of strategy seems to have made less progress during the last decade: "Managers today know much about how to embed quality disciplines, how to reengineer processes, and how to reduce cycle times, but they don't know how to foster the development of innovative wealth–creating strategies" (Hamel, 1998, pp. 8–9). A starting point for understanding strategic management practices in an ever-changing industry may be to identify and describe the factors that create uncertainty.

4. Conditions of Uncertainty

Some industry experts advocate that an Internet-year equals two "old-economy" months. Put differently, the new economy moves six to seven times faster (Zerdick et al., 1999, p. 13). Courtney, Kirkland, and Viguerie (1997) suggest coping with increased uncertainty by distinguishing four levels of uncertainty: In a "clear-enough future," traditional strategy tools such as regression analysis may work because the past is an adequate predictor for the future. On the next higher level of uncertainty, one may identify "alternative futures," such as capacity strategies for chemical plants. According to the authors, the strategy tools to apply are decision analysis, option valuation models, and game theory. The third uncertainty level consists of a "range of futures," when entering an emergent market, for example. No obvious scenarios can be identified and therefore latent-demand research, technology forecasting, or scenario planning may be adequate strategy tools. The fourth uncertainty level is "true ambiguity," where no basis for forecasting exists. The authors mention the choice of entering the Russian market in 1992 or the decision to enter the market for consumer multi-media applications as examples. In a situation of true ambiguity, the strategy tools that may be applied are analogies, pattern recognition, or nonlinear dynamic models.

In sum, Courtney, Kirkland, and Viguerie (1997) recommend first of all identifying the nature and extent of residual uncertainties and then applying the strategy tools that best fit the amount of uncertainty. A more comprehensive strategy tool kit should therefore include scenario planning (Heijden, 1996; Schoemaker, 1995; Schwartz, 1996), game theory (Dixit and Nalebuff, 1991), system dynamics (Senge, 1990), agent-based models (Casti, 1997), and a real options approach (Dixit and Pindyck, 1995). In addition to levels of uncertainty, we propose to distinguish types of uncertainties. *Levels* of uncertainty refer to the predictability of future events, whereas *types* of uncertainty describe the origins of uncertainty, i.e., the factors that cause uncertainty, such as technological changes or changes in customer preferences.

5. What Strategy Models Really Work in Uncertain Environments?

Beinhocker (1999) in his article on the "origins of strategy" suggests taking an evolutionary approach to mastering uncertainty. Strategy in an environment of true ambiguity may be seen as an "evolutionary search" on a "fitness landscape" (Kaufmann, 1995), where the strategic goal becomes to create options and open up new choices rather than shutting them down (Beinhocker, 1999, p. 53). The survival motto for an uncertain world suggested by Beinhocker therefore reads as follows: Invest in diversity; value strategies as if they were options; categorize the mix of strategies; stress-test your strategies; bring the market inside; and use venture-capital performance metrics.

In an empirical study analyzing 113 public limited U.K. companies, Glaister and Falshaw (1999, p. 115) discovered, however, that the most frequently used strategy tools are the most simple ones: "We therefore conclude that companies can obtain benefits from a classical approach to strategic planning and these benefits are apparent with the use of relatively unsophisticated tools and techniques." Among the most often used strategic tools are first spreadsheet "what if" analyses, followed by analyses of "key" or "critical" success factors, financial analyses of competitors, SWOT analyses, and core capabilities analyses. More sophisticated methodologies like soft systems methodology can be found in the last position of the ranking list.

What might surprise us is that although the environment has become increasingly complex, the strategic tools to cope with that complexity are the well-established and—at a first glimpse—simple ones. Option valuation, game theory, or models based on complexity theory do not seem to have a substantial impact on management practice (yet). The real option approach, for example, is not popular among management practitioners because academic discussion has so far centered around "arcane equations and models" (Amram and Kulatilaka, 1999, p. 104) and has thereby seemed to be too complex to be pragmatically applied to management issues. Even if the strategy tools are simple, the thinking processes taking place around the use of those tools, however, is rather complex and, in the end, decisive for the creation of a successful strategy.

What may reassure strategists is that Glaster and Falshaw (1999) conclude their empirical study on strategic management practices in the U.K. by saying that "...strategic planning is currently perceived to be of benefit and is still going strong" (p. 115). Other studies undertaken on the impact of strategic planning on company performance have, however, not always come to the same positive conclusion—for an overview of some forty studies, see Boyd (1991).

6. Viewing Strategy Formation as a Process of Organizational Learning

To boost the positive impact of strategic planning on performance, influential authors in the field of strategic management—such as Mintzberg (1994), Hamel and Prahalad (1994), or Wilson (1994)—have suggested shifting the focus away from strategic planning to strategic thinking and developing a theory of strategy creation (Hamel, 1998, p. 10). In Gary Hamel's view, the planning process may create a plan, but strategy is more than producing plans—it is about setting the preconditions for innovative ideas.

Frequently, strategy formation is described as a learning process. Henry Mintzberg (1990, p. 190) views strategy formation as "a long, subtle, and difficult process of learning." He accuses the "planning school" around Igor Ansoff (1965) of promoting "thought independent of action, strategy formation above all as a process of conception, rather than as one of learning" (Mintzberg, 1994, p. 182). Mintzberg's approach, on the other hand, might be described as "try something, see if it works and learn from your experience" (Goold, 1992, p. 169).

However, viewing the process of strategy formation as "organizational learning" may not necessarily imply a position within the "learning school" as described by Mintzberg and Lampel (1999). Cognitive processes, power, cultural or environmental aspects are not excluded by definition. If learning is perceived as taking information from the environment and relating these to the previously acquired frames of reference

(Varela, 1979), even planning may be described as a process of organizational learning.

Goold (1992, p. 170) therefore suggests not viewing strategy as making random experiments and using both strategy formation perspectives—planning and learning—to improve management practice. Similarly, Brews and Hunt's (1999) empirical study concludes that "good" strategic planning, especially in unstable environments, includes both planning and learning. Specificity of strategic ends and means served in their study as the decisive factor that distinguished planning from learning, and it is this specificity that may lead to the inflexibility of a plan in turbulent times. From a knowledge perspective, one could however interpret the specificity of ends and means as knowledge that has been made explicit in a written plan. Explicit knowledge may originate from a tacit basis, which is often called "intuition" or even "collective intuition" (Eisenhart, 1999). If the major difference between the learning school and the planning school is that intuition has been made explicit, the below described process of "organizational learning" may well include both the learning and the planning school.

Assuming now that strategy formation may be described as a process of organizational learning, the following sections outline a framework for organizational learning mainly based on the work of Crossan, Lane, and White (1999), including three core processes: intuiting, conducting strategic conversations, and institutionalizing.

6.1. Intuiting: Pattern Recognition from Past Experiences

Crossan, Lane, and White (1999, p. 525) refer to Karl Weick's definition of intuiting as "...the preconscious recognition of the pattern and/or possibilities inherent in a personal stream of experience" (Weick, 1995, p. 25). Intuition therefore is an individual rather than a group or even organizational phenomenon. It refers to a stock of knowledge that is tacit (Polanyi, 1966) and hard to express in words. Some authors (e.g., Shapiro and Spence, 1997) suggest using intuition and implicit learning as interchangeable. The attention for the role of intuition in strategic processes has centered around the question of whether intuitive decision making is leading to better organizational performance in highly turbulent environments or not.

Nonaka and Takeuchi (1995) claim that too formal and systematic thinking is outdated and should eventually be replaced by a more intuitive mode of thinking. "….Western managers need to 'unlearn' their old view of knowledge and grasp the importance of the Japanese view. They need to get out of the old mode of thinking that knowledge can be acquired, taught, and trained through manuals, books or lectures. Instead, they need to pay more attention to the less formal and systematic side of knowledge and start focusing on highly subjective insights, intuitions, and hunches that are gained through the use of metaphors, pictures, or experiences" (Nonaka and Takeuchi, 1995, p. 11).

Empirical studies in psychology have shown that individuals can learn complex rule structures without being able to articulate them (Shapiro and Spence, 1997, p. 63). In such instances, managers may refer to their gut feelings or intuition, defined as "…a non-conscious, holistic processing mode in which judgments are made with no awareness of the rules or knowledge used for inference and can feel right despite one's inability to articulate the reason" (Shapiro and Spence, 1997, p. 64). Inherent in this definition, one may find three main building blocs of intuition:

1. The source of intuition occurs at a nonconscious level and one is therefore unable to identify what caused it (intuition is therefore distinct from judgments with clear thought structures).

2. Intuition allows us to understand not only the variables involved in a complex situation but also their relationships.

3. Intuition often involves a feeling of being "right."

Similarly, Khatri and Ng (2000, pp. 59–60) describe intuition as a psychological function that allows us to see the totality of a given situation and to synthesize isolated data and experiences into an integrated group; intuition is subconscious, complex, quick, distinct from emotion, not affected by cognitive biases, and part of all decisions. Developing tacit knowledge based, on explicit knowledge is closely related to "learning by doing": "When experiences through socialization, externalization, and combination are internalized into individuals' tacit knowledge bases in the form of shared mental models or technical know-how, they become valuable assets" (Nonaka and Takeuchi, 1995, p. 69).

It is, however, most likely that the combination of both intuition and formal thinking plays a role in strategic processes. Research conducted by Khatri and Ng (2000) or Shapiro and Spence (1997) suggests that intuition should be cautiously used in combination with rational analysis in stable and moderately unstable environments, but should be used more often in highly unstable contexts. Well-structured problems to which established decision rules can be applied seem to occur less frequently in fast-moving industries than ill-structured problems for which no explicit and widely accepted decision rules exist. Intuition might therefore be more applied in managerial decision processes than in other industries.

6.2. Conducting Strategic Conversations: How Can a Language for "Gut Feelings" Be Developed?

Often, managers refer to their intuition when post-rationalizing important strategic decisions: "I just had a gut feeling." However, few top executives have the power to steer their companies based on their gut feelings. At a certain point, it may be necessary to communicate individual feelings about the company's future course of action—be it to get support from the shareholders or to facilitate implementation. In times of uncertainty and ambiguity where strategy may be reduced to a "gut feeling,"—hard to express in words—the communication process becomes challenging. Distributing leaflets with vision statements, the publication of an occasional article in the in-house magazine, or number crunching in strategy meetings may have to be complemented with other forms of communication. Developing a shared vision entails developing redundant information about the future, or shared meaning that is stored in more than one brain or body. Yet how can "gut feelings" become shared information? How can media moguls or individuals from distinct parts of the company communicate what is hard to put in words? How can one interpret one's own intuition?

In *strategic conversations*, intuition is interpreted (made explicit) and distinct meanings are then integrated into shared understanding. Winning strategies emerge from a decision process in which executives develop collective intuition, accelerate constructive conflict, maintain decision pacing, and avoid politics (Eisenhardt, 1999). Strategic conversations may be described as settings in which a management team develops a picture of a common future as well as strategies to reach the corporate objectives.

Several authors have recognized the essential role conversations play in today's business world. They argue that individuals create their realities through their everyday conversations (von Krogh and Roos, 1995). Strategic thinking on the organizational level therefore requires a capacity to link up these individual conversations (Liedtka and Rosenblum, 1996), especially in a network of individuals that hardly know each other, and create an environment where employees and other members of the organizational network can have productive conversations about the future of the company.

Interpreting may be defined as the process of "explaining through words and/or actions an insight or idea to one's self and to others" (Crossan et al., 1999, p. 525). Nonaka (1995, p. 72) calls the process of transferring tacit knowledge into explicit knowledge "externalization," whereas turning tacit knowledge into tacit knowledge requires "socialization." *Externalization* involves the use of "…metaphors, analogies, concepts, hypotheses, or models" (Nonaka and Takeuchi, 1995, p. 64) to uncover the explicit part of knowledge. *Socialization* on the other hand is "…a process of sharing experiences" through on-the-job training, in brainstorming camps (Nonaka and Takeuchi, 1995, pp. 62–63), or just managerial conversations.

Take the case of 3M, where managers recognized that their Power-Point presentations at strategy meetings did not facilitate the communication of strategic ideas in a way strategic stories do. Traditional business plans at 3M "…failed to reflect deep thought or to inspire commitment"; strategic stories on the other hand "…not only clarify the thinking behind their plans but also capture the imagination and the excitement of the people in their organizations" (Shaw et al., 1998, p. 42).

Throughout the interpretation process, words may help, but common experiences are central to the communication of one's own intuition to others. Meaning is generated if people look at what they have done and then try to make sense of these events: "Although people may not share meaning, they do share experience" (Weick, 1995, p. 188). The clue may be to generate memorable strategic experiences that people remember and continue to discuss. The more the message is afflicted with uncertainty and ambiguity, the more difficult it is to create similar interpretations among organizational members. Common experiences need to be created and new forms of communication such as visual thinking need to be developed (Sanders, 1998) to integrate divergent interpretations.

The process of integrating may therefore be perceived as "...developing shared understanding among individuals and of taking coordinated action through mutual adjustment" (Crossan et al., 1999, p. 525). Although intuition has been described as an individual rather than a collective process, *integration* attempts to develop what could be called "collective intuition" (Eisenhardt, 1999), "collective mind" (Weick and Roberts, 1993), or "collective tacit knowledge" (Leonard-Barton and Sensiper, 1998). To turn individual "gut feelings" into collective intuition, formal meetings (Eisenhardt, 1999) or informal conversations (Crossan et al., 1999) may play an essential role.

6.3. Institutionalizing: Creating Communities of Strategic Practice

Crossan, Lane, and White (1999, p. 525) define *institutionalizing* as " ...the process of ensuring that routinized actions occur. Tasks are defined, actions specified, and organizational mechanisms put in place to ensure that certain actions occur. Institutionalizing is the process of embedding learning that has occurred by individuals and groups into the organization, and it includes systems, structures, procedures, and strategy." Accidental learning is turned into systematic learning, or a "practice." On the one side, the "old" planning approach with the formal annual "creative" meetings followed by strategy workshops, mid-term planning rounds, and annual budgeting will most likely not disappear and will continue to systematize the strategic learning on the organizational level. On the other side, first field interviews have shown that informal groups discussing strategic issues have become increasingly important. Those groups may be labeled as "communities of strategic practice."

Whittington (1996, p. 732) proposes to look at strategy as a *practice:* "Practice is concerned with the work of strategizing—all the meeting, the talking, the form-filling and the number crunching by which strategy actually gets formulated and implemented." To study strategy as practice means to research into the process of strategizing on the level of managers or management teams. *Communities of practice* may be defined as "...groups of people informally bound together by shared expertise and passion for a joint enterprise—engineers engaged in deep-water drilling, for example, consultants who specialize in strategic marketing, or front-line managers in charge of check processing at a large commercial bank" (Wenger and Snyder, 2000, p. 139).

As the organizational learning model suggests, the strategic process seems to be less about the formulation of strategic decisions, and more about conversation and sharing of intuitive insights around key strategic issues. Leonard-Barton and Sensiper (1998) in their work on the role of tacit knowledge in group innovation suggest that tacit knowledge should be exercised in the service of innovation in three ways: problem solving, problem finding, and prediction and anticipation.

So far, two variables of the proposed theoretical model have been discussed, that is, uncertainty and strategic thinking modes. Intuiting, interpreting, integrating, and institutionalizing have been described as four distinct phases occurring during the learning process of strategy making. Institutionalizing means that accidental learning is turned into systematic learning. In other words, informal strategic thinking is captured in a formal strategy process.

7. Creating a Unique Strategic Position

The third component mentioned in the theoretical model in Figure 7-1 is the dependent variable, that is, the strategic position. Levels and types of uncertainty influence the way of strategic thinking, which, in turn, influence the strategic position of a company. A strategic position as perceived by Markides (1999, p. 1) is "… the sum of a company's answer to these three questions: *Who* should I target as customers? *What* products or services should I offer them? *How* should I do this?" Successful companies manage to develop a distinctive strategic position by making sometimes tough choices in those three fields: "There is no question that success stems from the exploitation of a unique strategic position. Unfortunately, no position can remain unique or attractive forever" (Markides, 1999, p. 8).

As indicated by the theoretical model introduced earlier, strategic positions change over time and companies attempt both "playing the game better" and "playing the game differently" (Markides, 1999, p. 14). The former consists of improving the current strategic position by practices such as restructuring, refocusing, process reengineering, quality programs, or employee empowerment. To play the game differently or to even play a different game means to search for fundamentally new answers to the "who," "what," and "how" questions.

Recently, well-known scholars in the field of strategic management have put more emphasis on the benefits of playing the game differently, or in other words, creating strategic innovation. The end of incrementalism has been announced by several authors in the field of strategic management. One of the major "revolutionaries" among them is Gary Hamel (1996, p. 69). He outlines how rule breakers such as IKEA, the Body Shop, Charles Schwab, Dell Computer, Swatch, or Southwest Airlines have managed to shape their industries; the process by which such innovative strategic thinking may be developed is described as inquisitive, expansive, democratic, prescient, inventing, inclusive, demanding, and subversive. Senior managers are more likely to prevent "revolutionaries" from developing and implementing innovative ideas: "To help revolutionary strategies emerge, senior managers must supplement the hierarchy of experience with a hierarchy of imagination" (Hamel, 1996, p. 70).

Strategic processes in most companies still seem to produce logical strategic behavior rather than identifying surprising sources of competitive advantage. Strategic innovation—as opposed to incrementalism—has, however, received much attention in recent research on strategic processes. Hamel (1996; 1998) perceives strategic innovation as change in the industry model. He claims that it is more difficult for established companies to strategically innovate and that strategists and senior executives need to set preconditions that could give rise to strategy innovation rather than developing strategies themselves—planning and strategizing are even seen as two distinct activities. Preconditions for strategic innovations proposed by Hamel include mechanisms to stimulate conversations and promote "new voices," "passions," "perspectives," and "experiments."

Similarly, Markides's (1998) way to strategic innovation is to identify gaps in the industry and to turn them into mass markets. His recipe for overcoming the structural and cultural inertia of success is to monitor the strategic health of the company, create a positive crisis, challenge the strategic planning process, and institutionalize a questioning attitude. Markides assumes that successful strategic innovators are faster at selling new strategic challenges to everybody. Firms that are able and willing to start their thinking at different starting points are more likely to escape existing assumptions and stereotypes and to see or discover something new.

To see or even create such industry breakpoints is, however, a challenging task. Strebel (1995, p. 11) defines industry breakpoints as: "…characterized by a new offering to the market that is so much superior in terms of the value perceived by the customer/consumer and the delivered cost of the offering that it changes the rules of the competitive game." Divergent industry breakpoints according to Strebel are usually product/market driven and lead to an increasingly innovative variety in the competitive offerings.

Organizational capabilities that are needed in order to create divergent industry breakpoints are direct innovation (strongly based on the creativity and market sensitivity of senior managers), spontaneous innovation as bottom-up initiatives, and stakeholder networking. Convergent industry breakpoints on the other hand involve improvements in the systems and processes employed to deliver the products or services. The main capabilities that may lead to convergent industry breakpoints are systematization (turning a task into mass production), continual improvement, and process re-engineering.

Kim and Mauborgne (1997) introduced the concept of "value innovation," which also refers to a change in the industry condition, regardless of what competitors currently do. High-growth companies, the authors argue, tend to focus less on competition than their less successful rivals do. To create value innovation, senior managers need to identify, articulate, and challenge the strategic logic of the company—and to think with the logic of a new entrant. This is, however, a difficult task as the work by Prahalad and Bettis (1986) on "dominant logic" shows.

The concept of *dominant logic* refers to "a mind set or a world view or conceptualization of the business and the administrative tools to accomplish goals and make decisions in that business" (Prahalad and Bettis, 1986, p. 491). The two main sources of dominant logic are the reinforcement of a worldview by market success and complex problem-solving behavior (cognitive simplifications by drawing on conventional wisdom or past experiences as well as cognitive bias due to inadequate or missing information). To overcome phenomena of dominant logic and to innovate strategically, companies need to develop the ability of the company—or its dominant coalition to learn (Prahalad and Bettis, 1986, p. 497)—or to "unlearn" (Hedberg, 1981) first so as to get rid of previously acquired mental models.

The concept of dominant logic as outlined by Prahalad and Bettis (1986) aims at showing the limits of diversification strategies. It is claimed that top managers are less likely to "respond appropriately" to situations where the dominant logic is different, as well as not respond quickly enough (p. 497). These difficulties caused by distinct dominant logics represent additional hidden costs of diversification. The insights on dominant logic can, however, be extended to any company—that encounters rapid change or aims at strategic innovation.

8. Bringing It All Together: In Search of Strategic Experiences

This chapter started off claiming that management teams often experience difficulty in sustaining conversations about the future. The dynamics of change have thickened the haze of uncertainty, and believing in traditional strategic forecasting tools becomes increasingly hazardous. As a consequence, strategy meetings often center on short-term issues. The desired output of most strategy processes, however, is reduced uncertainty and some kind of agreement on the long-term direction of the company. A shared vision of the future is nevertheless hard to find in most companies.

The communication of a picture of the future across the hierarchy risks becoming an organizational ritual without much value added. In times of uncertainty and ambiguity, where foresight may be reduced to a "gut feeling," hard to express in words, the communication process becomes challenging. Distributing some leaflets with vision statements, the publication of an occasional article in the in-house magazine, or some number crunching in strategy meetings doesn't do anymore. Developing a shared vision means to develop redundant information about the future, or shared meaning that is stored in more than one brain or body. Yet what does it take to create redundant information of a "gut feeling"? How can one communicate what is hard to put in words? How did Shakespeare's Romeo declare his deep love to Juliet?

Words may help, but common experiences are the clue for the creation of shared meaning. Meaning is generated when people look at what they have done and then try to make sense of these events: "Although people may not share meaning, they do share experience" (Weick, 1995, p. 188). The more the message is afflicted with uncertainty and ambiguity, the more difficult it is to create similar interpretations among organizational members. Therefore, what a member of a group has in common with other members of the same social group is not so much a set of shared beliefs or values as such, but a set of shared semiotic procedures or ethnomethods (Shotter, 1993, p. 46). Put somewhat more succinctly, groups may share a way of meaning creation and a certain set of ordered forms of communication.

This chapter suggests valuing personal intuition and integrating those "gut feelings" into formal and institutionalized strategy processes. We claim that:

1. The more uncertain the environment is, the more companies tend to rely on the intuition of single, powerful executives.
2. The biggest challenge within a strategy process of companies navigating in fast-moving industries is to link personal intuition with formal strategy planning routines.
3. Successful strategies emerge when a group of key decision makers manages to collaborate as a "community of strategic practice."
4. The stronger the link between intuiting, conducting strategic conversations, and institutionalizing, the more likely an organization is to develop revolutionary ideas and to change the rules of the industry.

Chapter 8

VIRTUAL KNOWLEDGE COMMUNITIES AND THE ISSUE OF INFORMATION QUALITY

Dr. Daniel Diemers
University of St. Gallen, Switzerland

1. Introduction

In previous publications I have investigated the issue of information quality (IQ) in the context of Knowledge Management (KM), and introduced a distinct perspective on the social dimension of these concepts. This perspective was based on the interpretative paradigm of the newer sociology of knowledge and the respective works of Alfred Schutz, Peter L. Berger, and Thomas Luckmann.

In these argumentations I've proposed a model of the basic transformational process in Knowledge Management, which turns external-

Original contribution to the IQ 2000 Conference at the Massachusetts Institute of Technology, Cambridge, Massachusetts. I owe thanks to Alfred J. Beerli, Martin J. Eppler, and Joerg Staeheli for their kind support.

ized information into internalized knowledge and vice versa. Within this basic model I've also developed a framework for information quality, which relates to earlier contributions in the field of IQ but nevertheless makes a proposition of transferring concepts from the interpretative paradigm into this field (Diemers 1999b; 2000a).

Although I've never focused entirely on the aspect of practical conceptualizations of KM in these works, and simply referenced to established theories of this discipline, this chapter now proposes a social conceptualization of Knowledge Management, and introduces the concept of virtual knowledge communities (VKCs) in the context of Knowledge Management and information quality.

This conceptualization of community-based exchange and management of knowledge in organizations is also based on strong sociological foundations. These include classical works by Ferdinand Toennies and Max Weber, the renowned community studies of the Chicago School of the 1960s, and recent ethnographic research within the increasingly popular discourse around virtual communities.

The goal of this chapter is thus to develop a general conceptualization of VKC based on the interpretative paradigm of the new sociology of knowledge, and to derive a respective framework for IQ, which connects and relates to established conceptualizations of information quality in knowledge and information exchange.

2. Challenges of the eConomy Environment

The new eBusiness environment can be characterized by high market volatility and an increasing uncertainty of decision makers about key market forces and trends. From a management perspective we have two important contingencies that will influence the performance of global companies over the next decades. The first is the evolution of Internet-based commerce and business, the second is the shift of negotiation and market power from producer to consumer. Both tendencies are obviously triggered by the development of virtual spaces, and both tendencies will definitely have a substantial impact on the way we will be doing business in the future.

The first contingency correlates to the emergence of virtual spaces. These spaces have evolved into a new interaction media to share information, communicate, express one's opinion, or settle contracts. As a very low-cost, time-effective communication platform, the Internet has become a major facilitator for shareholders, stakeholders, market makers, analysts, and contractors. But this development also includes specific dangers, for example, business misinformation or harmful rumors that may eventually spread and impact on exchange markets. A second issue is the challenge of information quality on the Internet in general or within a corporate intranet in particular; the third issue is the problem of information overload.

The second contingency is related to the shift of market power and the emergence of global virtual communities. Due to an increasing amount of available market information and the possibility to compare market prices, consumers have more options to choose from. This development is even more relevant within the eConomy, witnessing the fact that virtual communities are increasingly becoming new patterns of social practice. Virtual communities allow people to team up with likely minded consociates independently from time and place. Members of virtual communities share a common interest and use virtual spaces as a media platform, which is very low cost, may potentially have a broad impact, allows for anonymity, and is in many aspects uncharted territory from a legal point of view.

As a consequence, new modes of organizing have evolved, which allow companies to decentralize, share resources, or work on joint projects for a limited period of time. These new organizational forms are commonly referred to as virtual organizations, or virtual corporations. They have changed the level playing field in such a way that large companies are no longer in the position to dominate markets completely, but are increasingly being challenged by smaller, more agile companies. These small virtual organizations are able to easily adapt their structure to a specific project and change their market focus quicker than their larger counterparts (Davidow and Malone, 1994; Nohria and Berkeley, 1994).

Within this chapter, one important feature of the new eConomy is the rising importance of knowledge as a primary resource in companies, both in large, traditional companies and in small eBusiness companies. This argument is supported by three observations:

1. The transformation of economic structures in Western societies, that is, a shift from the industrial sector to the service sector, where immaterial resources are the most important and valuable asset of a firm.

2. Generally accelerating innovation cycles both in traditional industry segments and in the new economy, which lead to traditional, established knowledge and processes getting obsolete quicker and demand for renewal and faster innovation.

3. The rising importance of business intelligence systems, IT-based knowledge repositories, competitive intelligence, early-warning systems, and Knowledge Management for successful business models.

3. Knowledge Management and Information Quality

In the context of the eConomy we currently observe a wide scope of different business models. In most of them, practices of knowledge creation, processing, sharing, and distribution play a significant role. In general, an added value for customers within the eConomy can be offered either through virtual eBusiness services, or through an exchange of physical goods over virtual e-commerce platforms. Both types of business activities rely heavily on institutionalized processes of knowledge transfer and exchange.

An interesting point here is the observation that issues of information quality (IQ) are rarely conceptualized or included in new business models for the eConomy. This is even more astonishing given the fact that the epistemic dimension of new business models is typically conceptualized by Knowledge Management infrastructures and tools, which are in most cases very technical in nature. Within this chapter I therefore address both issues: a more social approach to Knowledge Management, which focuses on the exchange of personalized knowledge, and the related issue of information quality.

Let us now take a closer look at the implicit duality of Knowledge Management theory and practice, which differentiates a technical, IT-based approach to Knowledge Management (*processing and distribution perspective*), and a social, community-based approach to Knowledge Management (*sharing and socialization perspective*), as illustrated in Table 8-1.

Within this duality, we can generally divide activities under the notion of Knowledge Management into management of personalized and codified knowledge. Whereas the first is a soft-skill, social approach to generate and distribute knowledge within knowledge communities, the latter is clearly an issue of sound IT and database infrastructures. Traditional Knowledge Management theories are, from that perspective, more concerned with codified, externalized knowledge than with personalized, implicit forms of knowledge.

Personalized Knowledge	Codified Knowledge
Implicit/tacit knowledge	Explicit knowledge
Stored in cognitive brain structures Stored in personal notes, reminders, symbols, etc.	Stored/visualized/externalized on paper, in knowledge repositories, etc.
Personal networks, communities, experts	Hierarchies, libraries, IT infrastructures
Knowledge transfer by interaction	Knowledge transfer by media transfer
Sharing and socialization	Processing and distribution
Contextualized interpretation	Decontextualized interpretation
Remembering	Accessing/retrieving data
Forgetting	Forgetting loss of data, loss of index structure

Table 8-1. The duality of Knowledge Management.

Whereas early conceptualizations of Knowledge Management both in theory and practice have been focusing heavily on IT-based knowledge repositories and systems to manage codified knowledge, we currently observe a certain growth in popularity of approaches that focus or include sociologically influenced, community-based methodologies for management of personalized knowledge (Von Krogh, Ichijo, and

Nonaka, 2000; Nonaka and Konno, 1998; Von Krogh, 1998; Huemer, Von Krogh, and Roos, 1998).

This general tendency is in line with several experiences within contemporary Knowledge Management practice, where well-designed, technical Knowledge Management systems often failed to achieve the expected benefits. Most of these soft-factor impediments to Knowledge Management can be subsumed under four main paragraphs.

1. In almost all business activities, there is some specific knowledge that cannot be made explicit for a wide range of reasons, for example, high complexity, high degrees of automation, strong habitualization of practices, conflicts in time budget and priority, or inapt instruments for knowledge externalization.

2. In many cases there is no intrinsic willingness to externalize knowledge in the most adequate and optimal way. Typical reasons for this are often linked to individual strategic thinking, power relationships, lack of trust, or lack of emotional bonds.

3. People have only partial capabilities to interpret decontextualized external knowledge, for example, because of cross-cultural differences, semantic incongruencies, misinterpretations, and misunderstandings (Diemers, 1999a).

4. Externalized knowledge is too quickly becoming unusable, as too little context information is being included, or as classifications and indexes are misconceived.

The latter two points are obviously interesting issues within the context of information quality. The following conceptualization of community-based Knowledge Management addresses these impediments. Whereas a solid IT-based knowledge repository and corresponding Knowledge Management tools are important components of this distinct approach to Knowledge Management, the community-based model is an attempt to conceptualize the social aspects of knowledge exchange.

4. Virtual Knowledge Communities

My approach to community-based Knowledge Management is based on three theoretical discourses: the interpretative paradigm of the newer sociology of knowledge, the sociological understanding of and theory about communities in general, and the heterogeneous discourses around virtual communities, both from a sociological and business administration perspective.

The typical notion of community usually opens large patterns of diffuse associations, which might include social networks, family, neighborhood, clans, emotional bonds, and several more. Ferdinand Toennies (1922) was the first to approach the term community from a scientific, namely sociological, perspective. To Toennies, a community was the nucleus of social life, the very essence of living together with our consociates. He accordingly differentiated three types of communities:

1. Communities of blood comprise very close family relationships over a long period of time, with high levels of intimacy, trust, and emotional bonds.
2. Communities of place and proximity constitute themselves voluntarily or involuntarily as soon as people are sharing the same physical space. This type includes, for example, neighborhood communities, street gangs, cell mates in prison, campus communities, all of which evolve as a result of shared resources, repeated interaction, and processes of habitualization that facilitate and structure daily interactions.
3. Communities of mind are formed voluntarily on the basis of shared interests, common practices, intellectual exchange, likeliness, and friendship.

This basic typology was later enhanced by Max Weber (1914) and others, but may still serve as a basic differentiation scheme today. In the first half of the last century, the scientific discourse around communities was often accompanied by a morally biased critique of modern society.

That discourse, by the way, recently regained new attention as a result of the technologically induced transformation of society.

In the 1960s, however, the community studies of the Chicago School were a remarkable turning point, in that scientists started to research communities based on a purely ethnographic, descriptive empirical methodology (Bell and Newby, 1971; Foster, 1997; see also Hannerz, 1992; Cohen, 1985; LeVine, 1984; Cole et al., 1971; Geertz, 1973).

During the early years of the Internet a wide variety of virtual communities evolved in MUDs, chat rooms, and discussion boards. In this context, detailed ethnographic community studies became popular, but attracted only a small group of anthropologists, sociologists, and psychologists (Baym, 1995; 1998). After several years, however, the social phenomenon of virtual communities gained a certain level of popularity in broader media, a development that can be related to certain authors like Howard Rheingold (1993; 1995) or Sherry Turkle (1994; 1995; 1996).

Fueled by the euphoria about e-commerce, the discourse around virtual communities entered a new field, namely management practice and business administration theory, and the term became lately a popular buzz-word in business models for the new eConomy (Hagel and Armstrong, 1997; Pinchot, 1998).

In my understanding, a virtual community is basically a community that constitutes itself fully or to a major part in virtualized interaction spaces. Looking at it from a sociological perspective we can identify seven different factors of cohesion that characterize the social phenomena of community: shared interests, shared norms and values, common interaction platform, emotional bonds, continuity, reciprocity, and identity construction (Eppler and Diemers, 2000).

A virtual community, then, is a community that uses primarily virtual interaction platforms for communication. Of course, this also implies that members of a virtual community share a virtual space, but not necessarily a physical space. Within the scope of virtual communities, different spatial configurations may evolve, from hybrid forms, where community members meet regularly face-to-face, to completely virtual communities, where members have never met each other in physical space.

Komito (1998) made a distinct analysis of different facets of communities in the context of virtual modes of social interaction. Her basic distinction is between *proximate communities*, where a common interpretative space is constructed on the grounds of proximity in virtual spaces and involuntary membership; *moral communities*, where a common interpretative space is based on moral bonds, communal solidarity, and a sense of common purpose and commitment; and *normative communities*, such as communities of practice or communities of interest, which are usually directed toward economic or scientific goals, and share corresponding values and norms (Komito, 1998; Diemers, 2000b).

Virtual knowledge communities (VKCs), then, are normative virtual communities that have been formed with the purpose of facilitating Knowledge Management within a business context (Brown and Duguid, 1991). Such forms of VKC are typical for large consulting firms, where communities of practice exchange *best practice and lessons learned* in order to leverage knowledge across the firm.

Traditionally organizational forms of Knowledge Management have relied on IT-based systems for collection and distribution of packaged knowledge. Experience has shown, however, that such systems often reveal very low levels of performance and effectiveness, a fact that can be attributed to the above-mentioned soft-factor impediments to Knowledge Management.

As a consequence, a second, complementary approach has been undertaken with virtual knowledge communities, which were sometimes also referred to as sharing networks. Although these social forms of community-based Knowledge Management have proven to be very effective in business practice, only little scientific research has been carried out so far. What is even more striking is the fact that very few authors attempt a transfer of sociological knowledge on communities and virtual communities into this field.

The idea of VKC is a way of conceptualizing such a social approach to community-based Knowledge Management. I define VKC as follows:

Virtual Knowledge Communities (VKCs) are forms of temporarily constituted, social aggregations, which are committed to practical modes of generating, evaluating, exchange, and application of knowledge in companies. The manifold and regular interactions between community members are taking place both in virtual and nonvirtual spaces.

Thus, members of VKCs have interactions both in mediated forms of communication and face-to-face. Essential for the quality of these interactions, however, are not necessarily the type of communication media, but the enabling context of the interaction. I have analyzed this aspect of interaction in VKCs with the concept of common interpretative spaces (CISs), which are constituted between interaction partners through exchange of knowledge and a congruency of their cognitive spaces. The better these CISs are, the better the interaction within VKCs is being institutionalized and facilitated (Diemers, 2000b; 2001).

To describe and analyze VKCs we may use the seven factors of cohesion mentioned above and refer to the very essence of communities: the bonds and affiliations between members, and the feeling of oneness, of belonging together. These seven cohesion factors are now investigated in more detail.

4.1. Shared Interest

At the center of a VKC is a shared interest as a implicitly or explicitly formulated intentionality, task, object, idea, or vision. It can be understood as a collective, communal bundle of interests, which evolves and changes over time as the VKC evolves and changes. Some key interests might also be condensed into an explicit community goal or statement, and backed up by social practices, symbols, or narratives to sustain the commitment of the VKC members to that special set of key interests.

The aspect of shared interests within a community in general, or a VKC in particular, is also characterized by a delicate balance between the implicitly shared and explicitly published interests and goals of the community as a whole, and the various, individually configured interests, intentions, and goals of the community's members. These may eventually differ from the official community interests, and in some cases there is also a difference between the communicated, individual interests and intentions, and the hidden interests, strategies, and "hidden agendas" members might have.

4.2. Shared Values and Norms

A basic insight from sociological contributions to the field of community studies is the dual relationship that on the one hand, community in itself is impossible without commonly accepted and established norms and values, while on the other hand the mere being together in communal forms of sociality spontaneously leads to the emergence of common norms and values, which become institutionalized over time.

In a VKC, thus, there is always a set of implicit and explicit codes of conduct that regulate common practices and the way people interact with each other. It is a prerequisite that members share common knowledge about these norms and values, and new members internalize this elementary knowledge during the process of secondary socialization.

4.3. Common Interaction Platforms

A VKC is also dependent on common interaction platforms that allow members to exchange knowledge. The term platform should thereby not only be understood in a technical sense, but also in a more general, contextual interpretation.

A technical view on common interaction platforms includes physical, nonvirtual interaction spaces within clearly defined geographical boundaries. Where do community members meet? What interactions spaces do they use for working, collaborating, meetings, and informal discussions? A significant part of interaction platforms in VKCs also take place in virtual spaces, which have to be designed and conceptualized to meet the specific needs of computer-mediated communication.

In a broader sense, common interaction platforms of VKCs comprise the enabling context of knowledge exchange between community members. Through facilitated interaction they create common interpretative spaces among each other, which includes the common understandings of the symbols and representations through which they communicate. These CISs are based on a consensual configuration of semantic and contextual interpretations within relevant topics of the VKC.

4.4. Emotional Bonds

Emotional bonds are relevant for the general cohesion and stickiness of a community and are a significant differentiation criteria in respect to other forms of social aggregations like ad hoc teams, target groups, and so on. The so-called sense of community, that is, the common feeling of belonging together and being different from nonmembers, is at the very heart of communities in general, and VKCs in particular.

But in the context of communities other emotional bonds are also eminent, even if they are rarely discussed or analyzed, but are generally perceived in a diffuse mix of feelings like care, trust, affection, affiliation, sympathy, empathy, faithfulness, or solidarity. One major criterion among these for the success of VKC is the emergence of trust among community members. Intimacy and a personal relationship based on trust and care is essential for the knowledge exchange in VKC.

4.5. Continuity

Continuity, habitualization, and institutionalization are cohesion factors that emerge naturally when members keep on interacting with each other over time. As such they have a considerable impact on other cohesive factors, such as the emergence of emotional bonds, common norms and values, and reciprocity. Repeated interaction leads thus to a strengthening and facilitating of knowledge exchange patterns within VKCs, and the historic line of interaction becomes commonly shared collective knowledge, which influences future interactions and knowledge exchange in a community.

4.6. Reciprocity

A typical social phenomenon in communities are the high levels of reciprocity, that is, members of communities openly exchange and share material and immaterial resources among themselves. Interestingly, these social forms of solidarity are also observed in virtual communities, where direct and uncomplicated mutual assistance in spite of anonymous relationships is a typical phenomenon.

In VKCs, where the exchange of knowledge stands at the heart of the shared interest of community members, patterns of reciprocal exchange are an essential element, and also correlate to other cohesion factors, for example, emotional bonds and continuity.

4.7. Identity Construction

In the light of contemporary theories of identity, it is undisputed that the social context of our daily work plays a significant role in our individual construction of identity. In an increasingly fragmented and differentiated structure of society our membership and participation in professional or leisure communities are part of our various "self-narratives" that finally constitute our individualistic self-definition and identity (Giddens, 1991).

VKCs can thus be analyzed along these seven factors of cohesion. Such an analysis, however, is primarily static in nature, while VKCs are complex, spontaneous, and self-referential social systems, which develop and change over time. It is important to take this aspect into account and include a dynamic perspective on VKCs. Such a perspective could be developed along the concept of a natural lifecycle that differentiates various phases of emergence and development of VKCs (Diemers, 2001).

Furthermore, the concept of VKCs offers several interesting fields of research, both from an epistemological and practical perspective: How do these communities store, share, and refine their knowledge base? Which epistemologically relevant patterns of interaction have been established over time? How can we identify and observe social processes within virtual knowledge communities? What are typical roles that evolve over time? Which roles can be institutionalized within VKCs from a functional perspective? Which tools can be implemented to support members of a VKC? How can such communities actually leverage knowledge, and how are they able to solve complex, multidimensional issues? How can we measure the performance and quality of interaction within a virtual knowledge community?

Whereas all of these research questions are important for a conceptualization of virtual knowledge communities, the issue of performance and quality measurement is also of substantial relevance for managing VKCs in a business context. For this reason I'd like to focus in the last part of this chapter on a framework for information quality in virtual knowledge communities, which may serve as a starting point to develop tools and procedures for measuring and assessing performance and quality within a VKC.

5. A Framework for Information Quality in Virtual Knowledge Communities

Social interaction and exchange of knowledge are by definition key activities in virtual knowledge communities. From a general management or Knowledge Management perspective, the idea of measuring the quality of an information exchange process is crucial. This is obviously the point where the field of information quality becomes of primary relevance. In order to assess and value internal processes in virtual knowledge communities, we need a framework and respective criteria to measure information quality.

Recalling the duality of Knowledge Management, which is also reflected within VKCs, a framework for information quality has to include both the technical, IT-based level, and the community-oriented, social interaction level of knowledge exchange and transfer. A good starting point for such a framework is the basic model of the transformational process (Figure 8-1), which focuses on the cognitive processes that turn information into knowledge, as presented at the 1999 MIT Conference on Information Quality (Diemers, 1999b; 2000a).

That model tried to conceptualize the basic but complex question of how contextualized information is actually transformed into personalized, situated knowledge and vice versa, a question that has to be answered by any methodology on Knowledge Management. According to the epistemological foundations of Schutz, Berger, and Luckmann, information may or may not be sedimented in our cognitive structures

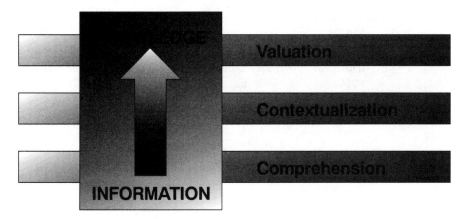

Figure 8-1. The transformational process of Knowledge Management.

during any interaction, but if it is, we can speak of an internalization of information. The chance of successful internalization depends on how certain information corresponds to our system of relevancies, that is, our prioritization and plans within the daily life-world, and to our already internalized typifications and objectivations, that is, the information's degree of connectivity to other, sedimented epistemic structures (Schutz and Luckmann, 1974; 1983; Schutz, 1982; Berger and Luckmann, 1966; Hall, 1997).

This actionable component is important, because generally an internalization of information will only take place when there is a possible and intended future action of the internalizing subject related to it. In this theoretical perspective, such individually internalized, actionable information is finally what we refer to as personalized knowledge. The introduced model then conceptualizes the stages from information to knowledge along the processes of comprehension, contextualization, and valuation.

Generally it can be said that the transformational process stands at the heart of a framework for information quality in VKCs. Accordingly, we need for every stage of the process appropriate criteria, which allow for measurement and assessment of the quality of information exchanged. In Table 8-2, different scientific conceptualizations of information quality have been assembled and integrated, namely the models

Levels of IQ	Model Components	Goals	Properties	4x4 PSP IQ Model
(Diemers, 1999a; Shanks/Darke, 1998)	(Diemers, 1999a)	(Shanks/Darke, 1998; Kahn et al., 1997)	(Shanks/Darke, 1998; Wand/Wang, 1996	(Kahn et al., 1997; Kahn/ Strong, 1998)
Valuation (pragmatic level)	Belief, system of relevance, attributions, labels	Usefulness (usability)	Reputable timely accessible concise	Usability
Contextualiz- ation (semantic level)	CIS, social context, synchronized typifications and representa- tions	Usability accuracy	Understood complete unambiguous correct	Usefulness dependability
Comprehension (semantic/ syntactic level)	Signs, meanings, syntax, language, protocols	Comprehen- siveness consistency	Meaningful well-defined syntax	Soundness

Table 8-2. An integrated view on different models of information quality.

and contributions of Kahn, Strong, and Wang (1997; 1998); Wand and Wang (1996); and Shanks and Darke (1998). The information quality goals and criteria have then been related to the respective levels of the 4X4 PSP IQ model by Kahn, Strong, and Wang, the respective levels of information quality in Shanks and Darke's contribution, and my own sociologically influenced conceptualization.

Please note a certain semantic incongruency within the useful/usable criteria. In the original 4X4 PSP IQ model, usefulness stood conceptually above usability. This corresponds fully to the sociological conceptualization of the transformational process, where only useable (level of comprehension/contextualization) information can be useful (level of contextualization/valuation) for someone, but not vice versa. The order of useful/usable was then, however, reversed as a result of empiric validation with information quality practitioners (Kahn and Strong, 1998). This incongruency, thus, only reflects the diffuse modes of apperception of information quality among practitioners, and is not a substantial semantic difference between the different information quality models themselves.

Based on this integrated conceptualization on information quality let us now further operationalize the respective measurement and assessment criteria. From a management perspective it would also be interesting to identify opportunities for pro-active management of virtual knowledge communities based on the underlying conceptualization of information quality. This conceptualization may principally be differentiated into a technical and personalized view on knowledge, an issue that has already been discussed in section 3 as the inherent duality of Knowledge Management.

Whereas this chapter addresses primarily the personalized dimension from a sociological perspective, the technical side is indisputably a necessary condition, a *conditio sine qua non*, for any conceptualization of information quality in the context of virtual knowledge communities. Several authors have elaborated various approaches to these prerequisites of data and information quality on the technical level (for an overview, see Naumann and Rolker, 1999). Typical criteria for such technically focused IQ measurement include accessibility, response time, latency, data integrity, and so forth.

In order to conceptualize IQ within management practices of personalized knowledge, I propose measurement criteria for each transformational level respectively. Then, some general opportunities for IQ management in the context of virtual knowledge communities are identified. The results of this conceptual framework are finally consolidated in Table 8-3.

On the comprehension level, quality information is related to correct syntax, which is meaningful to members of a specific culturally defined community in terms of individual socialization. Quality information, then, needs also to be concise and consistent over a longer peri-

Levels of IQ	Assessment Criteria	Opportunities for IQ Management in VKC
Comprehension	correct syntax meaningful concise consistent	✓ establishing standardized codes and symbols ✓ agreement on common interaction protocols ✓ assuring interactional continuity and consistency
Contextualization	usability interpretability semantic congruency unambiguous complete accuracy	✓ capturing and delivering social context information ✓ supporting correct, unambiguous interpretations ✓ agreement on semantic standards, e.g., glossary, definitions, "native terms," etc.
Valuation	usefulness relevance timeliness reputable trustful verifiable	✓ establishing common standards for reputation, e.g., labels, benchmarks ✓ supporting the emergence of emotional bonds and trust ✓ assessing relevance and usefulness of information ✓ ensuring timeliness of information ✓ measuring outcomes and performance of transferred knowledge

Table 8-3. A conceptualization of information quality in VKC.

od of time. Within virtual knowledge communities this level offers several opportunities for pro-active IQ management. First, we may establish standardized codes and symbols for interaction within the community. Second, commonly accepted interaction protocols, patterns, and codes of conduct allow for efficient and basically error-free interaction between community members. Third, we may eventually facilitate and improve the exchange of quality information by assuring interactional continuity and consistency within the community.

On the contextualization level, quality information depends on the general usability and interpretability of information. Completeness and accuracy of information are also very important to this end. Finally, a strong semantic congruency and unambiguousness are necessary conditions for common interpretative spaces that are a prerequisite for interaction in communities. Opportunities for facilitating knowledge exchange on the contextual level are:

❑ First, capturing and delivering social context information that facilitates interpretational efforts.

❑ Second, by supporting correct and unambiguous interpretation the evolvement of common interpretative spaces is positively influenced.

❑ Third, differences in interpretation among community members are significantly reduced by installing semantic and interpretational standards, for example, glossaries and commonly accepted definitions.

On the valuation level, finally, the subjective quality of information depends on the following criteria: usefulness, relevance, timeliness, reputability, trustfulness, and verifiability. The criteria usefulness and relevance point at the pragmatic aspect of knowledge, that is, we internalize knowledge always in relation to a possible, future action. In that sense our set of intended, projected action and our systems of relevance determine how we actually value certain information. The aspect of timeliness is related to this pragmatic element of knowledge in that only information that is made available to us in time may eventually lead to action. The probably most important differentiation of information is made along the subjective valuation of correct/incorrect, right/wrong, and appropriate/inappropriate. Accordingly, the trustfulness of information, the reputability of its source, and the verifiability of information make up very important criteria within virtual knowledge communities, which usually determine whether information is internalized during the transformational process or not.

Pro-active management of the valuation level within virtual knowledge communities is generally possible, but it requires a very sensitive, soft-factor based approach from a sociological and psychological perspective. First, inductive assessment methodologies can be applied within virtual knowledge communities that measure the subjectively perceived relevance and usefulness of information. Second, planning and evaluation tools may support the measurement of timeliness of information in knowledge exchange. Third, we can attempt to measure action outcomes or team and individual performance related to transferred knowledge by qualitative and quantitative social research. Here the primary question should be: how do we attribute a certain performance or outcome to the exchange of information within a virtual knowledge community? Fourth, the installment of common standards for reputation and trustfulness support the respective criteria at the valuation level of knowledge exchange, for example, by establishing commonly accepted labels, ratings, and benchmarks. Fifth, by means of coaching and organizational development initiatives we may eventually support the emergence of emotional bonds and trust among community members, which in turn influence the valuation level in a positive way.

6. Conclusions

This chapter elaborated a social perspective on Knowledge Management in the eConomy, based on the epistemological concepts of the newer sociology of knowledge, as represented by Schutz, Berger, and Luckmann. In the light of a new level playing field shaped by eBusiness and e-commerce, corporate practices of knowledge exchange and transfer are increasingly becoming critical success factors.

In this chapter the duality of Knowledge Management, which differentiates personalized and codified Knowledge Management, is taken as an argument in favor of a sociologically influenced conceptualization of virtual knowledge communities (VKCs), which form a primary organizational resource toward efficient practices of exchange of personalized knowledge.

This shift from traditional IT-based Knowledge Management to more socially biased conceptions of community-based knowledge exchange is elaborated along seven factors of cohesion: shared interest, shared norms and values, common interaction platform, emotional bonds, continuity, reciprocity, and identity construction.

Also, a strong case is made in favor of the view on VKC as complex, spontaneous, and self-referential social systems, which develop and change over time, and thus have to be looked at in a dynamic perspective. This understanding of VKCs also includes a clear negation of overly mechanistic views on knowledge exchange, and the idea that respective interaction processes can be controled and managed top-down.

In the final section of this chapter a distinct framework was presented on how to measure, assess, and identify information quality within VKCs. This framework is oriented along the three analytic levels of the transformational process of knowledge internalization: comprehension, contextualization, and valuation. At each level, respective assessment criteria are identified, and a first set of opportunities for pro-active IQ management in VKCs is proposed. Based on this initial conceptualization more elaborate tools and procedures could be investigated in a next step.

To conclude, this chapter presents a new, fresh look on a social conceptualization of knowledge exchange in companies. The introduced frameworks for VKCs and for the measurement of IQ comprise another brick in the wall of the theory and practice of community-based Knowledge Management. Further, it has also become clear that there remains ample space for further research within this newly emerging field at the intersection between applied business administration theory for the eConomy and the interpretative paradigm of the newer sociology of knowledge.

Part 3

Knowledge Worker:

Role of the Individual

in the eFuture

Chapter 9

ACCENTURE'S NEW OPERATING MODEL

Meeting the Needs of the Knowledge Worker

Susanne Alfs

1. Introduction to Knowledge Management at Accenture

Accenture is a global service provider in the areas of consulting, ventures, and technology. Knowledge Management processes have been designed already in the 1980s and have been developed since. A member of Accenture personnel is highly educated and a long-term user of leading-edge technology. A high affinity to technology is typical as the tasks and projects usually require hands-on experience with technology. Knowledge sharing is a strongly advocated and proclaimed value of the firm. Personal networking to exchange experience and knowledge is promoted through the mentoring process and additional initiatives, such as capturing, distributing, and reusing work products, are essential to the successful delivery of projects.

The Knowledge Management capability is globally developed and organized. Various industry analysts, such as, for example, IDC (International Data Cooperation), consider Accenture a leader. The current Knowledge Management structures can be characterized as follows: All employees around the globe are online, connected to a system of databases containing the firm's knowledge base, called Knowledge Xchange (KX). Access is given twenty-four hours a day, seven days a week. An Automated Library Ordering System allows remote access from almost everywhere to the repositories and asynchronous delivery of knowledge items. Since the beginning of the 1990s, Lotus technology has been used for collaboration, as well as for capturing, storing, and distributing knowledge assets.

There has been an increasing dissatisfaction with the structures provided, especially regarding the ease of access and the quality of content retrieved. The need for Accenture to invest in its knowledge management capability is evident, as the following trends show:

❑ Clients and the marketplace require faster mobilization and deeper insight, because the market has moved to just-in-time enablement. In the technology business the rate of appearance of new growth areas is rapidly accelerating and the life cycle of knowledge from first experience to maturity is more compressed.

❑ The practice people at Accenture demand improvements in the knowledge delivery capability, because they need easier, less-frustrating access to knowledge and experts. Technology expectations among the knowledge workers have increased in line with what they have seen on the Internet, at universities, or at their high-tech clients. They need knowledge capital that is more integrated and synthesized. Before the knowledge capital was distributed in much the same style as it was harvested.

2. Knowledge Management Today

So what has pushed the requirements of Accenture knowledge workers to higher levels? What has led to frustration among the knowledge workers, who are accustomed to using information technology not only to perform at the workplace, but also to retrieve all the information they seek for both private and professional life? Using Internet technology, knowledge workers have access to a wealth of information and knowledge, which they use autonomously.

The exposure to so much information triggers personalization; Knowledge workers get additional support in finding the content that is most relevant to them. This nurtures their expectation of an individualized and context-driven presentation of information. Only comprehensive knowledge pieces organized around a subject enable them to perform in today's quickly developing world.

The ability to connect virtually is now widely available and used. Being a member of a team that is not co-located, staying connected with distant friends, or playing an important role in a global organization, all are increasingly familiar roles for the typical knowledge worker. The inclusiveness of virtual groups involves knowledge workers in a two-way process: They are asked to participate and share their knowledge and expertise.

There is now a general expectation of speed when accessing and retrieving information. Knowledge workers demand easy access to information, as this is key to their success. They are at risk to fail when they don't have the necessary information in the quickly changing business context. An environment that offers such a structure is appealing to them, whereas complicated access methods and information overload are not motivating them to come back a second time.

With these expectations, knowledge workers are asked to play their role within the Knowledge Management structure at Accenture, where Knowledge Management depends on the knowledge workers' capability and motivation to contribute.

3. Pushing Knowledge Management to the Next Level

As the Accenture case will show, the expectations of the new knowledge worker push developments in Knowledge Management. All the expectations and new customs can be utilized to the benefit of Knowledge

Management. But how can the new attributes of the knowledge worker best be leveraged?

Knowledge workers expect knowledge processes—such as capturing, storing, and distributing knowledge—to be tailored to their individual needs. If they can have access to the Internet anytime and anywhere, they demand the same in the corporate environment. If the most recent information is available to them from external sources, they expect the same from the internal sources. Those already used to a personalized online banking Web site demand similar service to the corporate Knowledge Management repository.

Accessibility of external sources that are dynamically updated imposes the requirement of similar services in-house. And why access two separate systems, one for external know-how and another one for the internal know-how? Knowledge workers, used to having information at their fingertips, want a single point of access. In addition, they expect services from their in-house knowledge structures that would help avoid redundancies and simply search mechanisms by using the firm's typical vocabulary.

Today's knowledge workers are self-sufficient. They do not want an intermediary between the knowledge capital and themselves. They enjoy autonomy using the company's knowledge base. Powerful search capabilities should enable them to access many different repositories and find explicit knowledge in the documents stored, or to identify experts carrying the tacit knowledge that they might want to access. In their different roles within the Knowledge Management structures, knowledge workers are exposed to requests demanding just-in-time and comprehensive services. Self-sufficiency for them means that they can handle the vast majority of tasks without needing assistance from Knowledge Management staff. Unless they are surrounded by colleagues, they would expect to have a channel for personal assistance if they require it.

Further, knowledge workers are an integral part of the corporate knowledge base in the sense that their individually owned knowledge can be located and shared upon request by other members of the same knowledge community. Knowledge workers with the same area of interest should thus be empowered to build virtual communities on demand

and be provided with the support processes to smoothen the set-up phase of the community.

The new types of knowledge workers require a work environment that empowers them to play an influential role in the corporate knowledge structure, as opposed to being only a user of Knowledge Management systems. This will push Knowledge Management to a higher level, namely a much enhanced integration of technology with the other design fields of Knowledge Management (see Figure 9-1).

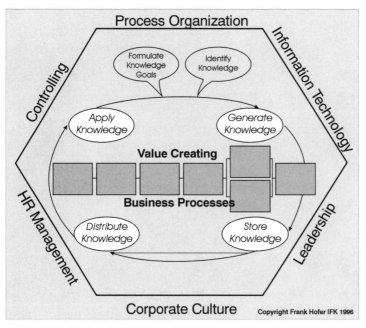

Figure 9-1. Design fields of Knowledge Management.

The schematic in Figure 9-1 shows the design fields building the framework for the Knowledge Management cycle. Knowledge Management-oriented actions in the design fields enable the Knowledge Management cycle, comprised of generating, storing, distributing, and applying knowledge. This will lead to sufficiently supported business processes, which are at the center of all Knowledge Management activities. This schematic is used to demonstrate how Knowledge Management professionals can utilize technology to address the requirements of the new knowledge worker in the next paragraphs. The Accenture approach is described in the following paragraphs.

4. Knowledge Management Getting Prepared

In the past, Knowledge Management was (and in many cases still is) dominated by collecting internally documented (explicit) knowledge. This is true especially for professional services firms, who rely heavily on reproducing existing knowledge assets. Repositories organized around organizational structures have been utilized to make this knowledge available to the knowledge worker. In many cases an opportunistic approach toward the content has been chosen: Selected documents that were generated upon client demand have been shared, and no customization or synthesizing was done. A lot of redundancy occurred and knowledge remained in the silos for which it was collected. Communities of practice have been centrally concerted and nurtured, and their importance has been rapidly growing recently.

The last few years have seen a movement toward distilling best thinking, consolidating, and synthesizing knowledge in the form of packages. An effort was made to include external references, thus enhancing the research capability. As a result, comprehensive knowledge packages are delivered to the knowledge worker, such as, for example, all information available to compete in a certain market segment or about a specific technology. The information is increasingly presented using personalized homepages that allow easy access to knowledge for a pre-defined group of customers, for example, knowledge workers in a company's marketing department.

What more is required to meet the demands of the new type of knowledge worker? Using the model shown in Figure 9-1, the following areas for action are evident.

4.1. Process Organization

The overall objective in this design area is to align all business processes with Knowledge Management activities. In order to identify knowledge, all created business documents should be made automatically available to Knowledge Management using an Integrated Document Management (IDM) solution. Capture all potential knowledge and prepare it for autonomous search and use by the knowledge worker. IDM further integrates Knowledge Management into, the business processes, because IDM is fully embedded in the companies' IT structures, such as the HR and collaboration systems.

To enhance the knowledge storing capability, Knowledge Management should move from maintaining repositories toward *content management,* which means managing content around subject areas as opposed to repositories typically organized around organizational structures. This movement is supported by technology that enables automatic categorization and thus helps in recognizing trends in content and building meaningful taxonomy.

The distribution of knowledge is supported in many ways by portals and their practical application. This delivery channel meets the needs of knowledge workers in becoming self-sufficient. When combined with automatic search agent technology, the knowledge worker enjoys a personalized knowledge service that is both relevant and timely. Depending on context, knowledge should be presented and displayed differently. Separation of content from presentation allows knowledge workers to access the same information in more than one way, depending on context and individual requirements.

Knowledge workers should be enabled with a powerful search capability. Personnel profiling technology allows them to build virtual communities on demand: The capability to locate not only documented (explicit) knowledge but also to locate experts greatly supports crucial components of communities of practice. Based on input from HR, but mainly based on the areas of interest identified by the system based on the work patterns of the knowledge worker, personnel profiling allows building interpersonal networks. Expertise profiles identify the staff that is most familiar with critical topics based on the authoring, editing, and assignment histories of personnel. Consider knowledge workers to be an active and integral part of the knowledge structures: They are playing a designated role for Knowledge Management, they are just a simple user of the Knowledge Management structures, and they are a knowledge source, all at the same time.

4.2. Information Technology

Technology evolves from a supporting tool to an enabler of Knowledge Management procedures. The most significant change is the opportunity to use technology to exploit the tacit knowledge existing in the heads of the workforce. Use technology to turn the knowledge worker into knowledge "nuggets." A prerequisite is the seamless integration of Knowledge Management technology into business processes. Technology can help overcome the organizational silos of the past and assist in directing Knowledge Management toward a more active management of the content provided.

4.3. Leadership

The autonomy enjoyed by the new type of knowledge worker unfolds to the benefit of the company only in an environment of trust and respect. This makes leadership a critical success factor. In the past, information denial was seen as a way to manage the workforce by exclusion. The modern knowledge worker will now becomes inclusive to the management process. The new Knowledge Management structures give more room for inspiration and creativity. The wealth of information made available enables surprising and refreshing solutions. A team has a broader variety of options for moving forward. The individual, being more self-sufficient, will grow to act more independently. As a leader, perform as a role model; encourage curiosity and autonomous use of knowledge. The speed of change and development requires a high level of responsiveness in management positions and timely decision making.

4.4. Corporate Culture

The successful implementation of personnel profiling technology depends on a knowledge-sharing culture. Otherwise the two-way exchange of knowledge between the experts fails. Teams must be perceived as a powerful structure to generate, distribute, and apply knowledge. Emphasize self-service as a concession to the individual work style of the new type of knowledge worker. Being used to working virtually, individual knowledge workers seek team member support on a just-in-time basis, using the technology provided to them. Depending on the needs of the knowledge workers, provide clearly defined Knowledge Management processes and define the access points to these services, providing support by the Knowledge Management department where necessary.

4.5. HR Management

HR matters should be involved in different ways to improve the Knowledge Management infrastructure. In order to support personnel profiling, cooperation with HR is crucial. Utilize HR structures to fully exploit the opportunities existing in the new Knowledge Management procedures and technologies. On the other hand, HR management benefits from enhanced Knowledge Management procedures, as it frequently needs to locate and manage experts. This is especially important during a period of quickly developing skill sets and changing skill requirements. Integrate the HR department in using the Knowledge Management framework to deliver e-learning components to the workforce. Instructional-type information should be incorporated in processes, because it provides an efficient and targeted way of learning.

Besides the general openness and motivation of the knowledge worker to use a modern infrastructure, the Knowledge Management structures depend on incentives, such as a bonus or social recognition. The provision of incentives to collaborate in the Knowledge Management structures should be incorporated in the overall incentive approach.

4.6. Controlling

Besides control mechanisms to make sure that the overall Knowledge Management strategy is being followed, the effectiveness of the Knowledge Management operations needs attention. Employ technology to evaluate the quality of content and contributors in an integrated fashion. The popularity of documents is a measurement that empowers knowledge workers because the documents that they retrieve are most often the ones most relevant to them. The same performance measure could be applied to a group of peers that are interested in a certain subject. Nobody other than the knowledge worker should make that choice.

5. Blueprint for the Future: A New Knowledge Management Operating Model

Knowledge management at Accenture has gone through the development stages described above. The structures evolved organically and managed to grow fast and well in line with the business units, whose value propositions were achieved. Over time, however, dispersed Knowledge Management responsibility tied to different organizational units made coordination of Knowledge Management services a challenge.

Various directories and homepages support the search functionality in the KX, but searches across repositories remain cumbersome, as the knowledge worker needs to know where to search. For contribution to the KX, the knowledge worker can use a Drop Box, which is used by Knowledge Management to further process the material. A rather opportunistic approach toward collecting knowledge assets is applied: Most contributions to the knowledge base remained as captured, and only a minimum of synthesizing and organization of content was done. The role of a "gatekeeper"—for example, performing a quality check on the material posted in the KX—was not consistently applied.

The combination of these factors led to increasingly inconsistent services and "Pockets of Excellence" rather than an integrated model, depending on the sponsorship for Knowledge Management in various units in the firm.

Currently two initiatives address the growing expectations of the knowledge worker at Accenture and the opportunities existing in the latest technology developments.

5.1. The New Knowledge Management Operating Model

Accenture currently implements a new Operating Model that, from the point of view of the knowledge worker, will deliver the following values:

- ❑ One user interface is provided for access and contribution to the knowledge base, and all content is stored in one logical store.
- ❑ The model has the ability to search across data repositories and organizational entities.
- ❑ The delivery channels are designed to be user-centric and self-service oriented, but are supplemented with hands-on support via help-desk.

To deliver that enhanced capability, the Operating Model is detailed as shown in Figure 9-2.

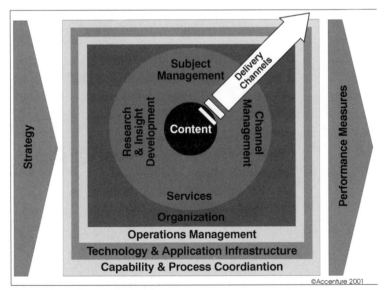

Figure 9-2. Knowledge Management operating model at Accenture.

A Content Architecture builds the core of the model. It is a framework that defines how content is stored, maintained, and accessed. Applying the Content Architecture, all knowledge assets are stored in one logical store. Each item is stored in one instance. The most significant change imposed by the Content Architecture will be the distinction of the logical store from the physical storage of knowledge. Before there was a logical framework connecting the content of the various databases, the physical databases were known to the user, and were owned and managed by the different organizational units in charge. The Content Architecture enables search and contribution mechanisms using a single user interface, and the user doesn't need to know where the knowledge assets are physically stored. At the same time the Content Architecture enables the Knowledge Management organization to support Subject Management Services effectively. A Content Architecture fosters consistency across the enterprise by defining rules for physical storage of content, access, and security. Physical storage is improved by imposing rules for the handling of attachments and rich media assets.

The architecture is supplemented with the establishment of a "managed vocabulary." At the same time "knowledge classes" will structure the knowledge base, as they build a hierarchy and relationships among different subjects. Both will enhance significantly the ability to coordinate management, storage, and presentation of related subjects across the organization. It helps Accenture professionals to navigate, as classes of knowledge will guide them to related items and widen their perception of the subjects they are working on.

The Knowledge Management organization establishes clear service levels and will make sure ownership for content areas is assigned independently from organizational considerations. In the future, Knowledge Management will concentrate on subject management, channel management, and Research & Insight development. Subject management will be greatly improved by the Content Architecture, because it is now possible to meaningfully aggregate and synthesize knowledge gathered from the client engagements. The Content Architecture enables classification of knowledge and allows focusing on the provision of knowledge assets in strategically important areas. Channel management enables Web-based access to content via a single point of entry. Portal technology is used to deploy that functionality. Content is packaged into smaller, more targeted objects for greater ease of use.

The operating model will greatly help Accenture to address the needs of knowledge workers. It is planned to achieve further improvements by combining the Knowledge Management Organization and the Learning Organization into a single, integrated entity.

Continuing on the road toward better leveraging the skills of the new type of knowledge worker in the future, a second initiative with impact for the Knowledge Management capability has been launched and is described in Chapter 10.

5.2. Opportunities Assessed for Integrated Document Management

With a further initiative, Accenture is currently investigating other opportunities that exist in the latest technology developments. To better integrate the operations that support the service delivery, Accenture is considering the implementation of Integrated Document Management (IDM). The solution suggested would supplement the Operating Model described above. A major element is the enablement for virtual teams, which is a style of cooperation that is used widely within Accenture. IDM supports simultaneous editing, viewing, and sign-off in a virtual team environment. Multilingual concept-based search would address the need of internationally operating teams and assist Accenture using local language for the benefits of its clients.

The repositories would be extended to include e-mail, which is important as more and more relevant information is contained in e-mails. Document and Records Management would make document-based operations more efficient. The incorporation of workflow in this system would ensure that documents are routed according to a predefined process, and employees would receive only relevant information at the exact time that it is needed. Retention schedules would be automatically applied to documents using a document-type sensitive approach.

IDM would be applied to a wide range of document types, including proposals and contracts, deliverables and reports, personnel files, and so on. That will significantly enlarge the number of potential knowledge sources, as all relevant documents would be captured and screened for further use. Knowledge workers will have much better evidence of what the company knows and how to access the knowledge, which will further empower them to perform their roles in the context of Knowledge Management. Uncertainty about information processes is reduced, which thus supports the cultural value to share knowledge. The major benefits Accenture expects from IDM would result from the reduced time required to manage the up-to-now decentralized managed documents and from the increased efficiency for virtual team collaboration.

6. Action Required

Knowledge Management needs to support the business model with a concise Knowledge Management strategy that addresses all design fields of Knowledge Management. Deriving that strategy, consider the following principles to make sure the needs of the knowledge workers are addressed:

- ❑ Understand business practices through an interviewing capability that focuses on possible improvements, given the increasing information literacy of knowledge workers and technology available.
- ❑ Capture the needs of the knowledge worker in order to adjust knowledge structures and provide enabling technology.
- ❑ Clearly define services and roles of Knowledge Management, with awareness of the level of self-service expected by and accepted from the knowledge workers.
- ❑ Given the borderless information landscape outside the company, move from maintaining repositories to content management.
- ❑ Utilize the knowledge workers' comfort level with technology and help each individual to perform in different roles: as a knowledge source, a knowledge seeker, a knowledge advocate, and a knowledge coordinator.

Chapter 10

THE KNOWLEDGE WORKER AS THE NEW PROBLEM SOLVER

Abilities, Competencies, and Needs

Betty Zucker,
Ruschlikon, Zürich, Switzerland

Welcome to the future!

It's broken.

I'm not writing this to spread gloom or depression. Rather optimism. Because being broken is productive. Conventional business structures, traditional perceptions about identity or about careers and choices in life—in short, all that gives spice to our lives—all these traditional views are changing.

The knowledge society is on the move. Fast. New abilities, new needs, and new demands of knowledge workers are coming into the workplace. Applying new rules. But which rule book?

1. Value Added Comes from Achieving

Technological change and innovation are so rapid that what counts is, first, getting things done, and second—and even more importantly— getting them done fast. Action instead of concepts. Do it, do it now. Those who count are those who get things done quickly and smartly. Not just are they able to do a job as quickly as possible, they also solve a problem while it's still a problem.

"Just in time" and "on demand" are indispensable in today's world of efficiency. That's what adds value to the individual. That's what pays.

2. The "Movers and Shakers" Create the Future

First, a word of warning: Don't confuse the movers and shakers with people generally labelled as "leaders" or "experts."

A psychology professor cannot *per se* relieve claustrophobia, and MBAs can't *per se* successfully execute a marketing strategy for Pampers. (MBAs were established in 1908 and revised in the 1950s; they focus especially on the B [business functions] and less on A [implementation]. As a study by H. Mintzberg [2001] shows, 40 percent of unsuccessful CEOs are MBAs, and some of them were star performers in school.) MBAs have been expensively educated, but—depending on context— their education is no guarantee of later success, nor is a director's position or title a guarantee that its holder can successfully implement change or even learn quickly. The new stars in the knowledge society are the achievers. Down-to-earth achievers, achievers with rolled-up shirt sleeves and well-developed common sense. Respect for hands-on knowledge wins over respect for formal authority.

2.1. Training Is a Result of Working, Not Preparation for Work

New times like these call for new forms of learning, of creating and exploiting knowledge, and for a new approach to training.

Traditional modes of learning—at school, at university, or even in corporate training courses—don't necessarily lead to the new kinds of abilities described above.

Pressures such as "just in time" or "on demand" increase the need to modify the way we learn. And how is learning to adapt to the biggest conundrum of all: the fact that 60 percent of the careers that are going to exist in ten years' time don't exist today?

Learning and training can no longer be seen as preparation for work. Learning becomes one new form of productive work per se: solving problems, pushing the limits (not always fun!), pushing the edge of the envelope. Learning itself becomes not the input, but part of the output. Afterwards you are always smarter.

Has our approach to learning caught up with this? Century-old traditions of learning have got to change. Training and education can no longer be seen as work and be treated accordingly. Chronic deficits are programmed into the system, we are permanently on watch, constantly on the edge, but never can we master it. We're never ready, or rather we never get things finished, we're always seen as trying to catch up, never having everything under control. The learner is morphed into an ever-shifting and never completed construction site. The learner's identity is under constant siege. He is pushed more and more into an infantile, child-like state of mind. Who likes this?

"Lifelong learning" around the world and around the clock has become a mantra. Chic and trendy, nobody dares object—at least not loudly. But it is seen by many, above all by those of the Baby Boomer generation, as an enforced obligation to learn. That isn't a helpful attitude for learning quickly nor does it provide the underpinning for rapid change.

3. What Characterizes Achievers Aside from Their Specific Areas of Expertise?

3.1. Coping with Quicksand

New technologies play an ever more important part in our lives, they penetrate every aspect of our lives, whether sport, sex, politics, or the workplace.

Eighty years ago Rainer Maria Rilke observed that the future enters us before it happens. This perception has since been transformed from stretched oxymoron to painful reality. Dinner tonight? Steak with DNA-styled tomatoes. A skiing accident? Your physician will prescribe "smart" protheses, such as artificial bones and skin transplants.

In the twenty-first century the six continents familiar to Columbus, Vasco da Gama, Scott, and Livingstone have been compressed into one: cyberspace. Nanotechnologies, artificial intelligence, robotics, and biotechnology are in the driver's seat. Technologies are no longer instruments or tools. They have become second nature, key elements in our environment.

We need to get used to this. Which means doing things in a way that's always new.

And that means learning without a sense of security, learning while being aware of a constant reality lag, operating in new, constantly changing terrain. Learning in quicksand.

Which animals survive in quicksand? Animals with well developed antennae for danger. Learners with a certain lightness of style, and of being. Learners who understand play as training for life. Play is not anymore a leisure activity, it becomes a crucial necessity in the "brave new work" accomplished on shifting sands. Play has become an essential constituent of professional careers for those who successfully navigate across quicksand.

In play you experiment with rules as well as the possibility of "bending" rules. In play we simulate behavior patterns and conflict resolution. In play emotional releases are possible.

Play frequently involves simulating attacks of fear, penetrating those parts of the brain affected by true fear, without generating adrenaline or any true stress. The purpose of many games is to test reactions, thus generating the extra confidence needed. So play along, it doesn't matter, just stay in the game. Ahead, of course.

It is no coincidence that kids' toys, which have always transformed the complexities of the world in tangible realities for children, have now become more and more intelligent, flexible, and closer to reality. (For example, the introduction of Playstation 3 is planned for 2005, and it is supposed to be 1,000 times faster than Playstation 2). Computer simulations of different worlds are an excellent way to prepare children for future worlds.

3.2. Passion and Curiosity

I'm deeply convinced that you're only on top, you're only first-rate, when you do something with a dose of 120 percent involvement, with a dose of curiosity because you yourself are genuinely interested. Only then you can conquer frustration, uncertainty, procrastination, time-wasting resistance, and whatever other daily business obstacles, and generate the necessary persistence to get through, to get things—innovative things—done. Involvement—I'd say even passion—and this curiosity—call it the urge to find out—is vital. What a shame it would be if all this energy gets reserved for when you're out of the office.

But this is what happens!

Have you noticed how, when other people ask questions about something that's supposed to be self-evident, or when they query taboos, they are seen as impudent or even indecent? Of course anyone else (who might have, but didn't think of it) could have asked the same question. "Always looking at something new." A living thirst for knowledge, the desire for something new, can rarely be inbred or purchased. Often, and with almost terrifying success, it will be cut down and killed. How often were we told as children: "Stop poking your nose into that"? The corporate jargon is different, superficially more polite, but the bottom line remains the same: "Mind your own business."

"Mind your own business" is costing more and more. The passion for knowledge, the search for the unknown, the ability to convert a crazy idea into business use, are getting lost.

Which leads us to the question: Where is all this creativity, where are all those desperately searched for unique ideas, going to come from?

We need to nurse curiosity and passion in our business lives, not just on vacation in Thailand. That spurt of adrenaline you get behind the wheel of a red Porsche belongs inside corporate life.

And why? To become, quite simply, the best.

Seeking to become the best means waging war on mediocrity; rejecting what others take as obvious; querying accepted procedures and (ruins of) routines, established products, self-satisfied colleagues; and above all stirring up the competition.

What is necessary for this to happen? Curious enquiries mustn't just be encouraged on all levels, they must be answered. Assumed barriers need to be torn down, not just in offsite training but in daily business practice.

Try these questions as part of searching for the best:

- ❑ What's the latest idea?
- ❑ What idea astonishes the most?
- ❑ What gives you a kick?
- ❑ What do you want to be recognized for?
- ❑ Who gets noticed?
- ❑ Who are the outstanding people? What support do they get?
- ❑ And last but not least: What's going on outside?

Today's eccentricity is perhaps tomorrow's mainstream. What's far off today may be already here tomorrow.

These questions help to define the answers that secure the future, lead to the information you need about tomorrow's markets.

Ask these questions with sufficient persistence and you will create a breeding ground that every business is looking for: the new and the unique. Thinking and learning become an everyday experience. There arises an inimitable mix of ideas, products, and services in a team of unique people. It's not processes but people who do the work, and smart working always pays.

But it has its price. There's no such thing as enthusiasm without pain. As the homey saying goes from across the Atlantic, it's okay to sit bravely on the nettles, but reckon with an itchy butt.

For those in management roles here are some questions to ask:

❑ Do you really like managing (or are you in a management position due to the lack of recognized and appreciated specialist careers in the company)?

❑ Are you really interested in people? In knowing what makes them tick, what drives them? Or is the question "how are you?" just a rhetorical ritual? Do you love people—because only then do you get access to their hearts, which is crucial in order that your people give their very best.

❑ Do you like looking in people's eyes? To establish trust, which means you'll need less control.

❑ Do you enjoy the dependencies you have with your employees, colleagues, and bosses? Being in the sandwich position?

❑ Are you a good politician? Lobbying, saving faces (and asses), securing, building alliances, and switching sides. Corporations are full of politics, and the higher up you are on the ladder, the more important are these skills. The masters of politics make careers.

❑ Do you want these responsibilities, which also include the necessity to respond to certain questions?

❑ Last but not least: Does the increasing loneliness at the top appeal to you? Growing individual self-interest means that open and honest conversations become a first-class rarity.

If it isn't your cup of tea, leave management alone. You won't be happy. Nor will your employees. The good ones will leave.

4. Developing and Building Collective Intelligence

Alas, the more complex the problem, the more complex the solution.

From the way adaptive complex systems operate, we know that within clearly defined boundaries, autonomous individuals and groups working together are able to come up with excellent solutions. Not as teams. Autonomous individuals and groups, experts in their very own specific areas, who collaborate on projects.

A kind of collective expertise, or system intelligence, gets developed as a result of the self-organization of the experts. An "invisible hand" is at work.

Network achievers understand this. They build reliable networks and in return get quick results when they need them. So the challenge remains: how to establish and use collective intelligence for a specified purpose.

In 1999 only 30 percent of the people working in Silicon Valley had permanent employment contracts, and 12 percent had more than one job (1999 California Work and Health survey).

Managing such a workforce requires different skills. Making connections and nurturing them are getting ever more important. This has also consequences for expense budgets, which too often get slashed. Virtual contacts aren't enough. You need face-to-face contact, looking in the workers' eyes to build confidence.

The use of social networks isn't just trivial. Constellations change constantly. Your partner of today can be your competitor of tomorrow. Competitors can suddenly start generating synergies when working together as partners. Overnight bosses can become colleagues and work next to you, or the other way around.

Social prestige also plays a role in network strategies. Your prestige is high when you are seen as cooperative and helpful, or if people think you have something to offer, and low when you are seen as just a follower or somebody who doesn't offer to contribute. Academic studies confirm the biblical phrase "to him that hath shall be given."

But for that you've got to build yourself a reputation, which gets us to the next point:

5. Self-Branding

Develop your personal abilities so that they become a "brand." That's how you can commercialize your know-how.

Some, mainly from the worlds of art, media, and show business, have taken the notion of branding to its legal conclusion:

❑ David Bowie, the rock star, issued ten-year bonds on himself and his twenty-five albums with 300 songs, on his own abilities. These bonds give the purchaser the right to a share derived from the sale of old recordings and future income from live concerts given by Bowie. The sale offer—worth $55 million—was taken up within one hour.

❑ Gilbert & George, the self-inverted pair of British painters, owe a lot of their success, not just to their posing always together, but to insisting that the press always refer to them as "Gilbert & George" complete with ampersand, a label they have registered.

❑ Martha Stewart, "Queen of Domestic Arts" (cooking and etiquette), went public with Martha Stewart Living Omnimedia in 1999 with an offering of several hundred million dollars.

These examples are early indicators of a trend. Yesterday's "employees" are going to take the message to think and act as entrepreneurs ever more seriously. Their knowledge—their real asset between their ears—will be capitalized, and they will manage to maximize profit, further develop it, further pass it on, and distribute it.

Developing the personal asset means defining your special qualities, and your competitive advantage versus others at work, versus a large crowd of people with similar basic training. Attention and attraction are simultaneously content and form. Profile should determine branding.

So, under what slogan will you be sold? To develop this, answering the following questions will be helpful:

❑ What are your special qualities and competences, what differentiates you from others?

❑ How would your colleagues/bosses/friends/customers/competitors describe you? And much more interestingly, how would your enemies and adversaries describe you?

❑ When is a difference a real difference?

❑ What are you most proud of?

❑ Where and in which context (in terms of task/scope/roles) are your personal qualities of use?

❏ Which roles do you like to take over? Which not?

You should also position yourself, for which you will need:

❏ A personal credo
❏ Who do you know? Who are the people who leverage your capabilities? Remember:

Your competitiveness = What you know x Who you know

That's how a CV becomes a "marketing brochure." Instead of a conventional list of credentials, titles, and former positions (with low-end content on the real capabilities), there's a portfolio of proven abilities, with relevant achievements and targets. That's what interests most, that's what pays.

This process of defining your qualities also builds self-confidence, which is more important than ever. Self-confidence creates a basis for certainty, inner strength, and stability, which no employer can provide. For—all too often—the employer has lost his own sense of security. This self-confidence is your best insurance policy when there is general chaos and loss of direction.

In today's environment of shifting sands, where not just products and markets but also partners and friends are changing, your ego remains your only true partner for life. Nourish it, nurture it, take care of it.

The danger is excessive egocentricity. But in business practice, this isn't unusual. Rational thinking often got shipwrecked on the rocks of egos. Nothing new about that.

5.1. Credible Visibility

But what help is a "brand" if you behave with traditional understatement and keep so quiet, that only few people hear about it? Become visible and within reach for others. Let them know your special gifts, expose them in projects, inside or outside the company. Visible credibility has the most extraordinary multiplication effects.

However, there are dangers here as well. The more your professional activities achieve public recognition, the more your private life will lose value as the boundaries between private and public erode. The danger of an uncontrolled excessive valuation of work against family life is getting bigger. Studies from California—where this development is very advanced—confirm this. The individual feels more at home at work. Most of his friends are from the workplace, the workplace provides the wider stage. The workplace organizes parties, open-air picnics, the soft drinks are free, and there's a fridge next to the coffee machine. The workplace provides outlets for jealousy, sexual attraction, or steaming anger, whereas the arena at home is more limited.

Workplace becomes home, home becomes workplace. That's one of the basic, but not fully recognized phenomena of our altered environment. A well-publicized debate is going on about globalization, but the biggest competitor is local. The local rival is called family. The family is also confronted with the spill-over of the efficiency cult from the workplace into the home, where it can even become a lifestyle. For example, in more and more families the upbringing of children resembles more an organizational and time management task than an educational issue.

5.2. Self-Protection

To our wired and world-wide audience, equipped with mobile phones and an e-mail address, you're available twenty-four hours a day, seven days a week.

An exaggeration? *American Demographics*, in its September 1999 issue, reports that on average, a U.S. office worker receives:

- ❏ 52 phone calls
- ❏ 36 e-mails
- ❏ 23 voice mails
- ❏ 18 postal mails
- ❏ 14 faxes

❑ 13 Post-it Notes

❑ 3 express mails

A gruesome workload? Alas, the National Mental Health Association (1997) reported that from 75 percent to 90 percent of all visits to physicians are stress related.

Even more important is the ability to provide a qualified "no" and the ability to draw boundaries. Being able to protect yourself against intrusion.

Being able to enjoy an evening at the opera without a mobile phone or being able to go to bed in the evening without reading the last twenty e-mails is for some a challenge. The areas of potential intrusion go up: The access channels need to be managed. Being available doesn't mean being at someone's disposal.

5.3. Resilience

Yesteryear's heroes were praised for their brave deeds—think of those "Magnificent Men in Their Flying Machines." The heroes of today are celebrated for their persistence in times of crisis and change. Their persistence derives from two sources:

1. *Awareness*
   ❑ That nothing is self-evident.
   ❑ That nothing is stable, that there is a perpetual novelty and constant surprise.
   ❑ That there are things that are beyond our control.

2. *Understanding*
   ❑ How the change will affect the individual.
   ❑ What should be done?
   ❑ How the change will be measured.
   ❑ The implications of change.

❑ What tools and support are available?

❑ What are the costs and benefits to the individual?

Here failure plays a critical, constructive part. Failure shouldn't be a taboo: If so, failure remains failure. But failure is just another step on the road to success and a chance for creative reinvention.

6. What Knowledge Workers Want and Need

❑ They view their career simultaneously as a test strip, and a means of developing and enhancing themselves.

❑ They see their careers as characterized by twists and turns, not by straight lines. Change, and the need to affirm their own lifestyle, dictate these twists and turns. The point merits amplification: Many HR professionals, faced with people whose careers are often interspersed with breaks and interruptions, characterize them as unreliable, or think "they don't know what they want."

❑ For knowledge workers, the desire for hierarchical positions is less an aphrodisiac than the freedom to turn their own plans and ideas into reality. They grew up in an anti-authoritarian mode. They had to do what they want—today they know what they don't want. They don't want to struggle against the various conventional work modes, to argue with the 1,000 good reasons why things won't work, with "well, it's not like that here," and with the favorite phrase of the moment, "Yes, and what's that going to generate? Bottom line? Today?"

Instead, knowledge workers want to develop their potential in a multihued variety of new possibilities—including new ways of working, such as working from home, or telecommuting—but also the possibility to learn through experiments, right from the start.

They look for meaningful, meaning-creating work with a future. Their nightmare is getting lost in a dreary career pattern with a management style as charming as a heap of statistics.

Money is important, as is a professional community. For they know that it's rare that hard-nosed egotism, the exclusive pursuit of one's own interest, can generate real change in the world. They need a group of fellow-thinkers and soulmates, who are used to working together. Which is why ever more frequently whole teams switch employers (such as CSFB's high tech group moving from DEC to Microsoft).

6.1. Knowledge Workers Want to Have Fun

They enjoy efficiency and results, especially when the going is hard (just like mountain climbers). If they get into areas of organized lack of achievement, where low achievers are in high positions and constantly "get up their noses," then—after a time—they will get frustrated and leave. They abandon poor leaders. They know that these days job-hopping won't damage careers; just the opposite, it is regarded as an investment in experience.

They want experience, results, and opportunities. They want to see their contribution acknowledged, to be recognized, appreciated, and to be—in the broad sense—cared for. Their vanities need stroking. The motto is "Love me or lose me."

In the Information Society, the true scarcity is getting noticed. The true indicators of success and riches are *recognition* and *attention*. These are the new tokens, the new currency of the Information Society, the primary reason for self-branding.

Capitalism has long been interpreted as a continuous process of creative self-destruction. Markets, currencies, selling strategies, industrial processes, products—all of these have been understood as areas of continuous change. As surely as the sun rises tomorrow, tomorrow's products or services will replace today's.

Less self-evident is the need for all companies, not just those with a traditionally high element of R&D or in the new industries, to adapt to the needs of the knowledge-driven corporation and their knowledge workers.

But the need is there. Just as the sun will rise tomorrow, so the smart will sweep away the dumb.

REFERENCES

Chapter 1

Beerli, A.J. "Facilitating Conditions for Effective Knowledge Transfer in New Business Models." Dissertation, Universität St.Gallen, Hochschule für Wirtschafts-, Rechts- und Sozialwissenschaften (HSG), 2001.

Clausen, S. "Ade ABB." *Financial Times Deutschland*, April 4, 2002, p. 25.

Christensen, C.M. *The Innovator's Dilemma.* Boston: Harvard Business School Press, 1997.

Edvinsson, L. and M. Malone. *Intellectual Capital.* New York: Harper Business, 1997.

Nonaka, I. and N. Konno. "The Concept of 'Ba': Building a Foundation for Knowledge Creation." *California Management Review* 40.3 (1998), pp. 40–54.

Rutherford, E. "Quick Poll Report: KM Catching O." *CIO Magazine,* 2001. http://www.cio.com/poll/041701_km.html.

Tapscott, D., D. Ticoll, and A. Lowy. *Digital Capital: Harnessing the Power of Business Webs.* Boston: Harvard Business School Press, 2000.

Von Krogh, G. "Care in Knowledge Creation." *California Management Review* 40.3 (1998), pp.134–154.

Von Krogh, G., K. Ichijo, and I. Nonaka. *Enabling Knowledge Creation: How to Unlock the Mystery of Tacit Knowledge and Release the Power of Innovation.* Oxford: Oxford University Press, 2000.

Chapter 2

Celsi, R.L. and J.C. Olson. "The Role of Involvement in Attention and Comprehension Processes." *Journal of Consumer Research* 15 (1988), pp. 210–224.

IATA Corporate Air Travel Survey: Europe, 1999.

Kiss, T. and H. Wettig. "Die Anzeigenwirkung in Abhängigkeit der Wirkungsfaktoren der Zeitschriften." *Marketing in a Changing World: The Role of Market Research.* Proceedings of the ESOMAR Congress, 1972.

Porter, M. "Strategy and the Internet." *Harvard Business Review*, March 2001.

Ryanair. "Die Rezepte eines Billigfliegers." *Manager Magazine*, February 2001, pp.104–113.

Sinus Sociovison (Hg.). *Sinus-Milieu*, 2000.
www.agmafu.de/kk/sinus2000/html/sinus_milieus1.htm).

Chapter 3

Alba, J., J. Lynch, B. Weitz, C. Janiszewski, R. Lutz, A. Sawyer, and S. Wood.
"Interactive Home Shopping: Consumer, Retailer, and Manufacturer Incentives to
Participate in Electronic Marketplaces." *Journal of Marketing* 61 (July 1997), pp.
38–53.

Bakos, J. Y. "Reducing Buyer Search Costs: Implications for Electronic
Marketplaces." *Management Science* 43.12 (December 1997), p. 1676.

Bakos, J.Y. "The Emerging Role of Electronic Marketplaces on the Internet."
Communications of the ACM. 41.8 (August 1998), pp. 35–42.

Benjamin, R. and R. Wigand. "Electronic Markets and Virtual Value Chains on the
Information Superhighway." *Sloan Management Review* 36 (Winter 1995), pp.
62–72.

Blattberg, R.C. and J. Deighton. "Interactive Marketing: Exploiting the Age of
Addressability." *Sloan Management Review* 33.1 (Fall 1991).

Christiaanse, E. *Strategic Advantage and the Exploitation of IT.* Amsterdam: Thesis
Publishers, 1994.

Culnan, M.J. "How Did They Get My Name?: An Explanatory Investigation of
Consumer Attitudes Toward Secondary Information Use." *MIS Quarterly* 19.3
(September 1995), pp. 341–364.

Culnan, M.J. and P.K. Armstrong. "Information Privacy Concerns, Procedural
Fairness and Impersonal Trust: An Empirical Investigation." *Organization Science*,
1998, www.msb.edu/faculty/culnanm/research/orgsci97.pdf.

Davenport, T.H. *Information Ecology: Mastering the Information and Knowledge
Environments.* New York: Oxford University Press, 1997.

Davenport, T.H. and L. Prusak. *Working Knowledge.* Boston: Harvard Business
School Press, 1998.

Davenport, T.H., J.K. Harris, and A. Kohli. "How Do They Know Their Customers
So Well?" *Sloan Management Review*, Winter 2001, pp. 63–73.

Davenport, T.H., J.G. Harris, D. DeLong, and A. Jacobsen. "Data to Knowledge to
Results: Building an Analytic Capability." *California Management Review*, Winter
2001, pp. 117–138.

Degeratu, A., A. Rangaswamy, and J. Wu. "Consumer Choice Behavior in Online
and Traditional Supermarkets: The Effects of Brand Name, Price, and Other Search
Attributes." Working paper, eBusiness Research Center, School of Information
Science, and Technology, Penn State University, University Park, Pa., 1999.

Department of Commerce. "Privacy Online: A Report to Congress." Washington
D.C.: Federal Trade Commission, 1998.

Duncan, T. and S.E. Moriarty. "A Communication-Based Marketing Model for Managing Relationships." *Journal of Marketing*, April 1998, pp. 1–13.

Eastlick, M. A. Predictors of Videotext Adoption. *Journal of Direct Marketing* 7.3 (Summer 1993), pp. 66–76.

Evans, P.B. and T.S. Wurster. "Strategy and the New Economics of Information." *Harvard Business Review*, September/October 1997, pp. 70–82.

Fahey, L., R. Srivastava, D.E. Smith, and J. Sharon. "Linking E-Business and Operating Processes: The Role of Knowledge Management." Working paper, IBM Institute for Knowledge Management, Cambridge, Mass., 2000.

Forrester Research. "Measuring Web Success." *The Forrester Report,* November 1999, pp. 2–3.

Frenzen, J. and K. Nakamoto. "Structure, Cooperation, and the Flow of Market Information." *Journal of Consumer Research* 20 (December 1993), pp. 360–375.

Godwin, C. "Privacy: Recognition of a Consumer Right." *Journal of Public Policy and Marketing* 12 (Spring 1991), pp. 106–119.

Hagel, J. and J. Rayport. "The Coming Battle for Customer Information." *Harvard Business Review*, January/February 1997, pp. 53–65.

Hof, R.D. and H. Green. "Now It's Your Web." *Business Week,* October 5, 1998, pp. 164–178.

Hoffman, D.L. and T.P. Novak. "Marketing in Hypermedia Computer-Mediated Environments: Conceptual Foundations. " *Journal of Marketing* 60 (July 1997), pp. 50–68.

Iansiti, M. and A. MacCormack. "Developing Products on Internet Time." *Harvard Business Review*, September/October 1997, pp. 108–117.

Jaworski, B.J. and A.K. Kohli. "Market Orientation: Antecedents and Consequences." *Journal of Marketing* 57 (July 1993), pp. 53–70.

Jones, T.O. and W.E. Sasser, Jr. "Why Satisfied Customers Defect." *Harvard Business Review*, November/December 1995, pp. 88–99.

Kambil, A. and E. van Heck. "Reengineering the Dutch Flower Auctions: A Framework for Analyzing Exchange Organizations." *Information Systems Research* 9.1 (March 1998), pp. 1–19.

Kannan, P.K., A. Chang, and A.B. Whinston. "Marketing Information on the I-Way." *Communications of the ACM* 41.3 (March 1998), pp. 35–43.

Kim, W.C. and R. Mauborgne. "Procedural Justice, Strategic Decision Making, and the Knowledge Economy." *Strategic Management Journal* 12 (1998), pp. 323–338.

Kohli, A.K. and B.J. Jaworski. "Market Orientation: The Construct, Research Propositions, and Managerial Implications." *Journal of Marketing* 54 (April 1990), pp. 1–18.

Lynch, J.G. and D. Ariely. "Interactive Home Shopping: Effects of Search Cost for Price and Quality Information on Consumer Price Sensitivity: Satisfaction with Merchandise and Retention." Working paper, Duke University, Durham, N.C., 1998.

McKenna, R. "Real-Time Marketing." *Harvard Business Review*, July/August 1995, pp. 87–95.

Menon, A. and P.R. Varadarajan. "A Model of Marketing Knowledge Use Within Firms." *Journal of Marketing* 56 (October 1992), pp. 53–71.

Meyer, M.H. and M.H. Zack. "The Design and Development of Information Products." *Sloan Management Review* 37:3 (Spring 1996), pp. 43–56.

Moorman, C., G. Zaltman, and R. Deshpande. "Relationships Between Providers and Users of Market Research: The Dynamics of Trust Within and Between Organizations." *Journal of Marketing Research*, August 1992, pp. 314–328.

Nahapiet, J. and S. Ghoshal. "Social Capital, Intellectual Capital, and Organizational Advantage." *Academy of Management Review* 23.2 (1998), pp. 242–266.

Nonaka, I. and H. Takeuchi. *The Knowledge-Creating Company.* New York: Oxford University Press, 1995.

Nunes, P. F. and A. Kambil. "Personalization? No Thanks." *Harvard Business Review*, April 2001, pp. 32–34.

Pazzani, M.J. "A Framework for Collaboration, Content-Based, and Demographic Filtering." Working paper, Department of Information and Computer Science, University of California, Irvine, Calif., 2001.

Peppers, D. and M. Rodgers. *The One-to-One Future.* New York: Currency-Doubleday, 1997.

Peterson, R.A., G. Albaum, and N.M. Ridgway. "Consumers Who Buy From Direct Sales Companies." *Journal of Retailing* 65.2 (Summer 1989), pp. 273–286.

Peterson, R.A., S. Balasubramanian, and B.J. Bronnenberg. "Exploring the Implications of the Internet for Consumer Marketing." *Journal of the Academy of Marketing Science* 25.4 (1997), pp. 329–346.

Pine, B.J. II, D. Peppers, and M. Rogers. "Do You Want to Keep Your Customers Forever?" *Harvard Business Review*, March/April 1995, pp. 103–114.

Reynolds, F.D. "An Analysis of Catalog Buying Behavior." *Journal of Marketing* 38 (July 1974), pp. 47–51.

Rifkin, G. "Stop Squeezing the Cyber Melons!: Shopping for Groceries Online." *New York Times,* June 14, 1997, p. 21.

Rumelt, R.P., D. Schendl, and D.J. Teece. "Strategic Management and Economics." *Strategic Management Journal* 12 (1991; Winter special issue), pp. 5–29.

Rust, R.T., A.J. Zahorik, and T.L. Keiningham. "Return on Quality (ROQ): Making Service Quality Financially Accountable." *Journal of Marketing* 59 (April 1995), pp. 58–70.

Sanchez, A.M. and L.N. Elola. "Product Innovation Management in Spain." *Journal of Product Innovation Management,* 8.1 (1991), pp. 49–56.

Sarkar, M., B. Butler, and C. Steinfeld. "Cybermediaries in Electronic Marketspace: Toward Theory Building." *Journal of Business Research* 41 (1998), pp. 215–221.

Shankar, V., A. Rangaswamy, and M. Pusateri. "The Online Medium and Customer Price Sensitivity." Working paper, eBusiness Research Center, School of Information Science and Technology, Penn State University, University Park, Pa., 1999.

Shapiro, C. and H.R. Varian. *Information Rules: A Strategic Guide to the Network Economy.* Boston: Harvard Business School Press, 1999.

Smith, H. J. "Information Privacy and Marketing: What the U.S. Should (and Shouldn't) Learn from Europe." *California Management Review,* Winter 2001, pp. 8–33.

Sterne, J. *Customer Service on the Internet.* New York: Wiley, 1996.

Szulanski, G. "Exploring Internal Stickiness: Impediments to the Transfer of Best Practice with the Firm." *Strategic Management Journal* 17 (1996), pp. 27–44.

Wellman, B., J. Salaff, D. Dimitrova, L. Garton, M. Gulia, and C. Haythornthwaite. "Computer Networks as Social Networks: Collaborative Work, Telework, and Virtual Community." *Annual Review of Sociology* 22 (1996), pp. 213–238.

Williamson, O.E. *Markets and Hierarchies.* New York: Free Press, 1975.

Chapter 4

Bartlett, C. *McKinsey & Company: Managing Knowledge and Learning.* Boston: Harvard Business School Press, 2000.

Duder, R. "Anforderungen und Potentiale des E-Business an die Gestaltung von Wissensportalen." Unpublished thesis, Hochschule St.Gallen, 2000.

Falk, S. (2000): "Knowledge Management bei Andersen Consulting." In U. Hasenkamp, (ed). Notes/Domino effektiv nutzen. München: Addison Wesley, 2000.

Goffin, K. and R. Pfeiffer. *Innovation Management in UK and German Manufacturing Companies.* Anglo-German Foundation Series, York Publishing Series, 2000.

Hansen, P., et al . "What is Your Strategy for Managing Knowledge?" *Harvard Business Review,* March/April 1999, pp.106–116.

Horgan, J. *The End of Science: Facing the Limits of Knowledge in the Twilight of the Scientific Age.* Boulder, Colo.: Helix Books, 1997.

IDC. "Knowledge Management: U.S. and Worldwide Forecast and Analysis: 1999–2004." IDC, 2000.

Ovum evaluates: Knowledge Management, Boston, London etc 2000.

Chapter 5

Ackoff, R. L. "Beyond Prediction and Preparation." *Journal of Management Studies* 20.1 (1983), pp. 59–69.

Alchian, A. "Uncertainty, Evolution and Economic Theory." *Journal of Political Economy* 57 (1950), pp. 211–221.

Allison, L. E. *The Essence of Decision: Explaining the Cuban Missile Crisis.* Boston: Little, Brown, 1971.

Amit, R. and P.J.H. Schoemaker. "Strategic Assets and Organizational Rent." *Strategic Management Journal* 14.1 (1993), pp. 33–46.

Andrews, K. R. *The Concept of Corporate Strategy.* Homewood, Ill: Dow-Jones Irwin, 1971. Reissued 1987.

Ansoff, H. I. *Corporate Strategy: An Analytical Approach to Business Policy for Growth and Expansion.* New York: McGraw-Hill, 1965.

Ansoff, H. I. "The State of Practice in Planning Systems." *Sloan Management Review,* Winter 1971, pp. 1–24.

Argyris, C. and D. Schon. *Organizational Learning.* Reading, Mass.: Addison-Wesley, 1978.

Astley, W. G. and A. H. Van de Ven. "Central Perspectives and Debates in Organization Theory." *Administrative Science Quarterly* 28 (1983), pp. 245–273.

Barnett, W. P. and R. A. Burgelman. "Evolutionary Perspectives on Strategy." *Strategic Management Journal* 17 (1996, special issue), pp. 5–19.

Barney, J. B. "Firm Resources and Sustained Competitive Advantage." *Journal of Management* 17.1 (1991), pp. 99–120.

Bartlett, C. A. and S. Ghoshal. "Beyond the M-Form: Toward a Managerial Theory of the Firm." *Strategic Management Journal* 14 (1993, special issue), pp. 23–46.

Berliner, P. F. *Thinking in Jazz: The Infinite Art of Improvisation.* Chicago: University of Chicago, 1994.

Bettis, R. A. and C. K. Prahalad. "The Dominant Logic: Retrospective and Extension." *Strategic Management Journal* 16 (1995), pp. 3–14.

Boltanski, L. and L. Thévenot. *De la justification.* Gallimard, Paris, 1991.

Bourdieu, P. *Esquisse d'une théorie de la pratique. Précédée de trois études d'ethnologie kabyle.* Genève: Minuit, 1972.

Bourdieu, P. *Le sens pratique.* Paris: Editions du Seuil, 1980.

Bourdieu, P. *Leçon sur la leçon.* Paris: Minuit, 1982.

Bourdieu, P. and L. Wacquant. *An Invitation to Reflexive Sociology.* Chicago: Chicago University Press, 1992.

Bourdieu. P. *Raisons pratiques.* Paris: Gallimard, 1994.

Bourgeois, L. J. III and K. M. Eisenhardt. "Strategy Decision Processes in High

Velocity Environments: Four Cases in the Microcomputer Industry." *Management Science* 34 (1988), pp. 816–835.

Bower, J. L. *Managing the Resource Allocation Process: A Study of Corporate Planning and Investment.* Boston: Harvard Business School Press, 1970.

Bower, J. L. and C. M. Christensen. "Disruptive Technologies: Catching the Wave." *Harvard Business Review,* January/February 1995, pp. 43–53.

Bruner, J. *Actual Minds, Possible Worlds,* Cambridge, Mass.: Harvard University Press, 1986.

Bruner, J. *Acts of Meaning.* Cambridge, Mass.: Harvard University Press, 1990.

Burgelman, R. A. "A Model of the Interaction of Strategic Behavior, Corporate Context, and the Concept of Strategy." *Academy of Management Review* 8 (1983a), pp. 61–70.

Burgelman, R. A. "A Process Model of Internal Corporate Venturing in the Diversified Major Firm." *Administrative Science Quarterly* 28 (1983b), pp. 223–244.

Burgelman, R. A. "Fading Memories: A Process Theory of Strategic Business Exit in Dynamic Environments." *Administrative Science Quarterly* 39.1 (1994), pp. 24–56.

Burrell, G. and G. Morgan. *Sociological Paradigms and Organizational Analysis.* London: Heinemann, 1979.

Chakravarthy, B. S. and Y. Doz. "Strategy Process Research: Focusing on Corporate Self-renewal." *Strategic Management Journal* 13 (1992), pp. 5–14.

Chandler, A. D. *Strategy and Structure.* Cambridge, Mass.: MIT Press, 1962.

Christensen, C. *Innovators Dilemma.* Cambridge, Mass: Harvard Business School Press, 1995.

Clancey, W. *Situated Cognition.* Cambridge, Mass.: MIT Press, 1998.

Clark, A. *Being There: Putting Brain, Body, and World Together Again.* Cambridge, Mass.: MIT Press, 1998.

Cockburn, I. M., R. M. Henderson, and S. Stern. "Untangling the Origins of Competitive Advantage." *Strategic Management Journal* 21 (2000), pp. 1123–1145.

Cohen, W. M. and D. A. Levinthal. "Absorptive Capacity: A New Perspective on Learning and Innovation." *Administrative Science Quarterly* 35 (1990), pp. 128–152.

Conein, B., N. Dodier, and L. Thévénot. *Les objects dans l'action.* Paris: Ecole des Hautes Etudes en Sciences Sociales, 1993.

Cyert, R. M. and J. G. March. *A Behavioral Theory of the Firm.* Englewood Cliffs, NJ: Prentice Hall, 1963.

Dosi, G. "Technological Paradigms and Technological Trajectories." *Research Policy* 11 (1982), pp. 147–162.

Dosi, G., D. J. Teece, and J. Chytry. *Technology, Organization, and Competitiveness: Perspectives on Industrial and Corporate Change.* Oxford: Oxford University Press, 1998.

Dreyfus, H. and P. Rabinow. *Michel Foucault: Beyond Structuralism and Hermeneutics.* Chicago: Chicago University Press, 1982.

Dutton, J. E. "Understanding Strategic Agenda Building and Its Implications for Managing Change." In L. R. Ponty, R. Bland, and H. Thomas (eds.). *Managing Ambiguity and Change.* New York: Wiley, 1988, pp. 127–144.

Dutton, J. E. and J. Dukerich. "Keeping an Eye on the Mirror: Image and Identity in Organizational Adaptation." *Academy of Management Journal* 34.3 (1991), pp. 517–554.

Dutton, J. E. and S. E. Jackson. "Categorizing Strategic Issues: Link to Organizational Action." *Academy of Management Review* 12 (1987), pp. 76–90.

Dutton, J. E. and S. J. Ashford. "Selling Issues to Top Management." *Academy of Management Review* 18.3 (1993), pp. 397–428.

Eisenhardt, K. M. and M. J. Zbaracki. "Strategic Decision Making." *Strategic Management Journal* 14 (Winter 1992, special issue), pp. 532–550.

Eisenhardt, K.M. and J.A. Martin. "Dynamic Capabilities: What Are They?" *Strategic Management Journal* 21 (2000, special issue), pp. 1105–1121.

Elkana, Y. *Anthropologie der Erkenntnis. Die Entwicklung des Wissens als episches Theater einer listigen Vernunft.* Frankfurt: Suhrkamp, 1986.

Fleck, L. *Entstehung und Entwicklung einer wissenschaftlichen Tatsache.* Frankfurt: Suhrkamp, 1935.

Foster, R. *Innovation: The Attacker's Advantage,* New York: Summit Books, 1986.

Foucault, M. *Les mots et les choses.* Paris: Gallimard, 1966.

Foucault, M. *L'ordre du discours.* Paris: Gallimard, 1971.

Galison, P. *Image and Logic. A Material Culture of Microphysics.* Chicago: University of Chicago Press, 1997.

Garfinkel, H. *Studies in Ethnomethodology.* Englewood Cliffs, NJ: Prentice Hall, 1967.

Garfinkel, H. and H. Sacks. "On Formal Structures of Practical Action." In McKinney, J.C. and E. A. Tiryakian (eds.). *Theoretical Sociology.* New York: Appleton Century Crofts, 1970, pp. 338–436.

Ghoshal, S. and C. A. Bartlett. "Linking Organizational Context and Managerial Action: The Dimensions of Quality of Management." *Strategic Management Journal* 15 (1994), pp. 91–112.

Giddens, A. *The Constitution of Society.* Berkeley: University of California Press, 1984.

Ginsberg, A. "Minding the Competition: From Mapping to Mastery." *Strategic Management Journal* 15 (1994), pp. 153–174.

Gioia, D. A. and K. Chittipetti. "Sensemaking and Sensegiving in Strategic Change Initiation." *Strategic Management Journal* 12 (1991), pp. 433–448.

Goffman, E. *Encounters.* Indianapolis: Macmillan, 1961.

Goffman, E. *Frame Analysis: An Essay on the Organization of Experience.* Boston, Mass.: Northeastern University Press, 1974.

Gomez, P.-Y. and B. Jones. "Conventions: An Interpretation of Deep Structures in Organizations." *Organization Science* (2001). http://www.unizh.ch/ifbf/orga/downloads/kommorga/grand.pdf

Grand, S. "Paradoxical Organization of Multinational Corporations." Unpublished doctoral dissertation, University of Zürich, 1997.

Grand, S., G. von Krogh, and A. Pettigrew. "Strategic Thinking and Acting under Ambiguity." Paper presented at the 15th EGOS Colloquium, Warwick, U.K., 1999.

Grant, R. M. "On Dominant Logic, Relatedness and the Link between Diversity and Performance." *Strategic Management Journal* 9 (1988), pp. 639–642.

Grant, R.M. "Toward a Knowledge-Base Theory of the Firm." *Strategic Management Journal* 17 (1996, special issue), pp. 109–122.

Hamel, G. and C. K. Prahalad. *Competing for the Future.* Cambridge, Mass.: Harvard Business School Press, 1995.

Henderson, R.M. and I. Cockburn. "Measuring Competence? Exploring Firm Effects in Pharmaceutical Research." *Strategic Management Journal* 15 (1994, special issue), pp. 63–84.

Henderson, R.M. and K.B. Clark. "Architectural Innovation: The Reconfiguration of Existing Product Technologies and the Failure of Established Firms." *Administrative Science Quarterly* 35 (1990), pp. 9–30.

Iser, W. *The Act of Reading.* Baltimore: John Hopkins University Press, 1978.

Joas, H. *Die Kreativität des Handelns.* Frankfurt: Suhrkamp, 1991.

Kahnemann, D., P. Slovic, and A. Tversky (eds.). *Judgment under Uncertainty: Heuristics and Biases.* New York: Cambridge University Press, 1979.

Knight, F. H. *Risk, Uncertainty and Profit.* Boston: Houghton Mifflin, 1921.

Knorr Cetina, K. *Epistemic Cultures: How the Sciences Make Knowledge.* Cambridge, Mass.: Harvard University Press, 1999.

Kogut, B. and U. Zander. "Knowledge of the Firm, Combinative Capabilities, and the Replication of Technology." *Organizational Science* 7.5 (1992), pp. 502–518.

Kuhn, T. S. *Die Struktur wissenschaftlicher Revolution.* Frankfurt: Suhrkamp, 1962. Reissued 1970.

Latour, B. *Pandora's Hope.* Cambridge, Mass.: Harvard University Press, 1998.

Latour, B. *Science in Action.* Cambridge, Mass.: Harvard University Press, 1987.

Leonard-Barton, D. "Core Capabilities and Core Rigidities: A Paradox in Managing New Product Development." *Strategic Management Journal* 13 (1992), pp. 111–125,

Levinthal, D. A. "Strategic Management and the Exploration of Diversity." In C. A. Montgomery, (ed.). *Resource-Based and Evolutionary Theories of the Firm.* Boston: Kluwer Academic Publishers, 1995, pp. 19–43.

Levinthal, D. A. and J. G. March. "A Model of Adaptive Organizational Search." *Journal of Economic Behavior and Organization* 2 (1993), pp. 307–333.

Levitt, B. and J. G. March. "Organizational Learning." *Annual Review of Sociology* 14 (1998), pp. 319–340.

Lewis, D. K. *Convention: A Philosophical Study.* Cambridge, Mass.: Harvard University Press, 1969.

Lindblom, C. E. "The Science of Muddling Through." *Public Administration Review* 19.2 (1959), pp. 79–88.

Lindblom, C. E. *The Policy-Making Process.* Englewood Cliffs, NJ: Prentice Hall, 1968.

Lyles, M. A. and C. R. Schwenk. "Top Management, Strategy, and Organizational Knowledge Structures." *Journal of Management Studies* 29.2 (1986), pp. 155–174.

Lynch, M. *Scientific Practice and Ordinary Action: Ethnomethodology and Social Studies of Science.* Cambridge: Cambridge University Press, 1993.

March, J. G. "Exploration and Exploitation in Organizational Learning." *Organization Science* 2 (1991), pp. 71–87.

March, J. G. *A Primer on Decision Making: How Decisions Happen.* New York: The Free Press, 1994.

March, J. G. and H. A. Simon. *Organizations.* New York: Wiley, 1958.

March, J. G. and J. P. Olsen. *Ambiguity and Choice in Organizations.* Bergen, Norway: Universitetsforlaget, 1976.

March, J. G., J. S. Sproull and M. Tamuz. "Learning from Samples of One and Fewer." *Organization Science* 2 (1991), pp. 1–13.

McCloskey, D. N. *The Rhetoric of Economics.* Madison: University of Wisconsin Press, 1986.

McGrath, MacMillan, and Venkataraman, 1995.

Menuhin, J. and J. McGee. "Strategizing Routines." Paper presented at the 15th EGOS "European Group for Organizational Studies" Colloquium, Warwick, U.K., 1999.

Meyer, A. J., P. J. Frost, and K. E. Weick. "The Organization Science Jazz Festival: Improvisation as a Metaphor for Organizing." *Organization Science* 9.5 (1998), pp. 540–542.

Meyer, J. and B. Rowan. "Institutionalized Organizations: Formal Structure as Myth and Ceremony." *American Journal of Sociology* 83 (1977), pp. 340–363.

Miller, D. "Configurations of Strategy and Structure: Towards a Synthesis." *Strategic Management Journal* 7 (1986), pp. 233–249.

Miller, D. "Configurations Revisited." *Strategic Management Journal* 17 (1996), pp. 505–512.

Miller, D. and P. H. Friesen. *Organizations: A Quantum View.* Englewood Cliffs, NJ: Prentice Hall, 1984.

Mintzberg, H. *The Nature of Managerial Work.* New York: Harper and Row, 1973.

Mintzberg, H. "Patterns in Strategy Formation." *Management Science* 24 (1978), pp. 934–948.

Mintzberg, H. *Rise and Fall of Strategic Planning.* New York: Free Press, 1994.

Mintzberg, H. and A. McHugh. "Strategy Formulation in an Adhocracy." *Administrative Science Quarterly* 30 (1985), pp. 160–197.

Mintzberg, H. and J. A. Waters. "Of Strategies, Deliberate and Emergent." *Strategic Management Journal* 6 (1985), pp. 257–272.

Mintzberg, H., B. Ahlstrand, and J. Lampel. *Strategy Safari: A Guided Tour Through the Wilds of Strategic Management.* New York: The Free Press, 1998.

Nath, D. and D. Sudharshan. "Measuring Strategy Coherence Through Patterns of Strategic Choice." *Strategic Management Journal* 15 (1994), pp. 43–61.

Nelson, R. R. "Why Do Firms Differ? And How Does It Matter?" In R. P. Rumelt, D. E. Schendel, and D. J. Teece (eds.). *Fundamental Issues in Strategy: A Research Agenda.* Cambridge, Mass.: Harvard Business School Press, 1994, pp. 247–270.

Nelson, R. R. "Recent Evolutionary Theorizing About Economic Change." *Journal of Economic Literature* 33 (1995), pp. 48–90.

Nelson, R. R. and S. Winter. *An Evolutionary Theory of Economic Change.* Cambridge, Mass.: Belknap Press of Harvard University Press, 1982.

Noda, T. and J. L. Bower. "Strategy Making as Iterated Process of Resource Allocation." *Strategic Management Journal* 17 (1996), pp. 159–192.

Nonaka, I. "A Dynamic Theory of Organizational Knowledge Creation." *Organization Science* 5.1 (1994), pp.14–37

Nonaka, I. and H. Takeuchi. *The Knowledge-Creating Company.* Oxford: Oxford University Press, 1995.

Ocasio, W. "Towards an Attention-Based View of the Firm." *Strategic Management Journal*, 18 (1997, summer special issue), pp. 187–206.

Penrose, E. T. *The Theory of Growth of the Firm.* London: Basil Blackwell, 1959.

Pettigrew, A. M. *The Awakening Giant: Continuity and Change in Imperial Chemical Industries.* Oxford: Basil Blackwell, 1985.

Pettigrew, A. M. "The Character and Significance of Strategy Process Research." *Strategic Management Journal* 13 (1992, Winter special issue), pp. 5–16.

Pettigrew, A. M. and R. Whipp. *Managing Change for Competitive Success.* Oxford: Blackwell, 1991.

Pharao, P. and L. Quéré. *Les formes de l'action.* Paris: École des hautes études en sciences sociales, 1990.

Pinchot, G. *Intrapreneuring.* New York: Harper & Row, 1985.

Pisano, G.P. "Knowledge, Integration, and the Locus of Learning: An Empirical Analysis of Process Development." *Strategic Management Journal* 15 (1994, special issue), pp. 85–100.

Porter, M. *Competitive Strategy.* New York: The Free Press,1980.

Prahalad, C. K. and R. A. Bettis. "The Dominant Logic: A New Linkage Between Diversity and Performance." *Strategic Management Journal* 7.6 (1986), pp. 485–501

Quéré, L. *Theorie de l'action. Le sujet pratique en debat.* Paris: CNRS, 1993.

Quinn, J. B. *Strategies for Change: Logical Incrementalism.* Homewood, Ill.: Irwin, 1980.

Ricoeur, P. *La métaphore vive.* Paris: Editions du Seuil, 1975.

Roos, J. and G. von Krogh. *Managing the Strategy Process in Emergent Industries.* London, 1994.

Rumelt, R. P. "The Evaluation of Business Strategy." In H. Mintzberg and J. B. Quinn (eds.) *The Strategy Process, 3rd edition.* Englewood Cliffs, N.J.: Prentice Hall, 1997.

Rumelt, R. P., D. E. Schendel, and D. J. Teece. *Fundamental Issues in Strategy: A Research Agenda.* Cambridge, Mass.: Harvard Business School Press, 1994.

Schelling, T. C. *The Strategy of Conflict.* Cambridge, Mass.: Harvard University Press, 1960.

Schoemaker, P. J. H. "Strategic Decisions in Organizations: Rational and Behavioral Views." *Journal of Management Studies* 30.1 (1993), pp. 107–129.

Schutz, A. "The Social World and the Theory of Social Action." In A. Schutz, *Collected Papers.* The Hague: M. Nijhoff, 1964, pp. 64–90.

Schutz, A. *Der sinnhafte Aufbau der sozialen Welt.* Frankfurt: Suhrkamp, 1974.

Schwenk C. "Cognitive Simplification Processes in Strategic Decision-Making." *Strategic Management Journal* 5.2 (1984), pp. 111–128.

Schwenk, C. "Information, Cognitive Biases and Commitment to a Course of Action." *Academy of Management Review* 11.2 (1986), pp. 298–310.

Schwenk, C. "The Cognitive Perspective in Strategic Decision-Making." *Journal of Management Studies* 25 (1988), pp. 41–56.

Simons, R. *Levers of Control: How Managers use Innovative Control Systems to Drive Strategic Renewal.* Boston: Harvard Business School Press, 1995.

Spender, J.-C. *Industry Recipes. The Nature and Sources of Managerial Judgment.* Oxford: Blackwell, 1989.

Spender, J. C. "Managing Knowledge: The Basis of a Dynamic Theory of the Firm." *Strategic Management Journal* 17 (1996), pp. 45–62.

Steiner, G. A. *Strategic Planning: What Every Manager Must Know.* New York: Free Press, 1979.

Stone, M. M. and C. G. Brush. "Planning in Ambiguous Contexts: The Dilemma of Meeting Needs for Commitment and Demands for Legitimacy." *Strategic Management Journal* 17 (1996), pp. 633–652.

Suchman, L. *Plans and Situated Action.* Cambridge, Mass.: Harvard University Press, 1987.

Szulanski, G. and K. Amin. "Strategy Making in Uncertain Environments: The Need for Disciplined Imagination." Paper presented at the Strategic Management Society Annual Conference, Berlin, 1999.

Szulanski, G. and Y. Doz. "Strategy Formulation as Disciplined Imagination." Working paper, Fontainebleau: INSEAD, 1995.

Teece, D., G. Pisano, and A. Shuen. "Dynamic Capabilities and Strategic Management." *Strategic Management Journal* 18 (1997), pp. 509–533.

Tsoukas, H. "The Missing Link: A Transformational View of Metaphors in Organization Science." *Academy of Management Review* 16.3 (1989), pp. 566–585.

Tushman, M. L. and P. C. Anderson. "Technological Discontinuities and Organizational Environments." *Administrative Science Quarterly* 31 (1986), pp. 439–465.

Utterback, J. M. *Mastering the Dynamics of Innovation.* Cambridge, Mass.: Harvard Business School Press, 1994.

Van de Ven, A. H. "Suggestions for Studying Strategy Process: A Research Note." *Strategic Management Journal* 13 (1992, special issue), pp. 169–188

von Krogh, G. and S. Grand. "Justification in Knowledge Creation: Dominant Logic in Management Discourses." In von Krogh, G., I. Nonaka, and T. Nishiguchi (eds.). *Knowledge Creation: A New Source of Value.* London: Macmillan, 1999.

von Krogh, G. and S. Grand. "From Economic Theory Towards a Knowledge-Based Theory of the Firm: Conceptual Building Blocks." In C.W. Choo and N. Bontis (eds.). *The Strategic Management of Intellectual Capital and Organizational Knowledge.* New York: Oxford University Press, 2001, pp. 163–184.

Wagner, P. "Die Soziologie der Genese sozialer Institutionen." *Zeitschrift für Soziologie* 22.6 (1993), pp. 464–476.

Walsh, J. P. "Selectivity and Selective Perception: An Investigation of Managers' Belief Structures and Information Processing." *Academy of Management Journal* 31 (1988), pp. 873–896.

Weick, K. E. *The Social Psychology of Organizing, 2nd edition.* New York: Random House, 1979.

Weick, K. E. "Theory Construction as Disciplined Imagination." *Academy of Management Review* 14 (1989), pp. 516–531.

Weick, K. E. *Sensemaking in Organizations.* Reading, Mass.: Sage, 1995.

Weick, K. E. "Introductory Essay: Improvisation as a Mindset for Organizational Analysis." *Organization Science* 9.5 (1998), pp.543–555.

Weick, K. E. and K. H. Roberts. "Collective Mind in Organizations: Heedful Interrelating on Flight Decks." *Administrative Science Quarterly* 8 (1993), pp. 357–381.

Williamson, O. *Markets and Hierarchies.* New York: Free Press, 1975.

Wittgenstein, L. *Philosophical Investigations.* New York: MacMillan, 1953.

Zollo, M. and S. Winter. "From Organizational Routines to Dynamic Capabilities." Working paper, University of Pennsylvania, Philadelphia, Pa., 1999.

Chapter 6

Alba, R. D. "Taking Stock of Network Analysis: A Decade's Results." In S. B. Bacharach, (ed.). *Research in the Sociology of Organizations.* Greenwich, Conn.: JAI, 1982, pp. 39–74.

Arora, A. and A. Gambarella. "Complementary and External Linkages: The Strategies of the Firms in Biotechnology." *Journal of Industrial Economics* 38 (1990), pp. 361–379.

Badaracco, J. L. *The Knowledge Link: How Firms Compete Through Strategic Alliances.* Boston: Harvard Business School Press, 1991.

Barney, J. B. "Firm Resources and Sustained Competitive Advantage." *Journal of Management* 17 (1991), pp. 99–120.

Brown, J. S. and P. Duguid. "Organizational Learning and Communities-of-Practice: Toward a Unified View of Working, Learning and Innovation." *Organizational Science* 2.1 (1991), pp. 40–57.

Conner, K. R. and C. K. Prahalad. "A Resource-based Theory of the Firm: Knowledge Versus Opportunism." *Organization Science* 7.5 (1996), pp. 477–501.

Davenport, T. H., D. W. De Long, and M. C. Beers. "Successful Knowledge Management Projects. Eight Key Factors Can Help a Company Create, Share, and Use Knowledge Effectively." *Sloan Management Review* 39.2 (1998), pp. 43–57.

Davenport, T. H. and L. Prusak. *Working Knowledge: How Organizations Manage What They Know.* Boston: Harvard Business School Press, 1998.

Fleisch, E. *Das Netzwerkunternehmen.* Boston: Springer, 2000.

Giddens, A. *The Constitution of Society: Outline of the Theory of Structuration.* Berkeley: University of California Press, 1984.

Grant, R.M. "Toward a Knowledge-Based Theory of the Company." *Strategic Management Journal* 17 (1996, Winter special issue), pp. 109–122.

Hansen, M. T., N. Nohira, and T. Tierney. "What`s Your Strategy for Managing Knowledge?" *Harvard Business Review* 77.2 (1999), pp. 106–116.

Högberg, C. and L. Edvinsson. "A Design for Futurizing Knowledge Networking." *Journal of Knowledge Management,* 2.2 (1998), pp. 81–92.

Kogut, B. and U. Zander. "Knowledge of the Firm, Combinative Capabilities, and the Replication of Technology." *Organization Science* 3.3 (1992), pp. 383–397.

Leonard, D. and S. Sensiper. "The Role of Tacit Knowledge in Group Innovation." *California Management Review* 40.3 (1998), pp. 112–132.

Leonard-Barton, D. *Wellsprings of Knowledge: Building and Sustaining the Sources of Innovation.* Boston: Harvard Business School Press, 1995.

Lodge, G. C. and R. E. Walton. "The American Corporation and Its New Relationships." *California Management Review* 31 (1989), pp. 9–24.

Mitchell, J. C. "The Concept and Use of Social Networks." In J. C. Mitchell, (ed.). *Social Networks in Urban Situations.* Manchester: Manchester University Press, 1969, pp. 1–12.

Nohria, N. "Introduction: Is a Network Perspective a Useful Way of Studying Organizations?" In N. Nohria, (ed.). *Networks and Organizations: Structure, Form, and Action.* Boston: Harvard Business School Press, 1992, pp. 1–23.

Nonaka, I. "The Knowledge-Creating Company." *Harvard Business Review* 69.6 (1991).

Nonaka, I., P. Reinmoeller, and D. Senoo. "The Art of Knowledge: Systems to Capitalize on Market Knowledge." *European Management Journal* 16.6 (1998), pp. 673–684.

Nonaka, I. and H.Takeuchi. *The Knowledge Creating Company: How Japanese Companies Create the Dynamics of Innovation.* New York/Oxford: Oxford University Press, 1995.

Peteraf, M. "The Cornerstones of Competitive Advantage: A Resource-Based View." *Strategic Management Journal* 14.3 (1993), pp. 179–191.

Pisano, G. P., M. V. Russo, and D. J. Teece. "Joint Ventures and Collaborative Arrangements in the Telecommunications Equipment Industry." In D. C. Mowrey, (ed.). *International Collaborative Ventures in U.S. Manufacturing.* Cambridge, Mass.: Ballinger, 1988, pp. 23–70.

Porter, M.E. *Competitive Strategy.* New York: Free Press, 1980.

Powell, W., K. Koput, and L. Smith-Doerr. "Interorganizational Collaboration and the Locus of Innovation: Networks of Learning in Biotechnology." *Administrative Science Quarterly* 41(1996), pp. 116–145.

Prahalad, C. K. and G. Hamel. "The Core Competence of the Corporation." *Harvard Business Review* 68 (1990), pp. 79–91.

Reich, R. B. *The Work of Nations: Preparing Ourselves for the 21st-Century Capitalism.* New York: Knopf, 1991.

Richter, F. J. and K. Vettel. "Successful Joint Ventures in Japan: Transferring Knowledge Through Organizational Learning." *Long Range Planning* 28.3 (1995), pp. 37–45.

Schmid, B. and K. Stanoevska-Slabeva. "Knowledge Media: An Innovative Concept and Technology for Knowledge Management in the Information Age." Paper presented at Beyond Convergence, 12th Biennial International Telecommunications Society Conference, Stockholm, 1998.

Seufert, A., A. Back, and G. von Krogh. "Towards a Reference Model for Knowledge Networking." Working Paper, Research Center KnowledgeSource, BE HSG/ IWI 3 Nr. 5/ IfB Nr. 34, University of St. Gallen, 1999a.

Seufert, A. and S. Seufert. "The Genius Approach: Building Learning Networks for Advanced Management Education." Paper presented at 32nd Hawaii International Conference on System Sciences, Maui, Hawaii, January 5–8, 1999.

Seufert, A., G. von Krogh, and A. Back. "Towards Knowledge Networking." *Journal of Knowledge Management* 3.3 (1999b), pp. 180–190.

Seufert, S., A. Back, and M. Häusler. *E-Learning: Weiterbildung im Internet.* Kilchberg: Smart Books Publishing, 2001.

Von Krogh, G., K. Ichijo, and I. Nonaka. *Enabling Knowledge Creation: How to Unlock the Mystery of Tacit Knowledge and Release the Power of Innovation.* New York: Oxford University Press, 2000.

Von Krogh, G., I. Nonaka, and K. Ichijo. "Develop Knowledge Activists!" *European Management Journal* 15.5 (1997), pp. 475–483.

Weisenfeld, U. and A. K. Chakrabari. "Technologie und Marketingstrategien in der Biotechnologie: Ergebnisse einer deutschen und amerikanischen Studie." *Die Betriebswirtschaft* 50 (1990), pp. 747–758.

Wenger, E., and M. Snyder. "Communities of Practice: The Organizational Frontier." *Harvard Business Review* 78.1 (2000), pp. 139–145.

Wernerfeld, B. "A Resource Based View of the Firm." *Strategic Management Journal* 5 (1984), pp. 171–180.

Winter, S.G. "On Coase, Competence, and the Corporation." *Journal of Law, Economics, and Organization* 4 (1988), pp. 163–180.

Winter, S.G. "Four Rs of Profitability: Rents, Resources, Routines and Replication." In C. A. Montgomery, (ed.). *Resource-based and Evolutionary Theories of the Firm.* Boston: Kluwer Academic Publishers, 1995, pp. 147–178.

Chapter 7

Amram, M. and N. Kulatilaka. "Disciplined Decisions: Aligning Strategy with the Financial Markets." *Harvard Business Review*, January/February 1999, pp. 95–104.

Ansoff, I. *Corporate Strategy: An Analytic Approach to Business Policy for Growth and Expansion.* New York: McGraw-Hill, 1965.

Barker, D. "Technology Foresight Using Roadmaps." *Long Range Planning* 28 (1995), pp. 21–28.

Beinhocker, E. "On the Origin of Strategies." *Sloan Management Review*, Spring 1999, pp. 95–106.

Boyd, B. "Strategic Planning and Financial Performance: A Meta-Analysis." *Journal of Management Studies* 12 (1991), pp. 449–461.

Casti, J. *Would-Be Worlds: How Simulation is Changing the Frontiers of Science.* New York: Wiley, 1997.

Courtney, H., J. Kirkland, and P. Viguerie. "Strategy under Uncertainty." *Harvard Business Review*, November/December 1997, pp. 67–79.

Crossan, M., H. Lane, and R. White. "An Organizational Learning Framework: From Intuition to Institution." *Academy of Management Review* 24 (1999), pp. 522–537.

D´Aveni, R. A. *Hypercompetition: Managing the Dynamics of Strategic Maneuvering.* New York: Free Press, 1994.

Dixit, A. and B. Nalebuff. *Thinking Strategically: The Competitive Edge in Business, Politics and Everyday Life.* New York: W.W. Norton, 1991.

Dixit, A., and R. Pindyck. "The Options Approach to Capital Investment." *Harvard Business Review*, May/June 1995, pp. 105–115.

Eden, C. and C. Huxham. "Action Research for the Study of Organizations." In S. Clegg, C. Hardy, and W. Nord (eds.) *Handbook of Organization Studies.* London: Sage Publications, 1996, pp. 527–542.

Eisenhardt, K. M. "Strategy as Strategic Decision Making." *Sloan Management Review* 40 (1999), pp. 65–72.

Glaister, K. and R. Falshaw. "Strategic Planning: Still Going Strong?" *Long Range Planning* 32 (1999), pp. 107–116.

Goold, M. "Design, Learning and Planning: A Further Observation on the Design School Debate." *Strategic Management Journal* 13 (1992), pp. 169–170.

Grant, R. M. *Contemporary Strategy Analysis. Concepts, Techniques, Applications.* New York: Blackwell, 1998.

Hamel, G. "Strategy as Revolution." *Harvard Business Review*, July/August 1996, pp. 69–82.

Hamel, G. "Strategy Innovation and the Quest for Value." *Sloan Management Review*, Winter 1998, pp. 7–14.

Hamel, G. and C. K. Prahalad. *Competing for the Future.* Boston: Harvard Business School Press, 1994.

Hedberg, B. "How Organizations Learn and Unlearn." In P. Nystrom and W. Starbuck (eds.) *Handbook of Organizational Design.* Oxford: Oxford University Press, 1981.

Heijden, K. v. d. *The Art of Strategic Conversation.* New York: Wiley, 1996.

Infante, D., A. Rancer, and D. Womack. *Building Communication Theory.* Prospect Heights, Ill.: Waveland Press, 1997.

Inkpen, A. C., and N. Choudhury. "The Seeking of Strategy Where It Is Not: Towards a Theory of Strategy Absence." *Strategic Management Journal* 16 (1995), pp. 313–323.

Kaufmann, S. *At Home in the Universe: The Search for the Laws of Self-Organization and Complexity.* New York: Oxford University Press, 1995.

Khatri, N. and A. Ng. "The Role of Intuition in Strategic Decision Making." *Human Relations* 53 (2000), pp. 57–86.

Kim, C. and R. Mauborgne. "Value Innovation: The Strategic Logic of High Growth." *Harvard Business Review,* January/February 1997, pp. 103–112.

Lechner, C., and G. Müller-Stewens. "Strategische Prozessforschung: Zentrale Fragestellungen und Entwicklungstendenzen." Institut für Betriebswirtschaft der Universität St. Gallen, 1999.

Leonard-Barton, D. *Wellsprings of Knowledge: Building and Sustaining the Sources of Innovation.* Boston: Harvard Business School Press, 1995.

Leonard-Barton, D., and S. Sensiper. "The Role of Tacit Knowledge in Group Innovation." *California Management Review* 40 (1998), pp. 112–132.

Liedtka, J. M., and J.W. Rosenblum. "Shaping Conversations: Making Strategy, Managing Change." *California Management Review* 39 (1996), pp. 141–157.

Markides, C. *All the Right Moves: A Guide to Crafting Breakthrough Strategy.* Boston: Harvard Business School Press, 1999.

Markides, C. "Strategic Innovation in Established Companies." *Sloan Management Review,* Spring 1998, pp. 3–42.

McDermott, B. "Foresight Is an Illusion." *Long Range Planning,* 29.2 (1996), pp. 195–202.

Mintzberg, H. "The Design School: Reconsidering the Basic Premises of Strategic Management." *Strategic Management Journal* 11 (1990), pp. 171–195.

Mintzberg, H. *The Rise and Fall of Strategic Planning.* Hertfordshire: Englewood Cliffs, N.J.: Prentice-Hall, 1994.

Nonaka, I., and H. Takeuchi. *The Knowledge Creating Company: How Japanese Companies Create the Dynamics of Innovation.* New York: Oxford University Press, 1995.

Parolini, C. *The Value Net: A Tool for Competitive Strategy.* New York: Wiley, 1999.

Polanyi, M. *The Tacit Dimension.* London: Routledge & Kegan, 1996.

Porter, M. E. *Competitive Strategy: Techniques for Analyzing Industries and Competitors.* New York: The Free Press, 1980.

Prahalad, C. K., and R.A. Bettis. "The Dominant Logic: A New Linkage Between Diversity and Performance." *Strategic Management Journal 7* (1986), pp. 485–501.

Roos, J., and H. von Krogh, G. *Managing Strategy Processes in Emergent Industries.* London: Macmillan, 1996.

Sanders, I. *Strategic Thinking and the New Science.* New York: The Free Press, 1998.

Schoemaker, P. "Scenario Planning: A New Tool for Strategic Thinking." *Sloan Management Review*, Winter 1996, pp. 25–40.

Schreyögg, G. "Strategisches Management: Entwicklungstendenzen und Zukunftsperspektiven." *Die Unternehmung* 53 (1999), pp. 387–407.

Schwartz, P. *The Art of the Long View: Planning for the Future in an Uncertain World.* New York: Doubleday, 1996.

Senge, P. *The Fifth Discipline: the Art and Practice of the Learning Organization.* London: Century Business, 1990.

Shapiro, S., and M. Spence. "Managerial Intuition: A Conceptual and Operational Framework." *Business Horizon*, January/February 1997, pp. 63–68.

Shaw, G., R. Brown, and P. Bromiley. "Strategic Stories: How 3M is Rewriting Business Planning." *Harvard Business Review*, May/June 1998, pp. 41–50.

Stacey, R. D. "The Science of Complexity: An Alternative Perspective for Strategic Change Processes." *Strategic Management Journal*, 16 (1995), pp. 477–495.

Strebel, P. "Creating Industry Breakpoints: Changing the Rules of the Game." *Long Range Planning*, 28 (1995), pp. 11–20.

Varela, F. *Principles of Biological Autonomy.* Amsterdam: North-Holland, 1979.

Vogel, H. *Entertainment Industry Economics: A Guide for Financial Analysis.* New York: Cambridge University Press, 1998.

Von Krogh, G., and J. Roos. *Organizational Epistemology.* New York: St. Martin's Press, 1995.

Webber, A. M. "What's So New About the New Economy?" *Harvard Business Review*, January/February 1993, pp. 24–42.

Weick, K. E. *Sensemaking in Organisations.* London: Sage, 1995.

Weick, K. E. and K.E. Roberts. "Collective Minds in Organizations: Heedful Interrelating on Flight Decks." *Administrative Science Quarterly*, 38 (1993), pp. 357–381.

Wenger, E. C., and W.M. Snyder. "Communities of Practice: The Organizational Frontier." *Harvard Business Review* 78 (2000), pp. 139–145.

Whittington, R. "Strategy as Practice." *Long Range Planning* 29 (1996), pp. 731–735.

Whittington, R. "The 'How' is More Important than the 'Where.'" *Financial Times*, October 25, 1999, p. 4.

Wilson, I. "Strategic Planning Isn't Dead—It Changed." *Long Range Planning* 27 (1994), pp. 12–24.

Yin, R. K. *Case Study Research: Design and Methods.* London: Sage, 1989.

Zerdick, A., A. Picot, K. Schrape, A. Atropé, K. Goldhammer, U. Lange, E. Vierkant, E. Lópes-Escobar, and R. Silverstone. *Die Internet-Ökonomie.* Berlin: Springer-Verlag, 1999.

Chapter 8

Baym, N. K. "The Emergence of Community in Computer-Mediated Communication." In S.G. Jones (ed.). *CyberSociety. Computer-Mediated Communication and Community.* Thousand Oaks, Calif.: Sage, 1995, pp. 138–163.

Baym, N. K. "The Emergence of On-Line Community." In S. Jones (ed.). *Cybersociety 2.0: Revisiting Computer-Mediated Communication and Community.* Newbury Park, Calif.: Sage, 1998, pp. 35–68.

Bell, C., and H. Newby. "Community Studies." In *Studies in Sociology (No. 5).* London: George Allen & Unwin, 1971.

Berger, P. L. and T. Luckmann. *The Social Construction of Reality.* New York: Doubleday, 1996.

Brown, J. S. and O. Duguid. "Organizational Learning and Communities-of-Practice: Toward a Unified View of Working, Learning, and Innovation." *Organization Science* 2.1 (1991), pp. 40–57.

Cohen, A. P. *The Symbolic Construction of Community.* London: Tavistock, 1985.

Cole, M., G. Gay, J. A. Glick, and D. W. Sharp. *The Cultural Context of Learning and Thinking.* New York: Basic Books, 1971.

Davidow, W. H. and M. S. Malone. *The Virtual Corporation: Structuring and Revitalizing the Corporation for the 21st Century.* New York: Burlinggame Books, 1992.

Diemers, D. "Knowledge and Culture: Introducing the Cross-cultural Dimension of Knowledge Management." Working paper, University of St. Gallen, Switzerland, 1999a.

Diemers, D. "On the Social Dimension of Information Quality and Knowledge." In Y. W. Lee and G. K. Tayi (eds.). *Proceedings of the 1999 MIT Conference on Information Quality.* Cambridge MA: MIT Press, 1999b, pp. 125–143.

Diemers, D. "Kontingenzmanagement, Frühwarnsysteme, & Virtualität." In M.

Henckel v. Donnersmarck and R. Schatz (eds.). *Frühwarnsysteme.* Bonn: Innovatio, 1999c. pp. 225–245.

Diemers, D. "Ein sozialwissenschaftlicher Beitrag zu virtuellen Gemeinschaften." Manuskript. University of St. Gallen, Switzerland, 1999d.

Diemers, D. "Information Quality and its Interpretative Reconfiguration as a Premise of Knowledge Management in Virtual Organizations." In Y. Malhotra (ed.). *Knowledge Management and Virtual Organizations.* Hershey, Pa.: Idea Group, 2000a, pp. 365–379.

Diemers, D. "Interpretative Spaces: How Interpretative Spaces Constitute Virtual Organizations and Communities." In *Proceedings of the 2000 Conference of the Association of Internet Researchers (AoIR 2000).* Lawrence, Kansas: University of Kansas, September 14–17, 2000b.

Diemers, D. "Virtual Knowledge Communities." In *Proceedings of the 2000 MIT Conference on Information Quality.* Cambridge, Mass.: MIT Press, 2000c.

Diemers, D. "Virtual Knowledge Communities." Ph.D. thesis, University of St. Gallen, Switzerland, 2001.

Eppler, M. J. and D. Diemers. "Reale und virtuelle Gemeinschaften im betriebswirtschaftlichen Kontext: Ansätze zum Verständnis und zum Management von Communities "Real and Virtual Communities in a Business Context: Contributions to an Understanding and Management of Communities"." *Die Unternehmung,* 55.1 (2001), pp. 25–42.

Foster, D. "Community and Identity in the Electronic Village." In D. Porter (ed.). *Internet Culture.* New York: Routledge, 1997, pp. 23–38.

Geertz, C. *Interpretation of Cultures.* New York: Basic Books, 1973

Giddens, Anthony. *Modernity and Self-Identity.* Cambridge: Polity Press, 1991.

Hagel, J. and A. Armstrong. *Net Gain—Expanding Markets Through Virtual Communities.* Boston, Mass.: Harvard Business School Press, 1997.

Hall, S. "The Work of Representation." In S. Hall (ed.). *Representation: Cultural Representations and Signifying Practices.* London: Sage, 1997, pp. 13–74.

Hannerz, U. *Cultural Complexity: Studies in the Social Organization of Meaning.* New York: Columbia University Press, 1992.

Huemer, L., G. Von Krogh, and J. Roos. "Knowledge and the Concept of Trust." In G. Von Krogh, J. Roos, and D. Kleine (eds.). *Knowing in Firms: Understanding, Managing, and Measuring Knowledge.* London: Sage, 1998, pp. 123–145.

Kahn, B. K., D. M. Strong, and R. Y. Wang. "A Model for Delivering Quality Information as Product and Service." In D. M. Strong and B. K. Kahn (eds.). *Proceedings of the 1997 Conference on Information Quality.* Cambridge, Mass.: MIT Press, 1997, pp. 80–94.

Kahn, B. K. and D. M. Strong. "Product and Service Performance Model for Information Quality: An Update." In I. Chengalur-Smith and L.L. Pipino (eds.).

Proceeding of the 1998 Conference on Information Quality. Cambridge, Mass.: MIT Press, 1998, pp. 102–115.

Komito, L. "The Net as a Foraging Society: Flexible Communities." *The Information Society* 14 (1998), pp. 97–106.

LeVine, R. A. "Properties of Culture. An Ethnographic View." In R. A. Shweder, and R.A. LeVine (eds.). *Culture Theory. Essays on Mind, Self and Emotion.* Cambridge: Cambridge University Press, 1984, pp. 67–87.

Nohria, N. and J. D. Berkley. "The Virtual Organization: Bureaucracy, Technology, and the Implosion of Control." In C. von Heckscher and A. Donellon (eds.). *The Post-Bureaucratic Organization: New Perspectives on Organizational Change.* Thousand Oaks, Calif.: Sage, 1994, pp. 108–128.

Naumann, F. and C. Rolker. "Do Metadata Models Meet IQ Requirements." In Y. W. Lee and G. K. Tayi (eds.). *Proceedings of the 1999 MIT Conference on Information Quality.* Cambridge, Mass.: MIT Press, 1999, pp. 99–114.

Nonaka, I. and N. Konno. "The Concept of 'ba': Building a Foundation for Knowledge Creation." *California Management Review* 40.3 (1998), pp. 40–54.

Pinchot, G. "Building Community in the Workplace." In F. Hesselbein, M. Goldsmith, R. Beckhard, and R. F. Schubert (eds.). *The Community of the Future.* San Francisco: Jossey-Bass, 1998, pp. 125–138.

Rheingold, H. "A Slice of Life in My Virtual Community." In L.M. Harasim (ed.). *Global Networks: Computers and International Communication.* Cambridge, Mass.: MIT Press, 1993, pp. 57–80.

Rheingold, H. *The Virtual Community: Finding Connection in a Computerized World.* London: Minerva, 1995.

Schutz, A. *Das Problem der Relevanz* "The Problem of Relevance." Frankfurt am Main: Suhrkamp, 1982.

Schutz, A. and T. Luckmann. *The Structures of the Life-World, Vol. 1.* London: Heinemann, 1974.

Schutz, A. and T. Luckmann. *The Structures of the Life-World, Vol. 2.* London: Heinemann, 1983.

Shanks, G. and P. Darke. "Understanding Data Quality in Data Warehousing: A Semiotic Approach." In I. Chengalur-Smith and L.L. Pipino (eds.). *Proceedings of the 1998 Conference on Information Quality.* Cambridge, Mass.: MIT Press, 1998, pp. 292–309.

Strong, D. M., Y. W. Lee, and R. Y. Wang. "Data Quality in Context." *Communications of the ACM* 40.5 (1997), pp. 103–110.

Toennies, F. *Gemeinschaft und Gesellschaft: Grundbegriffe einer reinen Soziologie* "Community and Society: Basic Terms of a Pure Sociology," *4th/5th edition.* Berlin: Curtius, 1922.

Turkle, S. "Constructions and Reconstructions of Self in Virtual Reality: Playing in the MUDs." *Mind, Culture and Activity* 1.3 (1994), pp. 158–167.

Turkle, S. *Life on the Screen: Identity in the Age of the Internet.* New York: Simon & Schuster, 1995.

Turkle, S. "Virtuality and its Discontents: Searching for Community in Cyberspace." *The American Prospect* 24 (Winter 1996), pp. 50–57.

Von Krogh, G. "Care in Knowledge Creation." *California Management Review* 40.3 (1998), pp. 133–153.

Von Krogh, G., K. Ichijo, and I. Nonaka. *Enabling Knowledge Creation: How to Unlock the Mystery of Tacit Knowledge and Release the Power of Innovation.* Oxford: Oxford University Press, 2000.

Wand, Y. and R. Wang. "Anchoring Data Quality Dimensions in Ontological Foundations." *Communications of the ACM* 39.11 (1996), pp. 86–95.

Wang, R. Y. and D. M. Strong. "Beyond Accuracy: What Data Quality Means to Data Consumers." *Journal of Management Information Systems* 12.4 (1996), pp. 5–34.

Weber, M. *Wirtschaft und Gesellschaft* "Economy and Society": *Reihe Grundriss der Sozialökonomik.* Tübingen: J.C.B. Mohr, 1914.

Chapter 10

Arnott, Dave. *Corporate Cults: The Insidious Lure of the All-Consuming Organization.* New York: Prentice-Hall, 2000.

Davis, Stan and Christopher Meyer. *Future Wealth.* Boston: Harvard Business Press, 2000.

Fortune Magazine. "Do MBAs Make Better CEOs?" February 15, 2001.

Harvard Business Review. *Work and Life Balance.* Boston: Harvard Business School Press, 2000.

Kauffman, Stuart. *At Home in the Universe.* Oxford: Oxford University Press, 1995.

Peters, Tom. "The Brand Called You." *Fast Company,* September 1997, www.fast-company.com/online/10/brandyou.html

Ridderstrale, Jonas and Kjell Nordström. *Funky Business, Talent Makes Capital Dance.* London: Sage, 2000.

Waldrop, Mitchell. *Complexity: The Emerging Science at the Edge of Order and Chaos.* New York: Simon & Schuster, 1992.

Zucker, Betty and Christof Schmitz. *Wissen gewinnt: Knowledge Flow Management,* Second Edition. Regensburg: Walhalla Verlag, 2000.

Zucker, Betty. "Der 2000Sassa." *GDI Impuls,* April 1999.

Zucker, Betty. "Die Generation X." *GDI Impuls,* February 2000.

Index

credible visibility, 204–205
credit card industry, 34–36
CRM, *see* Customer Relationship
  Management
CRM Capability Model, 22–24
culture
  of authentication and trust, 6, 10
  corporate, 189
  high-care knowledge, 119
curiosity, 199–201
customer behavior, 19
customer equity, 22
customer insight, 23
customer interaction, 23–24
customer knowledge, 43
customer knowledge management
  (CKM), 17–39, 41–60
  in airline industry, 32–34
  application of, 58–59
  in automotive industry, 30–32
  challenges to, 51–58
  cost of, to sellers, 54–55
  in credit card industry, 34–36
  and CRM capability model, 22–24
  and data mining model, 27–30
  definition of, 18
  e-commerce application of,
    58–59
  e-commerce challenges to, 51–58
  and fair disclosure, 55–56
  and involvement model, 24–26
  IT usage factors for, 21
  as model, 26–27
  and negative knowledge disclosure,
    58
  questions for, 21
  trends affecting, 19–21
  and utilization of knowledge, 57
  value of, for customers, 52–54
customer offers, 23

Customer Relationship Management
  (CRM), 22–24
customer service Web sites, 58

data mining, 27–30, 43–44
DEC, 208
decision making, 74
  behavior factor in, 25–26, 29
  cognitive, 26
  emotional, 26
  habitual, 26
  intuition in, 140
  rational, 74–76, 79, 80
Dell Computer, 56, 151
Delta Airlines, 34
digital abundance, 20
disclosure
  fair, 55–56
  negative knowledge, 58
"discover-codify-disseminate" model,
  65
discussion databases, 64
disintermediation, 50–51
documents, 65
  collection and storage of, 62, 66
  integrated management of,
    193–194
  retrieval of, 63, 64
dominant logic, 84–86, 153
Drucker, Peter, *ix*
dynamic capabilities, 75–77
dynamic perspective, 114, 115

e-commerce, *see* electronic
  commerce
"economic calculus," 53
eConomy, 93, 158–160, 164, *see
  also* new economy
8086(8) chips, 69

top management (*continued*)
  knowledge facilitation supported by, 9, 10
  and logical incrementalism, 82
trackability (of customer behavior), 19
training
  in knowledge facilitation, 11
  of knowledge workers, 196–197
  methodology repositories for, 64
transaction cost model, 50
transfer, knowledge, 102
transparency (of e-commerce), 47
travel industry, 34–36
Trilogy Software, 42–43
"true ambiguity," 142
trust, 6, 10, 13, 123

ubiquitous communications, 20
ubiquitous computing, 20
uncertainty, 79–81, 83
  conditions of, 142
  and decision making, 75–77
  definition of, 79
  and dominant logic, 85
  strategizing under conditions of, 139–140
  and strategy models, 143–144
United Kingdom, 67, 143
utilization of knowledge, 57

valuation level (of IQ), 175–176
"value innovation," 153

value(s)
  of CKM to customers, 52–54
  ideological, 89
  shared, 123, 167
virtual communities, 159
virtual knowledge communities (VKCs), 165–176
  common interaction platforms within, 167–168
  continuity within, 168
  definition of, 165–166
  emotional bonds within, 168
  identity construction within, 169
  IQ framework in, 170–176
  reciprocity within, 168–169
  shared interests within, 166–167
  shared values/norms within, 167
visibility, credible, 204–205
VKCs, *see* virtual knowledge communities
Volkswagen, 32

Weber, Max, 163
Weick, Karl
  on intuition, 145
  on sharing experience, 154
white blood cells, 68
Whittington, R., on strategy as practice, 150
wine shopping, 48–49

Zander, U., on knowledge, 99
Zurich Financial Services, 7–8

ABOUT THE EDITORS

Alfred J. Beerli, studied business administration, economics, and information management at the University of St. Gallen (HSG) in Switzerland and the ESADE in Spain. In 2001, he received his Ph.D. from the University of St. Gallen (HSG), based on his thesis at the chairs of Prof. Georg Von Krogh and Prof. Peter Gross. Dr. Beerli has worked since 1995 with Accenture as a strategy consultant in the area of strategy definition in the financial services industry. Dr. Beerli has published works on knowledge management as well as on e-business and coopetition. He lives in Winterthur, Switzerland.

Svenja Falk studied political science, sociology, and philosophy at the University of Giessen, Germany, and the University of Southern California, USA. In 1997, she received her Ph.D. summa cum laude from the University of Giessen. Falk is now heading Accenture's Knowledge Center and is responsible for operations in Austria, Switzerland, and Germany. Dr. Falk has published works regularly on knowledge management as well as on e-politics and e-democracy. She lives in Frankfurt.

Daniel Diemers studied business administration, economics, and sociology at the University of St. Gallen (HSG) in Switzerland, and the Rotterdam School of Management in the Netherlands. In 2001, he received his Ph.D. summa cum laude from the University of St. Gallen (HSG), based on his thesis on knowledge management and virtual communities at the chairs of Prof. Georg Von Krogh ("Enabling Knowledge Creation") and Prof. Peter Gross ("The Mulitoptional Society"). Dr. Diemers has been contributing in writing on the topics of knowledge management, virtual communities, society, and virtuality. He also works as a consultant in the areas of knowledge management, e-business, and strategy. Dr. Diemers works for zeb/rolfes.schierenbeck.associates, a German consultancy specializing in financial services, and lives in Zürich, Switzerland.